SUTTON STUDIES IN MODERN BRITISH HISTORY

SOCIAL
CONDITIONS,
STATUS AND COMMUNITY
1860–*c*. 1920

SUTTON STUDIES IN MODERN BRITISH
HISTORY
General Editor: Keith Laybourn
Professor of History, University of Huddersfield

1. The Rise of Socialism in Britain, *c.* 1881–1951
Keith Laybourn

2. Workhouse Children: Infant and Child Paupers under the
Worcestershire Poor Law, 1780–1871
Frank Crompton

3. Social Conditions, Status and Community, 1860–*c.* 1920
edited by *Keith Laybourn*

Forthcoming Titles

The National Union of Mineworkers and British Politics, 1944–1995
Andrew J. Taylor

Thatcherism and British Politics, 1975–1997
Brendan Evans

The Age of Unease: Government and Reform in Britain, 1782–1832
Michael Turner

SUTTON STUDIES IN MODERN BRITISH HISTORY

SOCIAL
CONDITIONS,
STATUS AND COMMUNITY
1860–c. 1920

EDITED BY

KEITH LAYBOURN

SUTTON PUBLISHING

First published in 1997 by
Sutton Publishing Limited · Phoenix Mill
Thrupp · Stroud · Gloucestershire · GL5 2BU

British Library Cataloguing in Publication Data
A catalogue record for this book is available from the British Library

ISBN 0 7509 1070 4 (hardback)
ISBN 0 7509 1501 3 (paperback)

Cover photograph: East End family, 1912
(The Hulton Getty Picture Collection Limited)

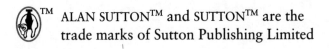 TM ALAN SUTTONTM and SUTTONTM are the trade marks of Sutton Publishing Limited

Typeset in 11/14pt Sabon.
Typesetting and origination by
Sutton Publishing Limited.
Printed in Great Britain by
Hartnolls, Bodmin, Cornwall.

CONTENTS

CONTRIBUTORS

Becky (Rebecca) Bryson has just successfully completed her Ph.D at the University of Huddersfield. She has written articles on health in Huddersfield in the late nineteenth century and is currently on a one-year contract working in archives at the University of Huddersfield Library.

Fiona Cushlow is a Ph.D student at the University of Huddersfield and is about to submit her thesis. She teaches history on a part-time basis in higher education.

Peter Gurney is a lecturer at the University of Huddersfield. He is the author of *Co-operative Culture and Politics of Consumption in England, 1870–1930* (Manchester University Press, 1996).

Margaret Jones has just completed an MA at the University of Huddersfield and teaches in Bath. Her dissertation is the basis for this chapter.

Keith Laybourn is Professor of History at the University of Huddersfield. He has written eighteen books and many articles. His books include *The Rise of Socialism in Britain, c. 1881–1951* (Stroud, Sutton Publishing, 1997), *The General Strike Day by Day* (Stroud, Sutton Publishing, 1996), *The Evolution of British Social Policy and the Welfare State 1890–1993* (Keele University Press, 1995) and *Britain on the Breadline* (Gloucester, Alan Sutton, 1990).

Tony Nicholson is Senior Lecturer in History at the University of Teesside. He has written many articles on the subject of community in the Cleveland area.

Stuart Robertson is a Ph.D student at the University of Huddersfield. He is about to submit his Ph.D and his chapter is based upon part of it.

Bertrand Taithe is a lecturer in History at the University of Huddersfield. He has written several articles and has published a book *The Essential Mayhew: Representing and Communicating the Poor* (London, Rivers Oram, 1996) and is the co-editor of *Prophecy: the Power of Inspired Language in History 1300–2000* (Sutton Publishing, 1997).

David Taylor is Principal Lecturer and Head of History at the University of Huddersfield. He has written many articles, a pamphlet on *'A Well-chosen, Effective Body of Men': The Middlesbrough Police Force, 1841–1914* (1995) and is currently completing books on policing for Manchester University Press and Macmillan.

Jack Williams is Senior Lecturer in History at Liverpool John Moores University. He has written many articles on sport and has just co-edited, with Jeff Hill, a book entitled *Sport and Identity in the North of England* (Keele University Press, 1996).

INTRODUCTION

KEITH LAYBOURN

The years between 1860 and 1920 saw dramatic changes in the lives of the English people and the attitudes of society towards poverty, community, voluntary activity and the role of the state. Indeed, in the 1860s the extended role of the state became evident with the more effective introduction of the New Poor Law resulting from a rising level of poor rate expenditure as the poor law communities geared themselves to a higher level of commitment.[1] That decade also saw the formation of the Charity Organisation Society in 1869. By the 1880s and the 1890s there was a greater concern being shown for the poor, children, the unemployed and the ill through a variety of public and private means, a body dedicated to the development and coordination of philanthropy.[2] The social surveys of London and York, conducted by Booth and Rowntree, did much to challenge the view that poverty was necessarily a result of personal failing and implied that society might do more for its unfortunates. By the beginning of the twentieth century the social reforms of the Liberal governments were beginning to reshape and extend the responsibilities of both the state and local communities.

Several dominant features emerged in these years and have been the focus of much contemporary and recent debate. In the broadest of ways the attitudes dominant in society were beginning to change. Philip Snowden, in a lecture to a joint meeting of the Reading Fabian Society and the Reading Independent Labour Party, in 1912, referred to an 'almost complete revolution in the mental attitude which had taken place towards welfare and poverty', emphasized that 'all political parties in the country today recognised the existence of what they termed the social problem', and added that 'it was not always so'.[3] Indeed, there had been a major shift in attitudes towards the poor between the mid-1880s and the First World War, most obviously in recognition that poverty was not necessarily a personal failing but a problem of the failures of society.

The main problem was how to deal with poverty and its root causes of unemployment, old age, ill-health and family size. Was it to be tackled through voluntary effort, local government initiative or state action? It is now clear that those historians who, in the 1950s, '60s and '70s, accepted the Whiggish assumption of the expansion of state welfare in dealing with these problems have played down the many other factors that were in operation.[4] However, recently, the pluralistic nature of the response has been noted by many historians, most obviously by José Harris who has recorded how welfare provision in late Victorian Britain was dominated by voluntary and philanthropic activity. She argues that most functions performed in other countries were assumed by 'coteries of citizens governing themselves' and that citizens were encircled at every level by 'a dense network of self-governing institutions'.[5] Indeed, she notes that as late as 1911 the gross annual returns of registered charities alone exceeded the public expenditure on the Poor Law, with unregistered charities, friendly societies, trade unions and other forms of institutional help excluded from the calculation. There has also been considerable debate as to whether the purpose of this philanthropy was to maintain social control, to offer reform or to ward off state expansion. But even more important has been the issue of the interrelationships and balance of interests between private and public activities and the resulting pattern of social welfare. Harris argues that there is no easily decipherable pattern of social policy and that British social policy often revealed conflicting tendencies and operated along distinct and separate routes. There is no obvious trajectory for the development of social policy in the late Victorian period and still a conflicting set of patterns is evident in the Edwardian years. What often emerged at any particular time, and on any specific issue, was a product of the balance between the interests and forces involved.

Inevitably, the tackling of social problems involves the 'community' or the 'local community'. Communities are now in the news, with constant reference being made to 'community schools', 'community leisure centres', the 'local community' and 'community policing'. However, the term community was, as it is now, a very vague concept in the late nineteenth and early twentieth centuries. It was normally used to denote a geographically specific area – a town, a village or a Poor Law area. Yet it could also be used to denote an occupational group of high or low status, or a middle-class or working-class community. More than thirty years ago Professor Herbert Finberg saw the local community as 'a social entity' and 'a closely integrated social formation which has been an ever present, not to say obsessive, reality for many thousands of people over the centuries'.[6] Since then sociologists and social historians have examined the shared attitudes and aspirations of groups who almost certainly worked, played and prayed together.[7] They have noted the sense of shared concerns but also recognized the tensions which divided occupational, religious, and other social groupings, within the community. Indeed, there are many recent writers who have argued that communities are imagined.[8] Joanna Bourke, for instance, has challenged the notion of the 'working-class community' which she feels has been the product of socialist writings and the work of people such as Richard Hoggart, who have elaborated on and romanticized their past experiences.[9] It is possible that the term community exaggerates the importance of certain features of 'organic' life but equally it may represent the sutures that held geographical, social and occupational communities together in some recognizable form. Indeed, some writers, such as Richard Colls, are not ready to give up the idea of community as readily as Bourke, even though they recognize the need for redefinition.[10]

This book attempts to address some of the major social and economic issues that occurred in the six decades between 1860 and 1920. It arose because a number of students and staff at the University of Huddersfield were working on broadly related themes, including poverty, community, crime, status and social conditions. It seemed appropriate to gather the fruits of their research and to supplement them with contributions from some outside scholars. Inevitably, given the specialist nature of much of the research, this cannot be a volume that examines the historiography of debate in a strictly systematic manner but it does offer to the reader new areas and angles of research, not least the work of the Guild of Help, voluntarism, policing and sport in the community – issues which have come to the fore of debate in recent years.

Some of the chapters in this book examine the way in which 'coteries of citizens' governed themselves. Fiona Cushlow deals with the Bradford Guild of Help in her piece on 'Guilded Help?'. Formed in

1904, the Bradford Guild developed a 'New Philanthropy', based on a personal help to the poor, the organization of a clearing house for relief and a partnership between public and private bodies. It offered a community response, in both a geographic and middle-class sense, to the problem of poverty in which it was considered the duty of every responsible citizen to become involved. In fact, the Guild of Help was a response by part of the middle-class community to the perceived social crisis of the Edwardian age. Using a sample of some of the 5,682 casebooks that survive for the Bradford Guild, Cushlow suggests that the Guild was making a serious attempt at operating a form of social control and challenges the view of Frank Prochaska that charity had little to do with social control.[11]

The Guild of Help saw itself as 'the practical expression of the civic consciousness and the end and the embodiment of new philanthropy'.[12] In his article on 'The Guild of Help and the Community Response to Poverty', Keith Laybourn examines the movement on a national scale. He suggests that the Guild played a part in the development of municipal and local action at a time when the duties of local public bodies were expanding greatly.[13] The Guild was particularly concerned with the urban environment and social conditions of the Edwardian age. It dealt with unemployment and ill-health but failed to check the move towards public service for several reasons: owing to the fact that only about one-fifth of the Poor Law districts of England and Wales had a Guild, because the movement lacked resources and as a result of the increasing professionalization of the local authority municipal services. In the end private and local initiative was not enough to check the centralizing tendency of the state.

The Guild took a keen interest in the issue of health, being particularly concerned with infant mortality and TB. Stuart Robertson's chapter focuses on some of the health work of the Bolton Guild of Help. He argues that there was a very close relationship between the Guild and Dr Gould, the Medical Officer of Health for Bolton, in tackling the problem of tuberculosis. In Bolton, indeed, the Guild was at the forefront of the new techniques to tackle TB (sanatorium and open-air treatments) and the attempts to campaign against the disease.

The improvement of the health of the nation was obviously one of the prime concerns of this period. The TB and infant mortality campaigns of the Guild highlight the concerns of the Edwardian years and some of the failures of the Victorian years. Becky Bryson's chapter on health in Huddersfield takes a broader sweep and examines the conditions of health in Huddersfield between 1870 and 1914. She suggests that Huddersfield's health improved substantially during the period, although there were still significant differences between the social classes. Huddersfield was, indeed, one of the healthiest towns in England by the Edwardian years, and its improvements were mirrored to a lesser extent by many other towns.

Although health was slowly improving in the late nineteenth and early twentieth centuries there is no doubt that old age remained a significant and potentially even more challenging problem in the continuation of poverty. Recent work by Pat Thane has suggested that old people have never been particularly dependent on their children for support but neither were they largely dependent on the Poor Law. Instead, she suggests that in the 'economy of makeshifts' people did their best to support elderly relatives but had to resort to the Poor Law when they could not do so. In the end, this can best be described as 'intimacy at a distance'.[14] As part of the process of relieving the increasing burden of the elderly on the Poor Law the Edwardian Liberal reforms introduced the Old Age Pensions Act of 1908. This measure offered a degree of relief which could not have been achieved by the previously inadequate and fluctuating attempts at pension provision made by the Charity Organisation Society and other philanthropic bodies.[15] The scheme was a compromise between central direction and local practice, although it strengthened the control of the state. Indeed, as Anne Digby has noted: 'coexisting with a continuation of the Victorian practice of central enactment but local implementation went an increased centralism in such measures as old age pension and unemployment insurance'.[16] Nevertheless, the provision of old age pensions was still locally determined by pensions officers who were responsible to the Inland Revenue, and, later, the Customs and Excise Board, but who reported to the local pension committee. Margaret Jones's article argues that the introduction of the 1908 Act was a genuine attempt to provide a state benefit for the deserving aged poor but that its similarities with the Poor Law became rather obvious. Even after changes to the rules in 1911, those who went to the workhouse would lose their pensions and the Poor Law philosophy and approach still left its imprint on the provision of old age pensions, where moral issues still counted highly.

The theme of community pervades this book and it raises the issue of whether or not historians have correctly interpreted the salient events of regional and local community life. The 'imagined past' has often been mentioned in recent writings, increasingly by post-modernist and post-structuralist historians who have continued to challenge the apparent certainties of the past, such as class and thus community structure. Even those of a more modernist perspective have challenged the 'mythology' of an idealized working-class community. This is not a view shared by Carl Chinn, whose book *They Worked All Their Lives: Women of the Urban Poor in England* (Manchester University Press, 1988) suggests a type of unity among the wives of the poor, based on matriarchy and the need to survive. Indeed, David Vincent's *Poor Citizen: The State and the Poor in Twentieth Century Britain* (London, 1992) and Carl Chinn's *Poverty amidst Prosperity: The Urban Poor in England 1834–1914* (Manchester University Press, 1995) suggest that the poor had strategies for survival which gave them a sense of cultural unity. The debate remains open as to whether the past was imagined or invented and whether the community and community relations have become part of some idealized myth.

This volume contains four different approaches to the issue of community. David Taylor's chapter on 'Policing and the Community' is very specific and suggests that the recent crisis in policing has encouraged people to look back to a mythological past when 'community policing' meant the happier days of the late Victorian village or district bobby who was firm but friendly, turned a blind eye to minor misdemeanours and whose status in the community was high. He argues that in reality policing the community rarely seems to have been a situation where a much respected bobby operated in a tranquil setting but one of immense variation where the community bobby may well have been in conflict with his local community and of major social conflict in communities such as London. In the final analysis the relations between policing and the community in late Victorian and Edwardian society appear to have varied according to person, place and situation.

Jack Williams, on the other hand, focuses on the impact of sport in defining loyalty to neighbourhood, village and town. He argues that 'Sport had a key role in the formation and expression of town identities.' Indeed, between 1870 and 1914 support for football and cricket clubs became part of the urban way of life and town clubs became the apex of a 'sporting pyramid' in the local community.[17] Sport emphasized town loyalties, political worthies of the town associated with their clubs, and sport could even temporarily overcome obvious differences of class. There is no doubt, to Williams, that some elements of community did emerge around the identification with sporting activities, whatever the doubts some sociologists hold about the existence of community ties.

Tony Nicholson investigates the defining of community and status through work and culture: examining the Cleveland ironstone mining communities he stresses that the work practices of the employers helped to ensure that these communities were male dominated and that they tended to establish work and social practices which guaranteed that status increased with age and trade union membership. Indeed, trade union lodges not only excluded women but they promoted, celebrated and empowered certain types of manliness. What gave many of these communities a sense of identity in areas where traditional forms of social control had broken down was the concept of masculine identity, which conferred social status.

Different aspects of community are raised by Peter Gurney. He is concerned with the 'imagined past' of D.H. Lawrence and, to a lesser extent, Raymond Williams in reconstructing their working-class experience of community. He maintains that their images of their idealized roots may have created an 'imagined past' but that their representations gave them a sense of rootedness as they moved out of the working-class life, of which they could no longer be a part, into literary and academic lives in which they felt isolated and rejected. In the case of both Lawrence and Williams the 'imagined' working-class communities of their youth shaped their thinking about future communities and, in Williams's case, the vision of organization for a future socialist society.

The last contribution to this collection is made by Bertrand Taithe. It returns to the issue of health by examining the nature of the opposition to the Contagious Diseases Acts. Taithe goes beyond the work of Josephine Butler and notes that the City of London Committee, the Working Men's League for the Repeal of the Contagious Diseases Acts, A.S. Dyer, old Chartist and other groups all campaigned for the repeal of the CDA, although their efforts were temporary since middle-class and working-class interests diverged on other issues.

This book is an attempt to bring together recent research on social history for the late nineteenth and early twentieth centuries. If there is one theme that unites most of the chapters it is that one must now adopt a pluralistic approach to explaining developments and changes in British society between the 1860s and the 1920s. There is much mythology to challenge and the old Whiggish narratives have given way to an awareness of the complexities and ambiguities of history. There is a danger that this alternative could produce numerous isolated case studies, but this can be overcome if one recognizes that the various events discussed – voluntarism, status and community relations – all had a part to play in shaping attitudes towards poverty, social control and the development of the state. A pluralistic rather than monolithic approach is now essential to the study of British history, whether it be of a social, economic or political nature.

CHAPTER

1

THE GUILD OF HELP AND THE COMMUNITY RESPONSE TO POVERTY 1904–c. 1914

KEITH LAYBOURN

The Edwardian years saw the emergence of rising concern about the problems of British society and most notably a debate about how to deal with poverty, raised so obviously by the detailed research of Seebohm Rowntree and the serious difficulties that many towns faced in dealing with their unemployed and poor during the early years of the century. Central to this debate was the work of the Guild of Help, an organization which offered a more community-based solution to poverty. The fact that this did not work and that the state had to take on an increasing responsibility for poverty does not discount the work of this organization which saw the middle classes attempt to operate through the local community, still the locus of power in Edwardian England, in order to establish a partnership between philanthropy, community and, ultimately, the state, in an attempt to stave off the prospect of state socialism in a climate of social crisis. Indeed, the work of the Guild of Help could be seen as a half-way house between the 'Old Philanthropy' of the Charity Organisation Society (COS), and the increased involvement of the state in social matters. It offered the 'New Philanthropy' which sought to enlist the full help of the local community in tackling poverty through helpers who showed a genuine concern in the welfare of those they sought to help. According to *Help*, the organ of the Bradford City Guild of Help:

The Guild of Help is the practical expression of the civic consciousness and the end and embodiment of the new philanthropy. The old was clearly associated with charity in the narrow sense, and between those who gave and those who received was a great gulf fixed; the 'lady bountiful' attitude has received its death blow, the Guild worker does not go in as a visitant from another world but as a fellow creature to be helpful.[1]

The Poole Guild of Help endorsed such views: 'The Guild was to be an expression of consciousness of mutual obligation within the borough of Poole, to gather into a well-organised body all who have an instinct for social service.'[2] The Guild of Help was thus an experiment to tackle poverty through the effective organization of the voluntary efforts of local community.

Beginnings

The movement was inaugurated in Bradford in 1904, but first emerged as an idea on 14 October 1903 when the Mayor of Bradford, Alderman David Wade, held a meeting 'for the purpose of discussing the question of Co-ordination of work and workers amongst the poor with a view to the adoption of some such system in vogue in Elberfeld as may be successfully carried out in this country'.[3] A central board of Bradford's charities was formed and met monthly to devise a scheme for coordinating their charitable provision. A provisional committee of ten people met regularly during the ensuing ten months and publicly launched the Bradford City Guild of Help on 20 September 1904, at a meeting addressed by Dr Boyd Carpenter, the Bishop of Ripon, and Seebohm Rowntree. One newspaper reflected that 'The experiment of applying to Bradford the system of poor relief and help which had been remarkably successful in Elberfeld was inaugurated yesterday.'[4] The idea was to form an alternative to the Charity Organisation Society, which had never been well represented in the north of England, and to gather into a well-organized body 'all the community who have a desire and more or less capacity for social services'.[5] 'Not alms but a friend' was to be the motto of the Guild, reflecting the emphasis that it placed upon personal service to individuals or families in need. In essence, then, the Guild had three main objectives. First, it wished to organize 'Helpers' who would exercise personal responsibility for the poor by visiting them and keeping a social casebook on each family visited, thus reaching into the 'darkest corners' of the local community through social casework. These Helpers would assess the family needs of the poor and contact their district, or head, office to consult the register of charitable and public organizations and call up necessary help. The second aim was that the Guild would act as a clearing house for cases of need, thus reducing the overlapping charitable effort and rooting out scroungers and beggars. Thirdly, the Guild aimed to form a partnership between the private and public bodies through which social work would flow. These three objectives were to be the basis of the New Philanthropy, and were considered to form a scientific approach to the assessment and treatment of want in the local community, replacing the indiscriminate relief that was considered to be the basis of Victorian charity. Philip Bagenal of the Harrogate Citizens' Guild of Help made this point when he informed the Halifax Guild that the town hall ought to be the home of every Guild and

> described the Guild as a core movement which was going to lay the foundation of a national movement for cultivating a more scientific interest in what they might call the problem of relief. It is impossible to meet the demand for public assistance merely by State aid. . . . Therefore to organise the voluntary and systematic charity of England was one of the great tasks which had been laid at the shoulders of the present generation.[6]

The Bradford scheme was based on one which operated in the German textile town of Elberfeld and involved the formation of a head office, four divisions and forty districts through which 400 to 500 helpers were organized. There were in fact some important differences, most obviously that Elberfeld was a municipal scheme while the Bradford one was voluntary, although Bradford and other guilds normally used the municipal boundaries as the basis for their districts. The influence of the Elberfeld scheme probably derives from the fact that in 1888 there had been a report on the *Elberfeld System and German Workmen's Colonies* by Charles Loch and others, and that some of the findings had been commented on by Bradford delegates at the COS conference held at Oxford in 1890. Also, five of the ten members of Bradford's provisional committee were of German origin and would have known of the scheme: these were Mr and Mrs Hoffman, Mr and Mrs Jacob Moser and F.F. Steinthal. In addition, others of German descent gathered to help the Guild, including C.C.

Leibreich, the Edelsteins, the Delius family, the Wolffs, the Mahlers and the Behrens. There was also the more immediate influence of Julie Sutter's book *Britain's Next Campaign* (1903) drawn from her articles in the *Daily News*, which resurrected the Elberfeld solution to poverty and emphasized that 'Even by individual action the great trouble could be put right.'[7] Yet, one should note that Sutter was not convinced by the Bradford voluntary version of the Elberfeld scheme: 'Let me, then, make one more effort to urge upon the promoters of this Bradford scheme that there is only one way to avoid disaster – namely, by municipalising the scheme . . . without authority and without access to the rates you can never be more than helpers.'[8] The Bradford Guild did not respond to this challenge, although there is evidence that there was some support for such a view in the Halifax Guild.[9]

The activities of the Bradford Guild were reported in the *Manchester Guardian* on 4 October 1905 and further outlined in a letter by Henry Brady Priestman, chairman of the Bradford Guild's executive committee, in the same paper on 21 October 1905. Much interest was stimulated by these reports and the citizens of fifty-six towns and districts contacted the Bradford Guild immediately for help and advice. There were requests from 106 towns by the end of 1906.[10] The Bradford City Guild of Help had caught the popular mood. There were six more guilds by the end of 1905, operating in Bolton, Eccles, Halifax, Heckmondwike, Salford and Swinton. In 1906 others were formed at Birmingham, Lewisham, Newport (Isle of Wight), Sunderland and Wallasey. Yet others were formed in 1907 at Chesterfield, Croydon, Egerton, Farnworth, Harrogate, Ilkley, Letchworth, Manchester, Peterborough, Plymouth, Poole, Sheffield and Wimbledon.[11] In 1908 ten more were formed, including ones at Bristol, Dudley and Wakefield.[12] In total there were seven guilds in 1905, twelve in 1906, twenty-five in 1907, thirty-five in 1908, sixty-one by the beginning of 1910, seventy with more than 8,000 members by 1911 and eighty-three in September 1917, adopting a variety of names such as City League of Help, Guild of Social Services, Guild of Personal Services, and Civic Aid Society.[13] These figures include the Birmingham Civic Aid Society formed by E.V.D. Birchall, but exclude the Hampstead Council organized by T. Hancock Nunn, the Liverpool Central Relief Committee, and the many social welfare councils, most of which had similar objectives, fulfilled similar purposes and often participated in the conferences of the guilds, even if they were more loosely organized than the Guild of Help.[14] The rapidity of its growth, which means that it was already larger than the Charity Organisation Society by 1909, reveals that it had caught the mood of the moment.

The movement mushroomed. Annual conferences were held from 1908 onwards, the first being at Bradford, and a National Association of the Guild of Help was formed in 1911. Nine guilds were publishing monthly journals by 1911 and the movement gained a *National Magazine* in 1917. However, the First World War changed its work and focus and the vast majority of the guilds disappeared into the National Council of Social Services when it was formed in 1919.[15]

THE PROBLEM

The Guild of Help had first emerged in Bradford to deal with the rising level of poverty that existed as a result of the trade depressions and rising unemployment of the Edwardian years. The COS, the Cinderella Club, other charitable organizations, and the city council found it impossible to cope with the high levels of poverty, ill-health, infant mortality and unemployment that resulted. These problems were common throughout the country. In Dorset, the Poole Guild of Help admitted that 'The problem we have to face is the impossible one of finding employment without employers: an isolated Labour Exchange could help but little, if at all. . . .'[16]

Nevertheless, the Guild of Help claimed much for its attempts to tackle poverty. It claimed to be scientific in its approach, emphasized the connection between private and public bodies, claimed to have obtained widespread support from both the working classes and the middle classes, and stressed the good relations which it had set up with the state to deal with poverty, ill-health and unemployment.

COMMUNITY

The Guild of Help always placed strong emphasis upon it being the civic duty of every individual to help the poor. Civic betterment by the community was the desire and intense localism was the result. Consequently, civic interests were paramount, a point noted by Stephen Yeo in his study of Reading, where he argued that the Guild 'in its early days was militantly local'. Its Central Board only emerged after a number of district committees were working and the Reading Guild was reluctant to join the National Association of Guilds of Help.[17] Yeo is absolutely right about the Reading Guild and his observations can be applied to practically every other guild in England. Indeed, the vast majority of guilds saw themselves as operating within the local community and encouraging citizenship rather than forming part of a coordinated national movement. They saw citizenship as anathema to the class antagonism which the socialist groups were fomenting. Indeed, the Guild of Help encouraged citizens to accept responsibility for their less fortunate brethren in the community.

Yet, this emphasis on local effort was both the strength and weakness of the Guild. While the Guild improved the efficiency of the local response to poverty it failed to form a lasting and effective alternative to the emergence of the welfare state, something recognized by speakers at the national conference.[18] The limitations of local action ensured that the welfare state would go much further than the Guild movement had anticipated and that the New Philanthropy would be a mere adjunct to the state, not its alternative or equal partner.

The emphasis of the Guild of Help was always placed on the family and local forces rather than the municipality and the state. This commitment was presented in concentric diagrammatic form on the back of every Bradford casebook, and in every Guild magazine, as a visual representation of its philosophy. At the centre of the diagram of social forces was the family. This was successively encircled by the personal forces of relatives, neighbourhood forces (including neighbours, employers, clergymen, doctors, trade unions), and civic forces (including teachers, police and health departments). Only when these had been exhausted would private charitable forces be called upon, bringing in the COS, benevolent individuals, district nurses, ladies' charities, charitable employment and the churches. The Guild emerged effectively at this stage, organizing charitable relief once other efforts had been found wanting. Finally, and only when all other efforts had failed, the state would be called upon to provide Poor Law hospitals and poor relief. At this stage, the poor would have become the destitute and the Guild would have failed in tackling poverty.

The Bradford casebooks reveal all these efforts to provide charity as the stopgap to state intervention. One after another, they record the efforts of the Helpers to obtain the support of parents, neighbours and landlords in providing assistance, deferring debt and finding jobs.[19] However, this structure does not appear to have operated exactly in this way since the guilds were clearly attempting to muster these earlier forces as part of their casework. Their assumption was that in helping the poor they had to try to activate these forces.

Obviously, the urgent need was for all these forces to work together and Seebohm Rowntree captured the intent of the Guild of Help when he wrote of 'the new spirit that needed to accompany the new social legislation that was being implemented. Without that spirit the new machinery for the relief of distress could not work.'[20] With a desire to create and to 'cultivate a more scientific interest in what they might call the problem of relief', the guilds worked with other charities to create general registers of the poor for each community.[21] It was registration that was seen to be the fundamental basis of working out a coordinated response to poverty.

Almost all the guilds associated, with moves towards the local registration of the poor. There were twenty-seven guilds operating mutual registration schemes in 1911 and upwards of sixty had declared that they saw these schemes to be of great value. Birmingham Civic Aid Society had already formed such an agency and 'It had registered in all 25,000, and in one month 855.'[22] In Birmingham, seven honorary registers in different districts had received lists from 140 charities from 1909 onwards. In Derby, a registrar was appointed to maintain a register for the Guardians, the Education Committee, the Distress Committee, the Guild of Help and the COS. Similar developments occurred in Bolton and Liverpool.[23] The Bradford Guild received weekly lists from the Guardians and the COS and monthly ones from other organizations. In the case of Bradford, the Guardians received 'an annual grant from the Guardians for the maintenance of a register, which is . . . systematically . . . kept in order to be open at all times to the inspection of the Board and others'.[24] The register numbered 10,000 in 1911 and 30,000 in 1918.[25] There were also moves towards establishing mutual registration in Croydon.[26] The Croydon Guild started a Register of Relief in 1909 open only to the Hon. Registrar and the Secretary of the Guild. Its influence was extended with the formation of the Central Council of Croydon Charitable Agencies in 1910 which took over the Guild register, although the Guild continued to pay the expenses. However, at the beginning of the war, as soon as the Soldiers' and Sailors' Families Association was set up, it was decided to enhance the value of the register by placing it in the town hall.[27] Indeed, most of the large guilds appear to have become involved in developing such schemes, although because of size there is little evidence of significant registration schemes occurring in the smaller guilds.

The immediate stimulus for such schemes came from the Appendix, volume XV, of the Poor Law Commission in 1909, where the majority of members strongly recommended the establishment of a 'Central register containing particulars of recipients of charitable and Poor Law relief'. Such a register 'would be of great value in facilitating the work of enquiry and investigation which lies at the basis of all wisely conceived systems of charitable relief, and without which waste, overlapping and imposture are inevitable.'[28] Obviously, this appealed to the Guild of Help which had always presented itself as the organization prepared to act as a 'clearing house' for local charity. Normally, it was the local Guild which took the lead in such moves. This was the case in Reading where the Guild of Help noted that the Mutual Register of Assistance was not socially connected with the Guild,

> which notifies cases just as does any other co-operating agency. It was undertaken by the Guild in March 1911, as a body which happened to have the best facilities for it, at the request of the Joint Committee of the Guild and the Charity Organisation Society. Forty-six agencies have already agreed to co-operate, and of these 25 are already doing so. The Register is not intended principally for the detection of fraudulent applications although this useful purpose is often served; but its primary object is the provision of a means of co-operation between two or more agencies which may assist one family.[29]

In Bolton a similar scheme was being prepared in 1910 by the Guild of Help in conjunction with the Board of Guardians, Bolton Education Committee, Bolton District Nursing Association, Bolton Infirmary, the NSPCC, a Charities Board and twenty-six other local organizations. The Bolton Guild undertook to pay the administrative expenses of the Council, suggested that there should be a central collection of the income of the charities represented and the keeping of a register, which would be financed partly by the Guardians – who were already partly financing the register already kept by the Guild.[30] Also, in Croydon, the mayor argued that 'the first step towards co-operation should be a Register. . . .'[31] Registration work was also being conducted in connection with the Liverpool Council of Voluntary Aid and the Hampstead Council of Social Services.

The justification for registration tended to be twofold. In the first place it was a way of controlling mendicancy. The anti-mendicancy movement was always strong in the Guild and registration helped to keep a check on the beggars. Secondly, as already indicated, registration met one of the main objectives of the Guild – the need for coordination of help in order to prevent overlapping of charity provision. The point was made by the Mayor of Croydon in 1910 when he announced that he thought 'the first step towards co-operation should be a Register. It was absolutely necessary that the Central Register should be recognized by all who were anxious to co-operate in the better distribution of charitable funds.'[32] Registration also provided the basis of a closer unity between charities along the lines of the Councils of Voluntary Aid proposed by the majority report of the Royal Commission on the Poor Laws and Relief of Distress. This idea had first been proposed by Mr Goschen, President of the Board of Trade in 1869 who, in his well-known Minute on Co-operation between the Poor Law and Charity, had suggested the need for cooperation and exchange of information to prevent the evils of overlapping. That Minute was quoted in a Local Government Board circular to the Guardians of the Poor in 1910 in which it was urged that the Guardians might work in concert with charities to provide a register of the poor. It also offered the possibility that the Local Government Board might encourage the proposal. As a result Liverpool, Derby and Bradford put this to the test. The Liverpool Voluntary Aid Council approached the three Boards of Guardians in their city and obtained sums of £300, £200 and £100 respectively. Furthermore, Liverpool City Council sought parliamentary powers to make an annual grant of £300 towards the Voluntary Aid Council.[33] Much smaller sums were obtained by Bradford, Bolton, Farnworth and other guilds. Bolton and Bradford received £25 each per annum and Farnworth £7 10s per annum.

Obviously the Guild of Help achieved some success in improving the coordination of charity, especially within large urban communities although, as Snowden suggested in 1911, it had a long way to go. It also reflected changes in attitudes between voluntary activities and the local authorities.

THE GUILD OF HELP AND MUNICIPAL AND LOCAL AUTHORITIES

At the national conference of the Guild of Help in 1913, L.V. Sharp, of Leeds, suggested that 'One of the difficulties in the way of voluntary service was a certain nervousness on the part of municipal and local authorities as the accepting co-operation with voluntary agencies.'[34]

G.R. Snowden also noted, in 1911, that while there were about sixty guilds in existence there were 600 Poor Law Unions and Parishes in England. 'Moreover, in no case has the Poor Law Union been adopted as the area in which a Guild is to act, and in very few cases are the services of the Guild available through the whole area of the Union.'[35] From these comments it is evident that the impact of the Guild of Help upon local administration was still limited on the eve of the First World War. Given that the records of only a small number of guilds, normally the larger ones, have survived it is easy to gain a misleading impression of the ubiquity of the guilds in municipal matters. Their success in Bradford, Bolton, Halifax, Croydon, Reading, and the like, undoubtedly exaggerates the true importance of the movement nationally. None the less, they did exert an impact in many areas of local politics.

The immediate association of the Guild of Help movement with the municipality resulted from the fact that local guilds always approached the local mayor to be the honorary president. That gave immediate access to the town hall and the council chambers, a connection that was strengthened in some communities where the Guild held its national conferences, for there was normally a Lord Mayor's address and a civic reception.

The mayoral route to municipal support ensured a link, often a continuing one, with the Guild. Alderman Wade, the Mayor of Bradford in 1903 and a founder member of the Guild, continued his association long after he ceased to be mayor, as did Councillor Henry Keatly Moore, Mayor of Croydon in 1907, and many others. This relationship was normally lubricated by the fact that the Guild often associated itself with the initiatives of town mayors. The Poole Guild helped raise money for the Mayor's Coal Strike Relief Fund between March and May 1912, and the Middlesbrough Guild offered 'willing and skilful assistance' to the Mayor's Relief Fund in connection with the national coal strike at the end of 1912 and early 1913.[36]

A similar local forging of links occurred in the case of the Poor Law. From the start, the chairman of the Bradford Board of Guardians, F.H. Bentham, was a member of the executive committee of the Bradford Guild. Bentham was later appointed as one of the commissioners on the Royal Commission on the Poor Law. This certainly eased the way for the creation of working relationships with the Bradford Guardians. Indeed, Miss Dorothy C. Keeling indicated these links at the National Conference at Birmingham in 1911. She described 'the cooperation working so successfully in Bradford where Guild representatives regularly attend each of several ward . . . committees, and where a system of allocation of Special Out Relief Cases prevails to both the advantage of the Guardians and the Guild.'[37] This arrangement had developed over the previous three years. In January 1908 the Guardians had granted the Guild the opportunity of sending representatives to sit at each of four relief committees of the Union where 'The representatives of the Guild (in each case a lady) is not only given full information and a careful explanation of the policy of the Guardians, but is permitted to make representations in regard to the cases which are under the supervision of the guild.'[38]

Elsewhere, the links between the guilds and the Guardians were well established. Indeed, Miss Keeling had communicated with

32 Guilds of Help and found that to seven the Guardians would furnish regular lists of all their cases, and to three others of special types of cases, viz, sick cases, out of relief cases, and cases with which they have all ceased to deal. Nine Guilds send regular lists to the Guardians, and another gives to the Guardians a regular report on all families receiving out relief. In 22 Unions the Guardians refer to the Guild, though of course there is a great variety as to type and number of cases referred.[39]

The Birmingham Guardians notified some cases to the Birmingham Society, to another guild the Guardians notified all their sick cases. Three guilds, including Bradford, were allowed to send representatives to the poor law relief meetings, and a fourth sent a representative to Guardians' Phthisal Committee. Indeed twenty of the thirty-two guilds mentioned had some definite connection with the local Guardians.

The fostering of good relations permitted the local guilds to make contact with many other local bodies and local government departments. By 1911 forty of the sixty or so guilds were acting in concert with health departments and education committees, 'most frequently by inter-representation', in some way or other.[40] This estimation came from Mr S.P. Grundy of Manchester, who conducted a survey of the guilds, asking them about the nature and extent of their relationship with the local authorities and the degree to which they were engaged in pioneer work which was the responsibility of the local authorities.[41] Of the forty guilds that replied, four had no relations with local authorities of the type under discussion. Of the rest twenty-five had unofficial connections, five had local authority representatives on their executive committees and five had no representation at all. Thus, the overwhelming majority of guilds had either official or unofficial links with the local authority health or education committees. Nevertheless, the relationship tended to be one way, with the local authorities providing information to the guilds, as in the case of Wakefield where the Medical Officer of Health provided monthly lectures and literature for the Guild Helpers.

Yet there were some indications that the Guild of Help was beginning to gain some recognition from local bodies. There was often close cooperation between the school attendance officers and the health visitors and Guild Helpers. Indeed, in Bradford, 'Co-operation with the Health Department had arisen almost entirely on case-work. The inspectors have notified 53 cases, in addition to the 141 on the Milk Lists, and their assistance has been invoked in many other cases, by helpers in difficulty with dirty houses or neglected infants.'[42]

In addition, many guilds had taken up health matters of urgent importance. The Bolton Guild had assumed responsibility for the promotion of a Tuberculosis Exhibition, the Bradford Guild had cooperated with the Health Committee in a similar exhibition and the Warrington Guild had conducted a campaign against Infant Mortality. Wallasey Guild provided free meals for schoolchildren before the Education Authority assumed the responsibility and the Birmingham City Aid Society pressed for the conversion of an unused smallpox hospital into a sanatorium for consumptives.

By the summer of 1911 the Guild of Help had contributed significantly to the awakening of the civic consciousness in those small number of communities where an organization was present. There is no doubt that the guilds, within their limited spheres of influence, did much to work and encourage local authority action in a period of rapid change in social policy. Indeed, S.P. Grundy suggested a number of ways in which this relationship could be strengthened: guilds could invite local authority representatives on to the executive committees, all guilds should inform their Helpers of the powers and responsibilities of local authorities, local authorities should help educate Guild Helpers, care should be taken with official cooperation until the Guild Helpers were experienced, and the proposed National Association should give guidance to the guilds.[43] Some of these suggestions were not implemented up to the First World War, except in the case of the larger guilds. Nevertheless, their role could be important.

THE RANGE OF MUNICIPAL AND LOCAL ACTIVITY

The larger guilds were clearly 'dove-tailed into civic administration' and closely linked with every aspect of local social welfare.[44] Health was one of the most pressing concerns. The Bolton Guild acted to tackle TB/consumption. It organized a TB Exhibition in 1911, inviting many representatives of local organizations.[45] The Reading Guild also organized a TB Exhibition which was visited by 15,264 people including 1,000 schoolchildren.[46] The Eagley and District Social Help Society constructed an outdoor shelter for the treatment of consumptives in the district to cater for those who could not immediately gain admission to sanatoria.[47] The Warrington Citizens' Guild, the Middlesbrough Guild and the Plymouth Guild were also all involved in the care of TB patients and sometimes helped to establish dispensaries.[48]

These actions had arisen partly as a result of the campaign mounted by the Agenda Club, an organization of men in all parts of the country, formed in February 1911, who realized that 'all is not well with England'.[49] Organized by E.V.D. Birchall, of Birmingham, who became honorary secretary of the National Association of the Guilds of Help, it began to see itself as the English Samurai, invited Japanese officials to its first annual meeting and proclaimed respect for 'these Samurai, careless of material gain' and reflected that 'This civic heroism, so much less common then, as experience proves, than the high ardours of military heroism is, we take it, the point which the Agenda Club wishes to symbolise.'[50] It was this body which appealed for guilds and other charity organizations to focus on health by holding a week in the year – 28 April–4 May – as a week when public health measures could be raised throughout the country. This idea was taken up by ten London boroughs and thirty provincial towns. In many cases, as in Bolton, the Guild of Help was involved.

Infant mortality, as already indicated, was also of prime concern to the guilds. An infant mortality campaign was led by the Bolton Guild and also by the Harrogate Citizens' Guild of Help.[51] It led to many offshoot campaigns, one of which was the 'No dummies admitted' campaign connected with the need for infant hygiene.[52] The Bolton Guild, as well as advising against the use of dummies, also suggested the need for fresh air and a proper diet for children.

The guilds built up important links with the health departments of local authorities, and particularly with the work of the lady health visitors. Indeed, cooperation with the municipal health visitors was seen as almost the pivot of the Guild's health work in Bradford:

If all the homes in Bradford were clean and wholesome, poverty would be robbed of half its misery; if all mothers were instructed in the care of their babes, disease and deformity would be reduced considerably even without a great economic change in conditions. During the past year more Helpers have received instruction from the Health Department. . . . Increased cooperation with this department will be possible only when Guild workers are more accustomed to their work, and realise how much may be done in that direction.[53]

The Middlesbrough Guild also instituted a voluntary health visiting scheme, based upon the ladies of the Guild.[54] Unlike any other guild, it also began work with the mentally deficient.[55]

The effectiveness of the Guild in dealing with health work in the community is open to debate. The decline in infant mortality might well have something to do with Guild activities in some areas, as might be some of the improvements in the TB death rates. Nevertheless, even the largest guilds did not have the resources to deal with any large number of cases in which local authorities might request their help. In Bradford, for instance, the Health Department passed on a list of 200 infants needing supervision but

Added to unusually heavy demands in other directions, this proved to be a task too heavy for our strength, and many of the cases could not be allotted. Although more good work has been done in this direction than perhaps has been recognised, it is evident that we must be content with a more modest beginning, say one of two wards in the city. Many workers are prepared to work hard and patiently, but they are not prepared for the demands made upon them in undertaking the work under the present conditions.[56]

The guilds also became deeply involved in working with young offenders and developing a probation system. In 1896 a Special Government Committee enquired into young offenders and concluded that they were not irredeemable and could be made into good citizens. Further enquiries noted that up to 18,000 prisoners between the ages of 16 and 21 were convicted, representing an enormous tax burden. In 1902, therefore, practical efforts were made at Borstal prison to prevent youths graduating to a life of crime. As a result Borstal Committees were set up throughout the country and in 1906 special rules were issued to separately classify juvenile offenders, who were now for the first time instructed in various trades. Moreover, a special appeal was made by the Secretary of State to the various local committees for a more definite and individual treatment for juvenile criminals on release. Largely owing to these efforts the number of convicted prisoners aged 16 to 21 fell from 16,000 in 1906 to 12,000 in 1909, revealing that unemployment was a cause of crime and that local efforts could do much to reduce criminality in this group.[57] Although the Borstal regime operated at various gaols was little to do with the Guild of Help the probation arrangements assumed by some guilds did play their part in rehabilitation. Indeed, Alexander Paterson stated that

> When we add together all the demands the State makes upon us to provide Probation Officers, to provide supervisors for children returning from certified schools, to look for boys coming from Borstal institutions, men coming from local prisons, men coming from convict prisons, we find that there are more people being dealt with in a reformative way outside the prison walls at the present time than there are being dealt with inside the prison walls.[58]

Shortly afterwards, addressing the Annual Meeting of the Bolton Guild, and speaking on behalf of the Prison Commissioners, he thanked the Guild for the help given to those discharged under the Borstal system.[59] The result was the more humane treatment of prisoners and help in getting the young ex-offenders back to work.

There was widespread support for a probation system within the Guild movement. A.W. Whitley of Halifax 'strongly advocated Guilds taking over the care of the lighter cases from the Probation Officer . . .' and the Mayor of Poole suggested that 'the new Probation Officers should be chosen from among the League Helpers'.[60]

Education was another area in which the Guild became largely involved. In the first year of its existence, the Bradford Guild proved to be a useful substitute for municipal action in education and, with the Cinderella Club, investigated the circumstances of 1,350 parents who required school meals for children, paid for out of the Lord Mayor's Fund and the funds of the Cinderella Club. Visiting was done by the 'Mayor down to the maidservant'.[61] Similar activity occurred with the Halifax Guild which offered to bear the cost of feeding necessitous schoolchildren during the Christmas holidays of 1908/9 and eventually spent £30 on feeding 300 of them.[62]

This link continued throughout the lives of the major guilds. For instance, the Bradford Guild cooperated with the city council in implementing the Education (Provision of Meals) Act of December 1906. This act allowed local authorities, of which Bradford was the first, to undertake school feeding, and encouraged the formation of a new type of cooperative venture between the guilds and the city council, whereby the School Feeding Committee regularly referred the children of poor families to the Guild. It is therefore not surprising that S.P. Grundy should reflect, in 1911, that 'His enquiry . . . showed that 40 Guilds were, in varied directions, acting in concert with Health Departments and Education Committees, most frequently by inter-representation.'[63]

All these were worthwhile activities and helped to alleviate poverty, but what the guilds were unable to do was to tackle the massive problem of unemployment that underlay much poverty. The Guild of Help, insofar as it tackled poverty, attempted to do so by minimizing its impact. In most guilds unemployment was the dominant cause of poverty, being responsible for almost half the cases in many guilds between 1905 and 1910. When all forms of unemployment are considered, the Halifax Guild was faced with 50 per cent being caused by unemployment between 1909 and 1912.[64] In order to deal with this problem the Halifax Guild worked closely with the public authorities in using the Unemployed Workmen's Act of 1905, which enabled the formation of 'Distress Committees' as part of the coming together of the Poor Law, the municipality and charity in dealing with unemployment. The Distress Committee could find work for the unemployed, funding it partly through the rates and partly through voluntary contributions. Yet such efforts proved futile. In his evidence to the Poor Law Commission, W.H. Beveridge considered the Act to be the final effort to deal with unemployment by means of temporary relief. He also concluded that local relief work 'generally degrades the name of the work and disregards the principle of relief'.[65] The experience of Halifax proves the point.

In the winter of 1908 the Halifax Guild agreed to administer the funds of the 'Distress Committee'. The Guild cooperated wholeheartedly: 'Last winter the Guild undertook to distribute the funds subscribed by the town . . . we threw our own funds into the extended work . . . relaxing our own system, we judged cases more by the measure of mere distress and less on preventive and curative principles.'[66] Yet there were many problems and the Guild recognized that the 'Distress Committee is labouring under considerable disadvantage and has considerable difficulties'.[67] The Halifax Guild was clearly concerned about many aspects of the mechanics of cooperation.

The concern of the Halifax Guild was heightened by the fact that there had been high levels of unemployment in the winter of 1908/9 which had provoked hunger marchers to approach the Guild and enquire why it was 'not relieving single men in lodging houses'.[68] The leading figures in the Halifax Guild appeared to be shocked by the potential for protest that unemployment provided and concerned that both the respectable and the not-so-respectable working classes were involved. It is therefore not surprising that they should reflect that:

We have no desire to see any more processions of so called 'Hunger marchers' in our times. We state with knowledge that a good proportion of the 'Marchers' were men of poor calibre; but at the same time we know that a proportion were good men thrown out of work through no fault of their own. We cannot but feel the disgrace of such processions of out-of-works in this well-to-do Borough.[69]

The Distress Committee and the mayor's action worked haltingly but the Guild hoped that the new Labour Exchange, opened in 1910 under the superintendence of Harry Smith from Bradford (ex-Guild member and a prominent member of the Independent Labour Party), would resolve the problem. It was stated that 'All Guild workers rejoice at the establishment of the Halifax Labour Exchange' and were encouraged to 'inform "out of work cases" to the Halifax Labour Exchange and get them to register'.[70] In 1911 there was also a debate between the Guild and the Juvenile Advisory Committee of the Board of Trade Labour Exchange. J.H. Howarth, the chairman of the Guild, summed up the issues: 'There is an Act of Parliament. There is a Board of Trade Advisory Committee. Somebody must do the work required. . . . Ought we to manage this work, can we, will we?'[71] When he put the question to a Guild meeting 'A large majority voted in the affirmative and the meeting discussed 'whether the work . . . should be taken up by the Guild as a body, or should Guild Helpers as individuals offer their services'.[72]

In effect, the Halifax Guild recognized that unemployment was the pressing problem, was frustrated at the ineffectiveness of local organizations to deal with it and hoped that its greater involvement would make some measurable impact. Yet it was the revival in trade immediately before the First World War, rather than the actions of the Halifax Guild, that reduced the problem of unemployment. Many other guilds also recognized the strain that unemployment placed on their resources but were unable to make more than a limited response.

THE VOLUNTARY WORKER: AMATEUR VERSUS PROFESSIONAL

Such local effort, of course, placed an enormous burden on the participation of the voluntary Helpers, who were amateurs in social work. There were many in the Guild movement who feared that social work might be left in the hands of a massive army of ill-informed amateurs while others felt that experience should be the basis of the work of the Guild. This disagreement, which was widespread, is best reflected in the conflict between H.B. Saint, of the Newcastle Guild, and J.H. Heighten, of Bradford and, later, Croydon guilds.

In 1911, Saint argued that the Helper was the crux of the Guild movement, that anyone should be prepared to act as the citizen Helper, and that 'Emphasis must be laid upon the equipment it furnishes for good citizenship and for the wider service of the nation'. Indeed, he argued that no MP, Guardian or City Councillor was 'fit for his duty unless he had served some time with the poor through the Guild of Help or some similar organization.'[73] While he felt that Helpers should be made aware of the aims of the Guild and that some committee meetings might be attended, he argued that experience was the best possible training and that the Helper 'will learn most by doing the work himself'.

Saint's views did not go unchallenged. J.H. Heighton, in his paper to the National Conference at Croydon in 1912, was concerned that many men and women Helpers 'soon found their lack of experience a serious handicap in dealing with the varied cases' and called for more guidance for them in the form of a handbook, lectures, the guidance of a more experienced Helper and a variety of other techniques.[74] In other words, he wanted more on-the-spot expert guidance than Saint demanded. A similar view had already been expressed by W. Milledge, Secretary of the Bradford Guild, at the First National Conference, held at Bradford in 1908, where he argued that the Central Office of a guild should be properly staffed and have at least one paid worker.[75] He also constantly emphasized the role of the professional, identifying the 'enlarging body of experts relentlessly exposing the material as well as moral needs of the city'.[76]

The reality was that most guilds were small and could not afford professional advice. They relied on their local volunteers who, by and large, were almost entirely drawn from the middle classes, and particularly dominated by the wives and the daughters of the local middle class.[77] Despite the suggestion of G.R. Snowden that 'The helpers are drawn from all classes of society; in a few societies half or more than half are men and women of the working classes', and the supportive statements of other writers, there seems to be little evidence of a significant working-class presence within the Guild of Help.[78] There appears to have been one guild, the small Farnworth Guild, near Bolton, with a significant working-class presence of about 50 per cent among its members.[79] It is not the purpose of this chapter to examine the origins of the membership of the Guild of Help. Nevertheless, it is worth noting that while the movement emphasized its all-embracing community nature this appears to have been a myth.

Returning to the theme of amateur versus professional, only a small number of larger guilds seem to have been able to afford to pay for professional guidance. The Bradford Guild employed W. Milledge, who had some social work experience, at £200 per year, in 1904.[80] On 11 February 1907, Miss B.D. Newcomb, 'a lady of experience in social work and professionally some training under the London Charity Organisation Society, was appointed as Assistant Organizing Secretary'.[81] She had taken Mental and Moral Science at Newnham College, Cambridge, where she displayed an interest in social questions, and had spent a year at the University Settlement, Canning Town, in a poor district of West Ham. She had moved on to the Dundas Service Union and then become private secretary to Margaret Sewell, who had for many years been head of the Southwark Women's Settlement and leader of social work in London.

Other professionals of a similar ilk were also appointed by the Bradford Guild and other guilds. In Reading, the local presence of University College meant that social course work was encouraged through lecture courses, often organized by Dr A.L. Bowley, statistician and professor at both Reading University College and the London School of Economics.

CONCLUSION

The Guild of Help played a part in the development of municipal and local action at a time when the duties of local public bodies were being expanded greatly. It played a part in tackling the high infant mortality rates that existed, in dealing with tuberculosis, and in tackling the multitude of other problems such as school feeding, probation work, unemployment and the like. In some areas, particularly in Bolton and Bradford, local guilds made an impact and won the confidence and cooperation of the local authorities. Nevertheless, the undoubted achievements of some of the larger guilds must not give a false impression of the success of the Guild of Help as a whole. There were many factors which undermined the effectiveness of the guilds in their local communities.

First, only about one-fifth of local authorities and only about one-ninth of Guardians had guilds in their areas. Secondly, there was still some hesitancy by the professionals in local authorities towards the amateurs which was only being eroded gradually by 1914. This was not helped by the fact that, for a number of reasons, many guilds focused on the amateur involvement of the Helper as opposed to the appointment of professional expertise. Thirdly, though the guilds may have contributed to improvements in health in some areas, and they were certainly about the campaign for improvement, they had to recognize their inability to deal with the major cause of poverty – unemployment. In most guilds this was the major problem they faced in dealing with poverty. Fourthly, they did not unite all of the community into a philanthropic effort for there was a significant absence of working-class support. In the end, despite its sterling work, the Guild of Help exerted only a marginal influence on a small number of local communities in England. As the major voluntary force in England on the eve of the First World War, the Guild helped to transform and improve charity. But in the end its failings only confirmed the need for the state intervention that was developing rapidly. As a result, both charity in general and the Guild of Help in particular had to try to come to terms with the rising demands of the state and to forge the new relationship which the New Philanthropy envisaged. In the end, local initiative was not enough to tackle the economic and social problems faced by most local communities in the Edwardian years.

2

GUILDED HELP?

FIONA CUSHLOW

The early twentieth century was a time of rapid change in the development of British social policy. The main studies of this period concentrate on topics such as the changing nature of the role of the state and the reforms of the Liberal government. Voluntary effort is mainly associated with the nineteenth century. The changing nature of voluntary effort during the Edwardian period has largely been ignored and yet it represented an important change in middle-class attitudes towards the poor, the state and welfare. To ignore the developments in Edwardian philanthropy is to dismiss the work of the Guild of Help and miss out on an important insight into early twentieth-century middle-class attitudes towards the poor and social welfare.

In an attempt to understand where the Guild of Help fits into the debate on Edwardian social welfare, the historical perspectives on the period need to be examined. At least five different approaches to the development of Edwardian social welfare have been identified.[1] The first suggests that the developments in Edwardian social policy and the failure of charity are almost inevitable stages on the road to the welfare state.[2] The second interpretation doubts the sociological and socialist theory that charity is a form of social control. It is made clear that charity was not always good done by one class to another, and cites the growth of working-class charity including official subscriptions to charities, as well as unofficial charity such as helping out neighbours in times of need. This stresses that charity strengthened the family unit and could bring about social harmony. It disputes the social control agenda.[3] The third approach examines the tensions between collectivism and individualism, in particular the tension surrounding the self-help debate.[4] The fourth approach examines the tensions between New Liberalism and the Labour Party.[5] There is some confusion on this theme as it is not clear whether the New Liberals were reacting to the socialist societies such as the Independent Labour Party or to the Labour Party which was radical but not socialist.[6] The fifth approach focuses on the development of the professionalization of welfare and the emergence of the professional social worker.[7] This chapter will discuss where the Bradford City Guild of Help fits into the historical debate. It will be argued that the survey and close examination of the casebooks rejects the hypothesis put forward by Prochaska that charity was not a form of social control. It also rejects Prochaska's view that the working class played a large part in organized charity. In the case of the Bradford Guild of Help, there is little evidence to support Prochaska's view. The evidence which will be put forward will show that the Bradford City Guild of Help was primarily a middle-class Liberal organization which attempted, albeit unconsciously, to enforce their own middle-class position.

EMERGENCE OF THE BRADFORD CITY GUILD OF HELP

The City Guild of Help emerged in Bradford in 1904, loosely based on a system set up in the German town of Elberfeld. This was organized by the municipal government, where members of the community visited and assisted those in need.[8] The Elberfeld system was brought to the attention of the Bradford community from two main sources. The first was a report carried out by C.S. Loch for the Local Government Board in 1887 which rejected the introduction of the Elberfeld system in England: it could not be incorporated within the national Poor Law because it was a locally based municipal system.[9] The second and most important source was a book written by Julie Sutter entitled *Britain's Next Campaign*, which put the case for a system of district visiting and local initiative to cope with the problems of poverty.[10] 'The loving sacrifices of men and women in united organised action alone can solve the problem of the poor.'[11] This was a major influence on the founders of the Guild of Help in Bradford; however, Sutter later criticized the Guild of Help as she had wished the initiative to be municipal rather than voluntary. She regarded the Guild of Help as nothing more than another COS which would be bound to fail: 'What is this newly started Bradford Guild other than a Charity Organisation Society under a different name. Yet another name cannot produce new results.'[12]

The Guild of Help emerged at a time of social crisis within the middle class. The Edwardian era saw the growing realization that Britain no longer had the economic means to sustain a large empire indefinitely.[13] The Boer War had highlighted the problems at home. As a colonial war it cost far more and took much longer than those in power expected. A sizeable proportion of those men from the cities and towns who applied to join the army were turned down on the grounds of poor health, and thus attention was firmly focused on problems of poverty and deprivation in cities and towns. The fact that the enemy were from farming stock further highlighted the deficiencies of the urban working class. Concerns about poverty and the problems of the poor were also brought to the fore by Rowntree in his study of York, conducted in 1899 and published in 1901. This emphasized the poor condition of the working class in York and also painted a picture of the drabness of life on the breadline. He found that 28 per cent of the population of York lived in some degree of poverty.[14] York was not one of the major industrial towns and yet it still had high levels of poverty. If this was the case for York, then it was clear that an industrial town like Bradford would have far higher levels.

The predominant fear was that the British race was degenerating and that measures had to be taken in order to prevent this. It was clear that many initiatives would have to be taken in order to improve the condition of the poor in England. The existence of such widespread poverty raised difficult and profound questions concerning the economic and political emphasis at the time, and in particular the role of the state and its relationship to the individual came under close scrutiny.

Large-scale social welfare reforms were largely unpalatable to many of the Edwardian middle class as they were seen as unnecessary interference which would undermine traditional class structure and values. Those involved with the COS still believed that poverty was a temporary condition caused by moral failure rather than economic circumstances and that the existing system was basically sound.[15] However, by the turn of the century it was more widely acknowledged that poverty was more likely to be caused by economic circumstances than personal failing. Yet the Poor Law, based on the principle of less eligibility, was geared up to deal with destitution rather than poverty. It was virtually incapable of dealing with the poverty caused by a capitalist, imperialist, *laissez-faire* economy which had produced a class of low paid, insecure or unemployed workers. The Poor Law would provide indoor relief in the form of the workhouse and occasionally test work in times of extreme distress, but this barely scratched the surface of the problem. Many officials, including F.H. Bentham in Bradford, were opposed to outdoor relief as a matter of principle and would obstruct moves to allow it.

The beginning of the twentieth century saw the reassessment of the Poor Law, as it had become evident to many that change was needed. Conflict arose between the socialists, Liberal progressives, old Liberals and Conservatives, each holding their own varying opinions on the subject as to what change was needed. The Webbs, writers of the Minority Report of the Royal Commission on the Poor Laws (1905–9), wished to destroy the Poor Law and replace it with a fairer system which did not penalize the unemployed nor stigmatize those who claimed. It is, however, significant to note that the Webbs still identified a certain section of the population who were to blame for their own poverty. The Majority Report, signed by the chairman and fourteen members of the committee, was largely influenced by Helen Bosanquet, the representative of the COS. The signatories wanted much of the Poor Law to remain intact; charity was to be given a role as a barrier through which only the poor and not the destitute could pass. This report emphasized moral failing as a cause of poverty. Charity was still very important to the middle class as it had been in the Victorian era and yet there was a growing awareness that charity, as practised by the Victorians, could not cope with the problem of poverty. Unwilling to concede that the only real solution to poverty was the massive extension of state welfare, some members of the Bradford community sought to help the poor in a manner that would endorse traditional class distinctions. One solution presented itself in 1904 in the form of the Bradford City Guild of Help.

The Bradford City Guild of Help was publicly launched on 20 September 1904. Within a year of its foundation 500 helpers were enlisted and it was dealing with approximately 2,000 cases.[16] At the public meeting held to launch the Bradford Guild, speeches were given by Seebohm Rowntree and the Bishop of Ripon.[17] During the early stages of setting up the Guild those involved were careful to exclude religious leaders in an attempt to avoid sectarian conflicts, which had been a feature of Bradford charity before the creation of the Guild of Help.[18] Although excluded from the initial planning of the Guild, the clergy of various religious denominations were actively involved, either in providing funds for cases with a connection to their particular denomination, or in recommending cases to the Guild.

The objects of the Guild were set out clearly by Walter Milledge, the secretary, appointed to give an air of professionalism in 1909. He stated that it would:

Unite citizens of all classes, both men and women, irrespective of political or religious opinion, for the following objects. To deepen the sense of civic or collective responsibility for the care of the poor. To provide a friend for those in need of help. To secure timely aid for the suffering and needy and to bring about lasting improvement in the condition of each case by patient study and wise methods of help. To keep a general register of relief and to provide a centre of information for social workers, so that overlapping may be prevented and personal beneficence wisely directed. These objects are to be attained by the promotion of co-operation between voluntary workers and public officials, clergy and charitable agencies of the city.[19]

One of the main aims of the Bradford Guild was to put welfare on a more scientific footing. Before the creation of the Guild of Help Bradford charity was indiscriminate and sporadic.[20] The Guild aimed to coordinate philanthropic effort and encouraged cooperation between charities and the state in order to prevent indiscriminate alms-giving.

The name Guild of Help was chosen to avoid any connotations of religious or class bias and was to reflect the personal service nature of the Guild. The Bradford City Guild set out to provide a community-wide response to the problems of poverty and to bring together citizens of all classes to help the poor; it would 'unite all citizens in a collective effort to deal with the problem of poverty'.[21] Cahill and Jowitt point out that the Guild of Help in Bradford owes much to the civic consciousness movement of the time and cite the name of the Bradford Guild as proof of this: the Guild of Help in Bradford is always referred to in contemporary sources as the City Guild of Help.[22] Cahill and Jowitt feel that this cannot be due solely to Bradford's new status as a city. The Bradford City Guild of Help regarded itself as a civic consciousness movement and explained its feelings in its journal, Help: 'The Guild of Help is the practical expression of the civic consciousness and the end and the embodiment of the new philanthropy . . . the Guild worker does not go in as a visitant from another world but as a fellow creature to be helpful.'[23] The Guild was launched with its motto

'Not Alms but a Friend', which reflected the nature of the Guild in that it was to be a movement dedicated to personal service. 'Personal responsibility for the poor is a key note of the Guild and it is by the effort of single workers that really useful work has been and will be done.'[24]

The Bradford City Guild of Help placed a great deal of emphasis on local effort. It saw itself as operating within the local community and encouraging responsible citizenship. Although guilds developed all over the country they were still autonomous bodies holding an annual conference but retaining strong individual identities. Local effort was part of the central philosophy of the Bradford Guild as it encouraged a strong sense of responsibility for the poor among the local community. It gave the guilds a distinct identity. In a sense, the strengths that it had in keeping the movement on a local basis also added to its downfall. By staying as a local movement the Guild ensured that it would never be an alternative to large-scale state welfare measures and it became progressively subservient to the state following the welfare legislation of the Liberal government. Although they welcomed many measures, stating that they could now deal with the categories best suited to the charitable sphere, their territory had been encroached upon and the extension of state provision was under way.

THE GUILD AND THE WORKING CLASS

It is, perhaps, no coincidence that the Guild of Help emerged in Bradford, the home of the Independent Labour Party. Much evidence suggests that the local Liberals were reacting in part to the demands of the Bradford ILP. Poverty was a major issue for the ILP and they campaigned long and hard to raise awareness. Many socialists regarded charity as an anachronism and opposed charitable support for initiatives which they considered so important to the public that they should come under municipal control. There was much antagonism between the two organizations. A debate arose in the local press concerning the Guild's claim that it counted among its members a diverse range of political and religious opinions. In reply, Councillor E.R. Hartley wrote two letters referring to the Guild of Help as 'Guilded Help',[25] 'The Guild of Help was started and is managed by the very people who, refusing justice to the poor, abuse them with charity.'[26] The Bradford Liberals, H.B. Priestman and F.H. Bentham, both members of the City Guild of Help, and their followers, had obstructed and opposed the ILP on many measures. For instance, F.H. Bentham was a whole-hearted opponent of changing the system of poor relief in times of unemployment to one where outdoor relief was more flexible. The Bradford Liberals under H.B. Priestman failed to provide much help for the unemployed able-bodied other than test work which was clearly not practical during a major trade depression, and were much criticized by the ILP for this. Yet it was clear that the Liberals could not continue to respond in a wholly negative way to ILP demands because humanitarian opinion would opt for the ILP solutions.[27] The ILP was hostile to the Guild of Help and actively discouraged its members from joining. This seems to have worked.

In her book on the National Council of Social Services, Margaret Brasnett states that:

> Indeed, this meeting [forming the Bradford Guild] must be regarded as a turning point in the history of social service, for it marked the end of the old order that rested on the implicit assumption that social service was good done by a favoured class to those less fortunate. Here was the first successful attempt on a large scale to enlist the support of every section and class of the community in a common endeavour to tackle the problem of poverty.[28]

She argues that the Guild of Help fulfilled its aim of enlisting members from all walks of life. She has been backed up to some extent by Michael J. Moore who, although he exhibits more caution than Brasnett, comments that, 'Guilds advocated the involvement of those more fortunate to relieve the distress of the poor. Solidly based in the middle class, their appeals, however, reached well into the ranks of the working class.' Moore does acknowledge that the Guild was viewed with suspicion by many members of the working class.[29] Most members of the Independent Labour Party viewed it with at best apathy, and at worst outright hatred. There has been little evidence found in the survey to back up the view of Brasnett. In Bradford there were three well-known members of the ILP who were also members of the Guild of Help. These were A.T. Priestman, a middle-class socialist and cousin of H.B. Priestman, Harry Smith who was district head of the C2 division and G.T. Meggison who was head of Bowling Back Lane for a time. All three had left the Guild by 1909, Smith leaving in

1908 probably due to the conflict on the creation of a general relief fund. There was no significant working-class presence in the Bradford City Guild of Help.

THE HELPERS

'In learning to give help which shall be of permanent value, the next great principle of the Guild has been rediscovered, i.e. the necessity of knowing the circumstances, or as we call it investigation.'[30] The Guild wished to create a professional welfare organization which investigated the circumstances of the applicants fully before attempting to relieve distress. Those who actually carried out the visiting and the casework were the Helpers, the backbone of the Guild's organization:

> Helpers shall be elected by the District Committees. They shall endeavour to become the personal friends of those whom they visit. . . . They shall ascertain the circumstances, difficulties and the needs of each case, fill in the particulars in the case-book and consult the District head as to the means to be used to secure permanent benefit. . . . Helpers shall not have more than four cases at one time but they should visit these at least once a week.[31]

As a Helper was expected to spend a great deal of time working for the Guild, this tended to preclude certain groups from taking an active part. A record of each case was to be kept and written up after every visit, and district meetings would be attended every week. This illustrates that the life of a Helper was very full and busy. It is likely that working-class men or women would not have had the time to take on the life of a Helper. Those members of the working class who would, perhaps, have been able to spare the time would have been the wives and daughters of the highest paid working-class men. Whether or not these women would have got involved with the Guild of Help is debatable. Many members of the highest paid working class would also have been members of a trade union, and as such would probably have been influenced to join the ILP which had reservations about the Guild of Help.

It was the Liberal elite of Bradford society who made up the members of the Guild, or more precisely their wives and daughters. Women dominated the lower echelons of the Guild, although some, such as Florence Moser, were founders. The composition of the

Bradford City Guild of Help was set out in the *Help* journal in March 1906. The four division heads in Bradford were men. Of the other forty districts seven were unorganized and two had not decided on a district head. Of the remaining thirty-one, thirty had men and one had a woman as its head: this was Miss M. Wade, the daughter of David Wade, the former Lord Mayor of Bradford. Of the Helpers, there were 152 men and 222 women, of whom half were single women.[32] They included many of the daughters of the Liberal elite such as Miss Lister, daughter of a leading industrialist.[33]

The Guild of Help gave many women their first experience of political matters, and produced an interest for some in the suffrage movement. In Bradford, Mrs Moser, one of the founders of the Guild, was also the driving force behind the Bradford women's suffrage movement. The Guild represented a gateway for middle-class women to become involved in social work. Jane Lewis points out that social work was a natural extension of the middle-class domestic world and was accessible through their local community.[34] It is ironic that the increase in state welfare following the First World War undermined the position of women when it removed the emphasis from voluntary action and placed it on the state.[35]

There was often a problem between the Helpers and those whom the Guild wished to help. In order to ascertain the circumstances of the case, a case had to be fully investigated, including checking on what an applicant had said. This caused mistrust between the parties. The Helper often found out that an applicant had not told the truth and therefore they distrusted other cases on the basis of their experience. Those in need of help felt that their lives were invaded, their word distrusted and their circumstances investigated. And yet the Guild of Help had set out to avoid this problem. Guidelines had been circulated in order to give advice on the best way to approach the applicant and alleviate distress. It was suggested that the Helper behaved confidently and did not take a superior or patronizing attitude towards the applicant:

> The practised helper, confident in his purpose, will simply say 'I have heard so and so, may I come in and speak to you?' The assumption that this is the most natural thing in the world begets a similar confidence and it will be generally found that by taking for granted the belief in the goodwill of the visit, even delicate questions may be discussed without a sense of trespassing.[36]

The guide suggested that the Helpers should try and put themselves in the position of the applicant in order to ascertain how they would react in the same circumstances. It also suggested that the Helper should try to put the applicant at ease. Methods suggested by the Guild were different for men and women. If the Helper was male, Milledge suggests that he should make jokes with the applicant and if he smokes, the Helper should ask permission before doing so. If the Helper was a woman, Milledge suggests that she should compare her children with those involved in the case.[37] It seems unlikely that the advice would have worked as it does not appear too tactful to tell jokes to a person when you are about to ask very personal questions. Milledge pointed out that 'it is the assumption of equality and friendliness that is so essential to success',[38] and yet the casebooks provide many examples of exactly the opposite attitude. A superior or distrustful position was often assumed. In one instance, the first comment of the Helper is that the case is 'undeserving',[39] while in another the Helper is unwilling to give advice at first because the woman is rude, but she relents when the woman expresses gratitude.[40] Many other cases show similar attitudes.

The Helpers were given advice on the best methods of giving help. The handbook set out three points on how to do this. The first states that help should be given in a way that would not stop the applicant from being self-dependent and that help should not injure the self-respect of the case.[41] The Guild did not want applicants to expect hand-outs, it was not a relief society and had no general relief fund. Many cases were given up by the Guild when it was found that they were unable to be self-dependent or would be referred to another organization. The second point states that the kind of help that was to be given should remove the temptation to beg or to seek help from any other agency.[42] What was offered by the Guild was to be comprehensive, to avoid the need for the applicant to go elsewhere to look for help. This suggests that the Helpers were allowed a certain amount of leeway in order to deal with each applicant. The third point states that 'material help shall be given in such forms as will be least likely to sap the self-dependence of the recipients'.[43] This included free school meals for children or material for clothes. The handbook does not say that the Helpers were forbidden to give money but it did encourage other forms of assistance and the casebooks are littered with references to small amounts of money or food being given for the applicant. It is clear that the Guild wanted its cases to practise self-help; it wished to change the behaviour of those who sought its assistance.

The Helpers attempted to enforce their own middle-class values on the working-class applicants, although most were probably not aware of this. The advice given to the Helpers by Milledge clearly shows that the Guild of Help wanted to bring about habits of thrift and self-help. The kind of help that was offered was designed to produce such habits. This was a central pillar of the Guild and those who did not show willingness or were unable to practise it often had their cases closed by the Guild. For instance, there is one case which started with a problem of old age and ended as an infant welfare case. The daughter of the applicant had an illegitimate daughter and although there was no outright condemnation by the Helper, Helen Lister, the case was dropped because it became clear that the case was not only unable to practise self-help but was also unwilling to try.[44]

The Guild placed great emphasis on moral as well as physical help. The *Bradford City Guild of Help Handbook* published in 1911 gave guidelines on how to provide moral help. The Guild emphasized that moral failing should be treated in the same way as physical or economic failing: 'The man loses his work because trade is bad, but also because he is a slack workman and is therefore the first to be discharged. The woman's home is in a deplorable state because there is not enough money coming in but also because she is thriftless.' It is clear from the casebooks that moral judgements were made almost every time an applicant was assessed. One of the first comments that appeared in a great many casebooks was whether or not the woman or the house was dirty. If either was, then they would generally be regarded with distrust. The above quotation is rather significant because it shows that the Guild regarded the house as the woman's responsibility. In the casebooks, the man was regarded as the main applicant but the Helper addressed most questions to the woman.

Although applicants were not always openly condemned for their mistakes, they were noted all the same and viewed with suspicion, and as such, Helpers were very rarely able to go into a person's house without a patronizing or superior attitude. However, many Helpers were very genuine in their desire to alleviate the problems caused by poverty and were sympathetic individuals who did try to put themselves in the position of the applicant. There were limitations on what could be achieved. For instance, a large family came to the attention of the Guild. Strong evidence of domestic violence was uncovered. The woman, who was the main applicant, was addressed in the records with a great deal of sympathy. However, when they address her husband they plead with him to change. They do not encourage the woman to take any action against him. There is no suggestion that domestic violence was in any way acceptable but they stress the moral reformation of the husband rather than giving practical help or advice to the woman.[45]

The recipients of the attentions of the Guild, aware of investigation and moral scrutiny, were often disinclined to be grateful. Many families perceived the proposed help as unwarranted interference, an attitude which puzzled many of the Helpers. The Guild of Help expected the applicants to respond with gratitude and were surprised when this was not the case. To view the system of visiting from the point of view of the working-class would-be recipients it is clear that many would have resented the intrusion into their homes. There is very little evidence of Helpers being asked to leave by the applicant. There is evidence which suggests that the applicant would protest with a campaign of non-cooperation. The tactics used included being out when the Helper was due to call or choosing not to open the door. Other methods included offering no, or no truthful, information about themselves in order to obstruct the work of the Helper. It may appear strange that those who were in poverty were unwilling to cooperate with the organization trying to help them but it must be remembered that many of those whom the Guild dealt with had been referred from other agencies. An applicant for free school meals or free milk may not have welcomed a visitor from the Guild knocking on the door every week.

SURVEY OF CASEBOOKS

A survey of 250 of the surviving casebooks of the Bradford City Guild of Help has been carried out. A random sample method was used, taking one in every twenty casebooks for examination. The results of this survey have been collated. This enables us to explore the work of the Helpers and the lives of the recipients.

The majority of cases, over 70 per cent of those taken on by the Guild, were married couples. There are several possible explanations for this. The first is that married couples, especially those with children, were more likely to be in poverty. Or perhaps it could suggest that married couples were seen as more deserving and more likely to have their cases taken up by the Guild. More married couples were referred to the Guild by people or organizations, concerned that they were in poverty; they would rather not resort to the Poor Law and separate the family. A further factor could be that married couples (particularly those with children) had to stretch their income further than single people, thus making poverty more likely.

The great majority of cases involved between one and three children. It is highly likely that the majority of these married couples were those with young children. As most children earned nothing it suggests that most of the children involved with the Guild of Help were not old enough to work, which further emphasizes that most of the families who needed help from the City Guild were families with young children. Of those children who were earning, most earned between six shillings and fifteen shillings, a relatively small amount. Families with a new baby would sometimes come under the care of the Guild. In certain areas, the women sanitary inspectors organized a scheme of visiting to help combat infant mortality. The Guild provided the Helpers to carry out the visiting and, although this scheme started in one ward, it spread to others.

Laybourn has suggested that the Guild was not interested in the destitute, and this has been borne out by this study.[46] The income of a family is an important measure of family circumstances and can be a somewhat deceptive one. It refers to the amount recorded the week the case commenced. This survey clearly shows that 41 per cent of cases had an income of under ten shillings when first referred. At first glance this might suggest that the Guild was helping those who were almost destitute. Yet this was not the case. The Guild wished to engender a culture of self-help. The approximate income at the start of a case was to some extent not a matter of great importance; what was paramount was the potential of the case to be self-supporting. In each casebook there is much evidence of income fluctuations throughout the duration. An applicant may have only had ten shillings during the first week of investigation, but the following week it was quite possible that an income of twenty shillings or more may have been attained. This was particularly true of those who were in poverty caused by casual work or illness. With casual work, wages were unpredictable and with illness or injury, recovery could be just around the corner. Because of this, the measure of income at the start of the case is not an accurate reflection of the status of the case. Those who were genuinely destitute were usually not the married couples who made up the majority of the cases of the City Guild of Help but the widows and the elderly, whose inability to practise self-help left them in a precarious position. It is clear that many of the cases were referred to the Guild when circumstances were at their worst for the applicant, and improvement in the situation of the case often happened week by week. The hypothesis that the Guild was not dealing with the worst cases of poverty is further emphasized by the fact that some of the poorest districts, for instance Bowling Back Lane, remained largely unorganized during the period and consistently found it difficult to attract Helpers.

Widows and the elderly were more likely to have a lower income than other groups and were also less able to practise self-help. Forty-three of the cases in the sample were widows and of these cases seventeen had an income of below ten shillings per week and ten had an income of between eleven and fifteen shillings per week. Widows (and widowers) needed to work in order to support themselves and their families. The work available to women in this situation was usually low paid and low skilled, such as washing or cleaning. Those who found work in the textile mills were usually better off financially as they were paid more than those occupied with washing, but they were paid less than men in the same jobs and the work was full-time and usually casual; therefore child care had to be paid for long hours and there was little job security. These were perhaps the most vulnerable of the cases of the Guild. A widow with children would also have to pay for child care, a further disadvantage, unless home work could be found. These were usually the worst paid jobs.

One causal or additional factor in poverty was described by the Guild as vice. This referred to a wide range of behaviours including drink, gambling or debt. There is little hard evidence to ascertain the amount of poverty dealt with by the Guild that was caused by drink. *Help*, the journal of the Bradford Guild of Help, asserted that vice only accounted for 15 per cent of cases.[47] One area where it is easier to gain details concerning vice is on the question of debt. Most cases had no debt at all and yet some had massive debts, up to £20 or £30. In cases of large debt the City Guild was unable to help the case. Those whose debt added to their poverty were regarded by the Guild as being in poverty due to vice and as such were classed as undeserving.

One of the peculiar features of the Guild of Help was that it continued to visit many cases long after they became able to support themselves financially. The founders' vision of the Guild was of a society of friends, providing advice and assistance for those in need.

The Helpers continued to visit many cases, even just once or twice a year to let them know that if they needed any assistance then the Guild was still there. Many cases dragged on for years. In certain circumstances a case might be closed only to open years later, even up to 20 or 30 years later. It would be inaccurate to record these cases as being helped by the Guild for many years, as in most cases there are no visits in the intervening years. The latest recorded case ends in 1942.[48] The average period of help was almost 5 years, giving support to the view that the Guild of Help continued to visit long after people became self-supporting. The minimum period of help was one month and this was in a case where the applicant would not accept any help at all and the case was immediately closed.

It has been of great importance to investigate the spread of cases throughout Bradford in order to examine whether the Guild was working within the poorest communities. Bradford was loosely divided into four districts based on those used by the Poor Law; these are referred to by the letters A, B, C and D. The divisions were then subdivided into districts, which are referred to by numbers. From the table it is easy to see that the cases were spread throughout Bradford. The largest number of cases recorded in this survey were in the White Abbey district. This area was divided into three separate districts, B1, 2, 3. In total twenty-one of the two hundred and fifty cases came from White Abbey. Girlington (B7) had eighteen cases and Manningham (B4) had eleven. What is perhaps surprising is that there were not more cases recorded for these areas, particularly White Abbey, which was a very poor district. It is also significant that Bowling Back Lane, another very poor district, had very few cases. The Guild found it very difficult to recruit and keep Helpers for these districts. *Help* is littered with appeals for Helpers in these poor districts. When volunteers were found for these areas they discovered that the problems of poverty and unemployment were so vast that little could be done.

CONCLUSIONS

The creation of the Guild of Help in Bradford was a final heroic attempt to make philanthropy more effective and sympathetic than it had been during the nineteenth century.[49] The Guild wanted to provide the poor with a friend in order to help with their distress.

The Guild was a moralistic society which wished to inculcate a response of gratitude in the recipients of help. It did not challenge the existing political and economic structure of capitalism and thus sought no solution to poverty, merely its relief. Unlike the ILP, they had a vested interest in preserving the status quo. The Bradford City Guild of Help was primarily a Liberal organization, mostly progressive rather than new. It was willing to accept small-scale social change in order to bolster its own position and remove the threat of socialism. The members of the Guild believed that poverty and all its incumbent problems could be solved without recourse to major social change. The Guild recognized that the poverty of the early twentieth century could not continue unchecked and it was feared that if nothing was done to ease it then the more radical solutions offered by the socialists would be advocated.[50]

The Bradford Guild expected gratitude and deference from those it helped. It offered moral help to its cases. It was intent on imposing the middle-class views of its own Helpers on the working class and had little or no regard for the moral standards of the working class themselves. The Helpers often condemned the moral character of those whom they were trying to help for reasons such as maintaining a dirty house; they often adopted a patronizing and condescending attitude to their cases and could be indifferent to their plight. The Guild distrusted those they were supposed to help. Rather than being a friend to the poor, the Helpers were often no more than an unwelcome interference to be avoided. The Guild thus failed to be a truly civic organization.

This is not to say that nothing positive came out of the Bradford City Guild of Help. It provided an opening for women in professional social work. The experiences many women had within the Guild politicized many of them, and some took their experience to the campaign for the vote. The Guild of Help allowed women a participatory role in society and it seems ironic that this role was taken from them as the influence of the state increased. Finally, the Guild provided a half-way house between state and charity and made state welfare more palatable to many members of the middle class.

'THE TERRIBLE SCOURGE OF CONSUMPTION IS AMONGST US'[1]:

THE GUILD OF HELP, VOLUNTARISM AND THE
PROBLEM OF TUBERCULOSIS IN EDWARDIAN
BOLTON

STUART ROBERTSON

INTRODUCTION

The framework of analysis for this chapter centres on the relationship between the public and private sectors, and the degree of
cooperation that existed between the 'official' (Medical Officer of
Health) and the 'voluntary' in terms of initiatives to combat
tuberculosis (TB) among Bolton's poor. I will argue that the locality
and voluntarism until at least 1914 played an important role in the
provision of health care initiatives, as the example of the Bolton Guild
of Help and its efforts to combat tuberculosis among the town's
poorest citizens illustrates.

In Bolton the Medical Officer of Health (MOH) between 1905 and
1914 was content to transfer a large proportion of the town's formal
effort to combat the disease on to the shoulders of the Guild of Help
and private wealthy benefactors. The Guild became an important
source of social education and measures of prevention which it
transmitted to the poor by way of home visiting. The MOH compared
the work of the Guild to that of Health Associations in other towns
and by interesting itself in such work it was, he noted, 'trying to solve
one of the most serious, if not the most serious problem of modern

life'.[2] He was happy to support the efforts of the Guild to 'rouse' the opinion of the general public on such an important health matter as TB because, he argued, the town council could not hope to undertake progressive sanitary initiatives unless Bolton's sanitary conscience was stirred. This was to be the task of the Guild. The objective of the partnership between the Guild and the MOH had to be to ensure that the 'Englishman's home', besides being his castle, became his sanatorium.[3] The Guild's role as a provider of information was further strengthened by its organization of 'health-weeks' and a TB Exhibition. These educational initiatives were further complemented by 'gifts' from its members in terms of open-air shelters and fresh-air schemes. In a more recognizable philanthropic manner members of Bolton's traditional ruling elite provided the funds necessary to give the town its own sanatorium where the MOH and the Guild of Help had access to its beds and could refer patients.

The chapter will be written from the perspective of the Bolton Guild of Help and the support which it gave to social education, sanatorium and open-air treatment, and dispensaries as solutions to tuberculosis. Between the expert medical opinion in Bolton and the voluntary enthusiasts of the Guild of Help there was a strong and broad consensus as to the best means of combating TB. This was based on five complementary solutions: compulsory notification, sanatorium treatment (including open-air shelters and fresh-air schemes) for curable cases, the improvement of housing conditions, a home for advanced cases, and the teaching of personal hygiene. Significantly the Guild's support for compulsory notification was part of a wider desire to see the powers of the MOH expanded, which in many ways was akin to the ideas of Fabianism and its support for the 'rational expert'.

For example the Guild was concerned to see legislation that would empower the MOH to be able to certify consumptives and have them removed compulsorily if necessary from their homes to an institution. As the Guild noted in its *Annual Report* for 1909–10, 'consistently and continually the workers in the Guild are being brought face to face with the results of this terrible disease'.[4] One function of the Helpers was to persuade a family with a consumptive member to make an application to the Sanitary Authorities for their home to be disinfected. The Guild believed that this measure should be taken further in the interest of public health with the compulsory disinfection of houses, and supported this position by citing the following example:

In a very small house in a poor quarter of the town, there resides a labouring man with his wife and family. For some time the wife has been practically dying of consumption, and at a [sic] time of writing this report, she is daily expecting confinement and her only attendant on whom she can depend is her daughter. Every effort has been made to induce the women to leave the house, but without avail, and but for the fact that the Guild, besides being the means of providing what is necessary in the way of nourishment, will also urge disinfection at the first opportunity, probably the latter would not take place and greater evil might result.[5]

The Bolton Guild of Help was part of a wider movement of organized voluntary social service movements that developed in Edwardian Britain.[6] The guilds represent a community-based response to the Edwardian social problem, at a time of widespread concern for all aspects of the national efficiency debate. The health of the nation, infant mortality, diseases of poverty, particularly tuberculosis, and the consequences of high rates of unemployment dominated the agenda of the movement. The Guild of Help was concerned with social, medical and economic factors which affected the well-being of the poorest members of the locality. Unlike the older Charity Organisation Society, the archetype of Victorian rational individualistic philanthropy, the guilds were concerned to reconstruct the partnership between the voluntary sector and the state at the national level, and between 'official' providers of welfare and voluntary organizations in the locality. In contrast to the COS the Guild sought to develop a cross-class community-wide solution to poverty and health problems. They sought to emphasize their civic credentials by stressing that 'they were there to serve everyone'.[7] Thus the intention of the Bolton Guild of Help was to 'dovetail' itself and its campaigns to fit the profile of civic administration in Bolton, in other words to be connected with every aspect of local welfare provision, so that it had a role to play in delivering health initiatives and the relief of poverty, that it worked closely with the Poor Law Guardians, and was involved in social and Borstal work. With these objectives in mind, the Guild set about meeting the challenges of TB and fulfilling the clarion call of the MOH:

. . . in order to bring success to the efforts which are now being made to prevent the spread of this disease, it will be an advantage for the educationist, the philanthropist, and the State to work in

47

harmonious co-operation, so that adequate assistance, as well as proper advice, may be given to those who are unable to help themselves.[8]

MEDICAL INNOVATIONS

From the 1870s onwards there was a shift in elite medicine towards a new form of scientific authority, namely germ theory. The earlier elite had been based in the dissecting room, in the clinic or the statistical survey; at the end of the century it increasingly became supplemented and replaced by the 'authority of the laboratory'. According to Lawrence, the bacteriological laboratory became one of the most significant statements made by the medical profession of its legitimate role in explaining and controlling epidemic disease.[9] The germ theory of specific infective conditions developed principally in Germany in the 1870s and '80s, and was quite unlike Lister's early germ theory which was based on putrefactive theories of public health. Its adoption in the last two decades of the nineteenth century is significant for a number of reasons. Germ theory was, compared to previous new theories, relatively uncontested which produced in itself an important focus of consensus within medicine; compared, for example, with the ideological battles that were fought over theorizing about epidemic disease in the 1840s.

The new germ theory proposed that biological agents, bacteria, were the cause of specific febrile diseases. The significance for this research lies in the consequences its acceptance had on the role and eminence accorded to the medical profession in late Victorian and Edwardian society. At the bedside and in the arena of public health, germ theory was developed and employed in such a way as to reinforce the trend of medicine becoming increasingly prominent in the political decision-making process and thus ever-increasingly an influence on the lives of ordinary people. The process was set in motion by Sir John Simon's department, with the medical profession becoming more influential in the politics of poverty. Concern was shifted from whole-scale reform of the kind seen in mid-century, to personal intervention (by a doctor, health visitor or midwife) at the individual level. It is here that the voluntarism of Edwardian personal service converges with the new-found status of the MOH. Slowly but unwaveringly in the public health sphere, doctors moved their attention from environmental manipulation to the question of the individual's role in the production of disease; education about personal hygiene and diet was perceived as crucial to the nation's health, or lack of it. As one MOH noted in 1896, 'Thousands, nay, hundreds of thousands, of young men and women with hereditary or acquired tendencies to various diseases are, owing to want of knowledge, brought up, enter upon occupations and lead modes of life which inevitably result in disease and early death.'[10]

The causes of tuberculosis were increasingly seen to lie in lack of personal cleanliness, irregular habits and moral laxity as well as bad housing.[11] Surveys which regularly revealed high morbidity and mortality rates among the poor were used by the medical profession as evidence of the necessity for intervention at the individual level. As the example of infant mortality in the Edwardian era illustrates, this was primarily dealt with by the provision of health visitors, maternity services and infant welfare centres; in other words the focus of those providing assistance, in this instance largely educative, was individual mothers. The clinic, informed by the findings of the laboratory, was being installed as the solution to death and disease among the poor.[12]

The perceived potency of germ theory led to the view that the best medicine was intervention at the individual level to prevent or cure a specific disease process.[13] More generally, endorsement of this view followed from the respect the Victorians and Edwardians increasingly accorded the medical profession. In an era absorbed by notions of evolution, the claim that individual intervention had become scientific and effective was quickly coupled to the promise of social progress, and the expectations of doctors began to be shared by reformers. Lawrence argues that we should not underestimate the confidence some Edwardians were beginning to have in the power of the clinic (as the Broadbent anti-infant mortality scheme in Huddersfield serves to illustrate).[14] Equally Fabian criticism of the inadequacy of Poor Law medical services noted that tuberculosis, some forms of cancer, heart conditions and diabetes were all diseases which could be prevented by early medical intervention (backed up by a more proactive role for the state). This was the context in which the Bolton Guild of Help in partnership with the local MOH, Dr Gould, set about tackling TB.

THE EXTENT OF THE PROBLEM

Consumption was the largest single cause of death and chronic illness in Britain during the nineteenth century. When figures became available in 1838, they showed an annual mortality rate of 380 deaths per

100,000 population. Although the figure had fallen to 148 by 1900, consumption remained the second largest cause of death, producing an annual toll at the turn of the century of 50,000 deaths and an estimated 250,000 sufferers.[15] For most victims it was a lingering illness, where one's condition worsened over months or years and ended almost certainly with death.

In the first decade of the twentieth century TB was responsible for approximately one death in every eight in Britain.[16] It was the single greatest killer of males, causing a death rate of almost 2 per 1,000 population per annum in England and Wales. Among females the death rate from TB equalled 1.4 per 1,000. It accounted for more than one death in three among men aged 15–44, one-half of all female deaths in the age group 15–24, and one-quarter of all female deaths in the age group 25–44.[17] While TB was primarily a disease of adults, it was not completely absent among infants and children. The death rates from TB in the age group 5–14 were only 0.7 and 0.6 per 1,000 population respectively among both sexes in the first decade of the century. Nevertheless, it was the single greatest cause of death in this age group at the time, causing 24 per cent of male deaths and 20 per cent of female deaths. For infants (those under the age of a year), there were greater dangers to life such as infantile convulsions, pneumonia, diarrhoea and enteritis.[18]

Modern understanding of the aetiology of tuberculosis stems largely from the work of Robert Koch, a German bacteriologist, and his discovery of the tubercle bacillus, in 1882. As a result of the discovery it became clear that tuberculosis was not a hereditary condition as was formerly asserted but an infectious disease caused by the tubercle bacillus. It was shown that it could affect all parts of the body, although the dominant and commonest form was respiratory or pulmonary tuberculosis conventionally known in Victorian Britain as consumption or phthisis, in which the disease affects the lungs. Nevertheless, non-pulmonary forms assumed a greater importance than is statistically indicated, as these were the forms to which children were susceptible. Almost 85 per cent of all forms of the disease in those under the age of five were of a non-pulmonary nature, and 70 per cent of deaths of those between the ages of 5 and 14.[19] The major forms of non-pulmonary tuberculosis include tuberculosis of the bones and joints, the lymph nodes (known by the late Victorians and Edwardians as Scrofula), the abdomen, the meninges and central nervous system, and the skin (*lupus vulgaris*). Infection was largely due to spread by droplet infection, generally by coughing or sneezing; this applies to pulmonary and non-pulmonary alike. The remainder was due to infection with the bovine variety of the bacillus. Bovine infection could be caused by consuming infected meat and more commonly contaminated milk. Related primarily to the non-pulmonary form of the disease, bovine infection was associated in particular with children and infants.[20]

It was shown in the early twentieth century by the use of newly developed tuberculin skin tests, and by biopsies and autopsies, that the infection with the tubercle bacillus among the population in an urban community was as high as 90 per cent, but only around 1 per cent went on to develop the disease. It was never determined exactly who was most likely to contract the disease. The question of the influence of a hereditary predisposition remains largely unresolved but to all appearances environment has been a far more important factor. As Linda Bryder notes, the historian investigating the epidemiology of TB often discovers more about the assumptions and prejudices of the enquirers than about disease patterns themselves. Nevertheless, there appeared to be certain indisputable trends. Indicators were based on mortality (deaths and death rates) rather than morbidity statistics (incidence of the disease) as the latter were too undependable and incomplete in this period to form the basis of a sound investigation. Studies suggested that the geographical distribution of the disease coincided with less prosperous areas, generally with higher rates in Scotland and Wales than in England. Death rates by class showed the highest rates at the bottom of the socio-economic scale.[21] Tuberculosis was therefore recognized as a disease of poverty; the point of dispute was over which particular aspects in the lives of the poor were responsible for the disease – for example, overcrowding, insanitary conditions, a poor diet, or 'bad habits'.

Rather significantly many of the physical symptoms of the disease including fever, dyspnoea (difficulty in breathing), haemoptysis (blood-spitting), and weight loss were not wholly exclusive to tuberculosis, and might be absent from a particular case, making diagnosis problematic. A state of continued ill-health was probably the most constant symptom, but sometimes cases were discovered by chance through X-ray examination. The disease was somewhat unpredictable; cases which appeared to be advanced might recover spontaneously. The disease might also take a fulminating course, as was common among young adults, or it might linger on for many years, as was often the case with older sufferers, causing confusion between tuberculosis and chronic bronchitis. At its final stage, it was often marked by haemoptysis. Tuberculous meningitis was, before the chemotherapy of the 1950s, almost always fatal, the course of the disease running no more than three to six weeks, with the patient entering a deep coma. Tuberculosis of bones and joints led to crippling, while tuberculosis of the skin resulted in skin blemishes, often of the face and neck.

Patients with tuberculosis in the early twentieth century had more than the physical symptoms of the disease to contend with. With the newly acquired knowledge of the infectious nature of the disease, 'enthusiastically promulgated' by the National Association for the Prevention of Consumption and Other Forms of Tuberculosis (NAPT) (founded in 1898), and in the absence of an effective treatment, tuberculosis sufferers often found themselves cut off from the wider community. Securing a job following a period in an institution was difficult, and patients were even ostracized by family and friends. A short period in a sanatorium did not ensure that sufferers were no longer infectious, and so ex-patients were often stigmatized. Moreover, there was a persistent belief in some form of hereditary predisposition which led some patients to conceal their medical histories from future marriage partners and in-laws. The social consequences of the disease were often far worse than merely its physical symptoms, thus 'in the first half of the twentieth century Tuberculosis was not only a major killer, it also became a social problem'.[22]

A NATIONAL AND A LOCAL PROBLEM, 1898–1914

The foundation of the National Association for the Prevention of Tuberculosis marked the start of a national campaign to eliminate TB from Britain. This was to gain increasing momentum in the early twentieth century and eventually attract state involvement after 1911. As Bryder notes, the organization attracted the support of leading physicians, politicians including the prime minister, Lord Salisbury, and the Prince of Wales, later Edward VII. It aimed to attack TB in three ways: 'by educating the public in preventive measures, by campaigning to eliminate tuberculosis from cattle, and by promoting the establishment of institutions for treatment'.[23] Points one and three are of particular importance because they directly informed the approach of Bolton Guild of Help to TB. The NAPT was concerned to provide sanatoria for the working class and the poor, who they considered to be a danger to themselves, their families and society. It was in this context and with full support for the open-air treatment that the Guild set about making consumption the most important public health disease in Edwardian Bolton.

Robert Koch's significance, then, to contemporary medical opinion is illustrated by Sir Robert Young, a leading expert on respiratory disease, who argued that 'once the cause was known, the problem of prevention and treatment became concrete instead of nebulous. There was no longer any justification for a hopeless, fainéant or resigned attitude to the sufferers from this disease.'[24] This major shift in understanding was not only in terms of the growing acceptance of the infectious nature of the disease, but also in terms of immunological ideas. The infectiousness of tuberculosis meant that as much stress was placed on building up human resistance to the 'soil' as on attacking the seeds of the disease. Many of the new immunological theories were resonant with the older notions of a tubercular constitution or diathesis, either inherited or acquired. Many leading experts seemed to have assumed a kind of circumstantial contagionism, whereby TB was only infectious to certain people, in certain environments, behaving in certain ways. In reality this meant the poor, who put themselves, their families and communities in danger because of the unhygienic conditions in which they lived and their irresponsible behaviour. Thus within the context of the relationship between Helper and sufferer and their families, TB became a social disease of human contact, and indeed class contact.

The isolation of the bacillus suggested that 'preventive' measures could successfully combat the problem. The propaganda of the NAPT encompassed all aspects of health education and notions of personal hygiene. Education was seen as the solution to the problem, causes were viewed within a framework of ignorance on behalf of the poor, who made up the majority of sufferers. In an exhibition organized by the NAPT, the behaviour of consumption was explained by analogy with the parable of the sower: the seed was everywhere, it was the soil that was important. This soil, it was argued, was affected by three 'bads': bad food, leading to poor nutrition; bad air, the product of overcrowding; and bad drink, alcohol.[25] This explanation of the 'behaviour' of the disease suggests a movement committed to social reform, and an attack on living and working conditions and environment as fostering the tubercle bacillus, and therefore ultimately an organization interested in attacking poverty. However, the NAPT, as

Bryder maintains, showed itself to be very much a product of middle-class society and its fixed assumptions about the poor. Thus according to Robert Philip, a leading figure in the anti-TB movement of the Edwardian period:

> Individuals and communities must be shown that the disease is maintained through ignorance and folly, and that its removal lies completely in their hands . . . the people must be taught from day to day that tuberculosis comes of their disregard of physiological law for themselves. . . . Thereby a higher standard of national and personal cleanliness will be evolved, in presence of which the tubercle bacillus will be gradually discounted.[26]

It was within this framework of causes and solutions that the Bolton Guild developed initiatives to combat TB. The reason is clear, with the focus having shifted to the family and the individual the Guild was able to employ their Helpers to influence the habits of the poor by befriending them. The Guild and its Helpers assumed an important role; were they not the only bridge or link between poor families and the official apparatus of the MOH and the sanitary committee, but also with voluntary institutions such as the Wilkinson sanatorium? Their function was to be emissaries of what constituted good and bad habits. By visiting the homes of the poor, Helpers sought to promote messages extolling the virtues of cleanliness, good ventilation, fresh air, a good diet and moral responsibility. Through this process of domestic visiting and its philosophy of befriending it was believed the Helper could encourage and advise families and individual sufferers as to the best methods of preventing the disease from taking hold. The objective was to construct and pass on to sufferers, their family and friends as far as possible the idea that the home should be a healthy and clean place to live, and that in partnership with Helpers, other medical and health visitors, the sanatorium could be translated to the home.[27] In a sense this was the central plank of the Guild approach, to transfer as much as possible the ideological framework of the sanatorium treatment to the homes of Bolton's poor. It was an ideology based on restraint and self-control, in an environment which would be sustained by the Helper. Solutions were therefore focused on the individual; the notion of self-help and the power of education was to be delivered via domestic visiting, institutional contact between sufferers and experts, and the clinic. As one Guild Helper argued:

. . . there is absolutely no existing machinery to compel families to live healthy lives, and this can best be effected by personal influence. If the Helpers of the Guild could convince their cases and the public generally of the necessity for obeying the laws of Health as far as possible in matters of air, cleanliness, food, clothing, and sufficient sleep for children, a real permanent improvement in the health and consequent welfare of the town might reasonably be expected.[28]

Efforts to combat TB began in Bolton as early as 1901 when a delegation from the town council was sent to an international congress on tuberculosis held in London under the patronage of the Prince of Wales. As a result of the congress the sanitary committee of the town council established a Tuberculosis Sub-committee on 3 March 1902. By the end of the year the town had in operation a voluntary notification scheme, based on general practitioners informing the committee of cases, which were then placed on a register. As part of the scheme leaflets detailing advice on how to avoid contracting the disease were distributed to the town's population via GPs. On receipt of notification, a visit was made to the home of the sufferer by one of the MOH's lady health visitors and details of the sanitary conditions present were noted and advice as to what further precautions a family could take to arrest the spread of the disease was given.

As Table 3.1 illustrates, the number of consumptives brought to the attention of the MOH increased as the notification scheme shifted from being voluntary to compulsory first because of the Bolton Corporation Act, 1905, and then the nationally enforced Public Health Regulations, 1911.

Over the Edwardian period the TB mortality rate experienced increases and falls, as Graph 3.1 indicates. When these figures were set against national rates the MOH found that in 1903 they were equal, in 1904–6 they were lower and in 1908 higher. Since 1900 the MOH also noted that 200 deaths per annum from pulmonary TB appeared to be the norm. Of these deaths 83 per cent occurred in the 15 to 55 age range.[29] However, while there was a small downward trend, as Graph 3.2 illustrates, in the poorest and most densely populated areas of Bolton mortality was above the average for the period. Equally, mortality was spread across genders and age ranges, with certain key industries, particularly the textile trades, affecting incidences of death from TB. In the view of the MOH the statistical facts as regards Bolton 'may in the main be taken as representative of other manufacturing towns engaged in the cotton industries'.[30] The occupational distribution of TB can be better understood by looking at Table 3.2,

Table 3.1. TB cases brought to the attention of the MOH because of notification

| | Voluntary Notification | | |
	Institutions	GPs	Total
1902	14	66	80
1903	17	75	92
1904	37	55	92
1905 (9 months)	11	43	54
	Compulsory Notification		
	Institutions	GPs	Total
1905 (3 months)	19	76	95
1906	36	216	252
1907	45	143	188
1908	35	165	200
1909	58	177	235
1910	27	218	245
1911	36	209	245
1912	70	251	321

Source: *Bolton Medical Officer of Health Annual Report*, p. 35

Table 3.2. Occupational Instances of TB, 1908–9

	% of working population
Cotton Spinning	1.6
Cotton Weaving	1.0
Bleaching and Printing	1.6
Metal and Machine Work	3.0
Coal Mining	2.5
General Labourers	9.0
Domestic Work	0.9

Source: John Gould (Medical Officer of Health for the Borough of Bolton), 'Consumption. Preventive Measures adopted in Bolton', *County Borough of Bolton Guild of Help Magazine* (*Tuberculosis Exhibition Number*), 5/11 (December 1910), p. 10

produced by the MOH for a paper he gave at the TB exhibition organized by the Guild.

The links with age, occupation and working-class TB are further confirmed by statistics from MOH Annual Reports after 1910. For example, of the 321 cases notified to the MOH in 1912, 67 were under the age of 14, 175 were males and 146 females. Of those notified, 26 per cent died within a year of their notification. In terms of the occupational incidences of TB, 60 were employed in the textile trades (spinning, weaving and bleaching), 29 were general labourers, 52 were schoolchildren and 52 were listed as employed doing housework.[31] By contrast in 1914 the total registered mortality rate for Bolton was 2,721 deaths, of which 1,336 were male and 1,385 female. The majority of deaths occurred between the ages of 25 and 55 years, with 111 out of a total of 167 deaths or 66.4 per cent in that age group.[32]

Graph 3.1. The extent of TB mortality ('000s) in Edwardian Bolton, 1900–14

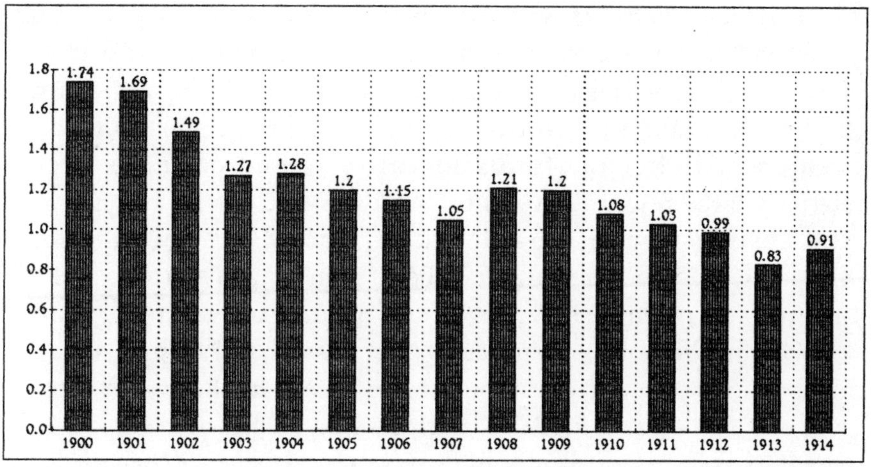

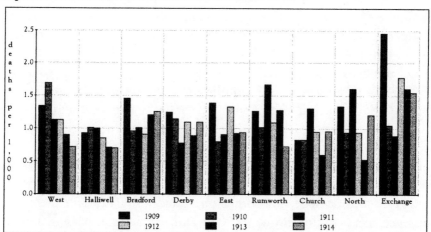

Source: Bolton Medical Officer of Health Annual Report for 1913–14, pp. 8–12

Graph 3.2. A residential breakdown of the incidences of TB

Source: Bolton Medical Officer of Health Annual Report for 1913–14, p. 28
Note: The average TB mortality rate over the period was 1.06 per 1,000 inhabitants. The wards listed in the graph relate to the oldest and most crowded areas of the town, where a majority of Bolton's textile and heavy industries were located.

The efficiency of home visits was limited because of the lack of resources and only became effective after the introduction of compulsory notification in 1905. After notification a visit to the home of a sufferer was made by the sanitary inspector and information was gathered as to the health of other family members or occupiers; a note was also made if there was a history of TB. In regard to the patient, if sanatorium treatment was considered necessary an application had first to be made to the MOH who would examine the case and determine whether such treatment was appropriate.[33] However, visits were often made without a 'medical man' being in attendance, and in these instances advice was given and the case would be subsequently brought to the attention of the MOH. This aspect of the scheme was strengthened after the formation of the Guild of Help, when its relatively large reserve of volunteer workers (Helpers) was deployed to take up domestic visiting duties. As the MOH noted, since its formation in 1905 the Guild had been of great assistance to the local authority. Patients' expenses were often paid to and from the sanatorium, the homes of sufferers were visited and help was given in the form of food and money where required. In the period between 1906 and 1912 alone the Guild Helpers had identified and reported to the MOH 379 cases, all of whom were found places in sanatoria and convalescent homes.[34] By the end of 1912, the Guild owned three open-air shelters, to which it could refer cases directly. The Guild estimated that when they were in regular use up to six cases a year could be dealt with there.[35] But most important of all was the fact that Helpers gave advice 'both generally and as to precautions to be taken to prevent the spread of the disease and to assist in the cure'.[36]

Significantly, for the first time efforts were also made to encourage 'influential members of the community' to consider the question of providing a sanatorium for Bolton's poorest citizens. A joint conference of Bolton Corporation and neighbouring authorities passed a resolution which asserted that 'a sanatorium for consumptives was highly desirable' and committed the council to 'take steps for carrying out such provision and invite contributions towards that object from public bodies, societies and other interested in its attainment'.[37] In the absence of a sanatorium of its own and in common with other local authorities the TB committee sought to find an alternative source of sanatorium beds. Between 1906 and 1908, the committee secured the use of eight beds at the Meathop Sanatorium in Grange-over-Sands. This was subsequently increased to a further ten beds by the Bolton

Guardians, at a cost of £90 per bed per annum.[38] However, as in some other instances the council was slow to act in relation to initiatives to combat TB, leaving voluntarism and private benefactors to step into the breach. Thus 'efforts' to recognize the needs of poor consumptives were not successful until 1908 and the opening of the Wilkinson Sanatorium. This had been achieved after Thomas Wilkinson, a wealthy benefactor, had entrusted to a set of trustees his house, 7 acres of land, together with £50,000 as an endowment.[39]

By the end of 1912 the Bolton MOH had access to 84 beds at three separate locations, 25 at the Meathop Sanatorium, 35 at the Wilkinson Sanatorium, and 24 at the Bolton Borough Hospital and Poor Law Infirmary.[40] Significantly the Wilkinson Sanatorium had expanded to accommodate 35 patients, which represented an increase of 15 beds. Between July 1906 and October 1912, 130 cases had been referred by the MOH to the Meathop Sanatorium, of which 61 cases (46 per cent) had been arrested, 42 cases had seen some 'improvement', 7 only slight improvement, and 20 had seen no improvement whatsoever.[41]

THE SANATORIUM AND THE GUILD

Sanatorium treatment for pulmonary TB was developed in Germany around 1860 and was introduced into Britain after 1890. Sanatorium provision grew rapidly during the years 1900–10, though the treatment was surrounded with some controversy over its efficacy. In 1911, however, the treatment was endorsed by the state, when provision for 'Sanatoria Benefit' was surprisingly included in the National Insurance Act.[42] After 1900 the NAPT launched an extensive nationwide campaign to stimulate interest in sanatoria and spread the gospel of social education. The campaign sought to emphasize the need to provide treatment for the consumptive working man and the poor. In order to reach this class, new methods of propaganda were developed, including touring exhibitions and films. There were some expensive private institutions that attempted to attract wealthy patients away from Europe, where they continued to go 'to take the cure', but for the most part British sanatoria were charitable institutions for the working class and lower middle classes. The Pinewood Sanatorium, Berkshire, was established with voluntary funds in 1900, the Blencathra Sanatorium, Lanark, in 1904 for male patients of the 'artisan and commercial classes', and by 1911 the NAPT reported that it had 27 branches in Britain, many with their own sanatoria.[43] Others were established as the result of private charities: Maitland Cottage Sanatorium, again in Berkshire, was founded by Esther Carling in 1899 as the result of a donation for 'the treatment of working class patients'.[44] Some Poor Law Guardians established purpose-built sanatoria – Liverpool in 1902, Bradford in 1903, and the Manchester Guardians developed property in north Wales and opened a sanatorium the following year. A few local authorities also became involved: by 1906, Sheffield Corporation had established a sanatorium, and Bristol and Manchester had purchased beds in private sanatoria.[45] Indeed the boundaries between the two are difficult to discern, given that voluntary sanatoria usually enjoyed some degree of local authority support and many local authorities relied on the availability of voluntary beds. For example, the first two 'public' sanatoria in Westmorland (the Meathop Sanatorium) and Durham and which were opened in 1900 both had beds subscribed to by the local Poor Law authorities.[46]

The most conspicuous example of social education and in many ways the culmination of the Bolton Guild's efforts to combat TB was the Exhibition it organized on behalf of the NAPT. As Worboys has noted, sanatoria were promoted as advanced, curative institutions, but they were also powerful symbols. The Bolton Guild was attracted to sanatoria because of their educative function: their regimes were working examples of hygienic living. They represented the antithesis of working-class life. They were spacious and clean, rather than overcrowded and dirty. The diet provided was wholesome, recreation was 'decent' and everywhere was open to observation, in contrast to the hidden unseen world of the poor. The significance of these themes is confirmed by the range of papers delivered at the Bolton Guild TB Exhibition, all of which capture the essence of the Guild approach to TB. All preached the gospel of pure air and the sanatorium cure, which as one delegate described was: '. . . the healthiest life possible, the one which enables the system to develop the maximum amount of vitality, and therefore that which best fits it to repel the invasion of disease. The essentials of sanatorium life are pure-air, good and suitable food, and properly regulated exercise. All the rest is mere detail.'[47]

The expansion of sanatoria can be located within the context of the wider growth of social institutions in general. From the second half of the nineteenth century to the outbreak of the First World War there was a considerable proliferation of institutions designed to serve or protect society, which included prisons, asylums, workhouses and hospitals. They were a product of a new faith in the medical profession and the social value of institutions, and significantly by the beginning of the twentieth century they had assumed the status of something close to a universal panacea.[48] This was certainly the case in Bolton, where a coalition of the medical profession, the Guild of Help as the town's leading organizers of voluntarism, and a number of wealthy benefactors cooperated to promote the value of sanatorium treatment. Of equal importance was the fact that TB and sanatoria also became an attractive object of philanthropy, for as Bryder rightly notes this was because donors could see the result of their charity. The Wilkinson Sanatorium in Bolton was a conspicuous example of charity. As the editor of the Guild *Magazine* noted, 'so much has been reported through the local press with regard to the gift, that our readers are doubtless now well acquainted with many of the details'.[49] But of importance also was that the idea that sanatorium treatment as well as fresh-air schemes should attract philanthropic support. This was because of the image of it being a modern cure to an economically important disease, while at the same time benefiting medical progress and the social good.

THE DISPENSARY

The Guild, heavily influenced by initiatives in Glasgow, was also concerned to see the foundation of a TB dispensary or clinic in Bolton but owing to a lack of resources and the reluctance of Bolton Corporation to become involved the idea never got off the ground. The issue of a dispensary was the one area of dispute between the Guild and the MOH and the Sanitary Committee of the town council. The Guild's support for such a clinic is perhaps not so surprising given its commitment to the social education ideal; indeed the idea of a dispensary can be seen as the natural extension of its support for sanatorium-related treatments. Rather significantly, the issue of a dispensary also saw the Guild begin thinking about what happened to working-class consumptives after they had completed a course of treatment either in a sanatorium or at an open-air shelter. As Mrs Haslam asked, 'Could not dispensary treatment in a small way be given at our Sanitary Office, as Glasgow began this, and followed up with advice at the patient's home?'[50]

In 1908 the Guild noted that the Corporation had taken additional beds at the Meathop Sanatorium, but 'admirable though these efforts are, they are not of themselves sufficient, and much more remains to be done'.[51] The Guild had ascertained that there were about 750 consumptives in the town and that the existing provision for them was utterly inadequate. Significantly the Guild noted the helplessness of Helpers when dealing with TB cases. In its view closer ties had to be established with the civic authorities: 'Sanatorium treatment for consumptives, immediately following notification, would appear to be of great service, but even this must be accounted a failure if patients on their discharge are allowed to return to the old conditions where they speedily lose all the advantages previously gained.'[52]

The Guild in other words was concerned to influence and become part of the 'after-care' process, a process it considered the town council had a role in also. The Guild did have access to three open-air shelters which it had obtained through generous benefactors, including the Haslam family. The usefulness of these shelters was according to the Guild undoubtable as the following case served to illustrate. A young male patient who having spent two periods at the Meathop Sanatorium after his discharge returned home to the conditions he had originally left, with the perhaps not too surprising result that his health worsened to the point that the Helper involved with the case doubted whether he would ever work again. A local benefactor became interested in the case and presented to the Guild a shelter for assisting the patient back to good health again. The Guild reported that this cause of treatment appeared to have some success, and the patient was said to have improved and had returned to some light work.[53] However, such victories were only slight, in the Guild's view even stronger ties had to be established between voluntarism and the MOH.

The question of how to deliver effective after-care would in the Guild's view be solved by the foundation of a dispensary jointly with the civic authorities. The Guild was drawing on the pioneering work of Robert Philip, a leading figure in Edwardian community medicine. He had established the world's first TB dispensary in Edinburgh in 1887. Patients were registered, while their family and friends were subjected to an examination to determine whether they, too, were infected. 'Early' cases were sent for sanatorium treatment, while advanced cases were separated and sent to another institution. By 1912, there were eleven dispensaries in London.[54] In common with infant welfare centres and Schools for Mothers TB dispensaries stressed that their functions consisted of diagnosis and health education, not treatment. The parallels with dealing with working-class infant mortality are quite striking, as this was clearly a conscious policy not to encroach upon the 'territory' of GPs.

While not successful in convincing official agencies of the worth of the dispensary, the Guild was able to convince another voluntary provider of TB care of the value of its after-care proposals. In 1911 the Guild received a request to undertake the after-care of Wilkinson Sanatorium patients, and the care of the families of breadwinners who were inmates there. After this request the Guild reworked its procedures for dealing with consumptives, and undertook: (1) to keep a special register of persons notified to the Guild suffering from consumption; (2) that all cases dealt with by the Helpers in the Sick Nursing and Cripple Section of the Guild worked in close cooperation with the Trustees of Wilkinson Sanatorium; and (3) to carry out points 1 and 2, a Committee of Nursing Sisters be attached to each division of the Guild (St John Ambulance).[55]

Building on these themes the Bolton Guild saw the framework of the dispensary as a means of advising patients and their families about questions of household cleanliness and the need to improve their living conditions. The focus of advice that a dispensary could give was to reinforce the work already being carried out by the Guild's Helpers. This idea can be seen as an attempt to complement the institutional treatment of TB in Bolton. In the national context there was an attempt to reach a wider public through the development of a TB dispensary movement, with staff going into the homes of patients. This was clearly an extension of the wider domestic 'visiting' culture that had grown in urban areas since the mid-nineteenth century, a culture that the Guild of Help movement itself was a part. The faith the Bolton Guild placed in dispensaries can also be located within the wider Edwardian interest in the 'clinic' and its instructive qualities. The attachment to the clinic draws further parallels with the anti-infant mortality movement of the period. Both movements had solutions that were devised with the individual in mind. In terms of infant mortality this meant measures were aimed at mothers; in the fight against TB initiatives were focused upon the consumptive. In the context of Bolton the value of 'class treatment' had already been proved by the 'Bolton School for Mothers' established by the local branch of the Women's Co-operative Guild. In the view of the Secretary of the Guild, its classes had been very successful and were a boon to all mothers who were privileged to attend them.[56] The same would be true of those attending a TB clinic because, as the NAPT maintained:

While caring for the individual in whatever way may be needful, the dispensary regenerates physiologically the dwelling – however humble. It makes the home of the poor man become the nursery of healthy children and cease to be the breeding ground of tubercle-tainted wastrels. Each recreated home is an effective preventorium against tuberculosis.[57]

CONCLUSIONS

It is clear from the experience of the Bolton Guild of Help and its efforts to combat TB that the idea of medical progress, the prize of reforming the habits and lifestyles of the poor and the influence of civic pride were a potent combination after 1900 in the fight against TB. Thus the Guild of Help, in partnership with the MOH, set about tackling TB based on the following three objectives: (1) to apply the most up-to-date and advanced techniques (sanatorium and open-air treatment) to cure and remove the threat of TB from Bolton; (2) to exploit the wider social role of sanatoria in educating the poor in self-discipline and attention to hygienic ways of living; and (3) to keep up with the activities of other towns and cities. The faith the Guild and the MOH shared in the value of social education and the sanatorium was unshakeable. As the medical officer of Wilkinson Sanatorium maintained, 'no treatment ever devised has yielded such satisfactory results in the treatment of consumption'.[58]

Equally initiatives to combat TB cannot be viewed in isolation from the wider health movements which developed and flourished in the period up to 1914. It is clear that the NAPT's ideological framework and approach had much in common with the infant welfare movement established after 1900. By emphasizing the infectious nature of TB and associating it with ignorant, feckless behaviour, 'the campaign against consumption . . . ended in a war against the consumptive'.[59] This kind of attitude contributed to the twentieth-century stereotype of TB sufferers as being dangerous and deficient individuals. This is a framework that the Bolton Guild certainly operated in, as its interest in compulsory disinfection of homes and the forcible removal of consumptives to isolation institutions illustrates. Given the extent of TB, the public fears about the disease, the degree of anti-consumption propaganda, and the fact that the campaigns of the NAPT were so eagerly embraced by such influential organizations as the Guild of Help, it is perhaps not over-stating the case to argue that initiatives designed to combat TB represented one of the most powerful attacks on working-class lifestyles in the Edwardian period. It is therefore quite valid to argue that the 'war' against TB was equal, if not greater in importance, than the better-known 'improvement' campaigns directed at motherhood and all aspects of physical degeneration.

Given all of this, what was the legacy of the Guild's contribution to combating TB in Edwardian Bolton? The Guild's relationship with the MOH, Dr Gould, was certainly a good one and it did all it could within its powers to answer his call for the educationist, the philanthropist and the state to work together. It displayed throughout this period total commitment to the idea that the community and organized voluntarism could in partnership solve the difficult problem of TB among the poor. The Guild took its lead from the NAPT and was unwavering in its support for the expertise of the medical profession. Moreover, as its support for a TB dispensary or clinic indicates, it was often ahead of the MOH in seeing the potential of new developments in anti-TB techniques. Its messages to the consumptive were a mixture of the negative and the positive; emphasis was always on the need to avoid dangerous behaviour and places, stress was on the individual pursuit of a healthy lifestyle. In different ways sufferers were held to be responsible for their conditions, while at the same time, the means of avoiding and overcoming the disease were seen to be in their own hands. As Mrs William Haslam, the architect of the Guild's anti-TB strategies, argued, because of the Guild: 'The present generation has learnt three important things about consumption: (1) that it is not hereditary; (2) that it is infectious; (3) that it is curable if attended to in its early stages, and what has to be done is to protect every outpost of the human body against attack from the outside at any vulnerable point. . . .'[60]

CHAPTER 4

HEALTH AND ENVIRONMENT IN LATE VICTORIAN AND EDWARDIAN HUDDERSFIELD

BECKY BRYSON

High rates of mortality, particularly age-related mortality, in highly populated industrialized towns like Huddersfield appeared to be among the most intractable public health problems of late Victorian and Edwardian Britain. Indeed, the rapid growth of the country's population, especially after 1870, has stimulated a whole series of historical research into the trends, associated problems and explanations for this sudden growth in population. National studies by A.S. Wohl and F.B. Smith, for example, have focused in detail on the state of public health in the country as a whole, examining important social and economic determinants like housing, sanitation and the cost of living on the well-being of the population.[1] More importantly though, many local studies have emerged which have examined health and sanitation in industrial towns and cities such as Manchester, Birmingham, London, Bradford and Middlesbrough.[2] It is the neglect of any complete examination into social conditions in the West Yorkshire region that has encouraged this study into health and environment in Huddersfield in the late Victorian and Edwardian period. These other regional studies find that there were improvements for most of the working classes in terms of health, particularly in the early years of the twentieth century. The situation in Huddersfield tends to follow the ameliorative line with there being a concerted effort made by a number of different authorities in Huddersfield to improve the health and sanitary facilities in the town.

It is the intention of this chapter first to examine selected aspects of health in Huddersfield, namely the issues of birth, mortality and infant mortality, and secondly to analyse possible environmental explanations for fluctuations in the course of these different variants in the period under consideration.

PART I

In the late Victorian and Edwardian period, Huddersfield was a rapidly developing town with the growth in population within the borough rising by almost 35 per cent between the census years 1871 and 1911, from 70,253 to 107,821. It was the arrival of a superior system of public transport and the extensive building of woollen and worsted mills and engineering factories that led to many of the town's population leaving the cramped streets of the town centre for the rapidly growing suburbs. This unprecedented migration towards the outskirts of Huddersfield led to the problem of slum areas due to shortages of drainage and clean water in the outlying districts, and this dearth of the basic sanitary amenities threatened to have grave consequences on the state of health in Huddersfield. However, despite this pressure on resources, the local council coped well when compared to its counterparts, showing much initiative and foresight. So much so that at a time when infant mortality rates were high in England and Wales, Huddersfield's standard death rate had fallen from 22.3 per 1,000 living in 1877 to 13.8 in 1912; families of all classes in Huddersfield were progressively limiting the number of children they had, thus reducing the birth rate to 18.1 between 1911 and 1914 from 35.1 in 1877–81. Huddersfield had reduced its number of deaths in infants under five from a peak of 794 in 1882 to just 303 by 1912.[3]

Birth Rate

The second half of the nineteenth century saw the birth rate of Great Britain entering what has been termed as a 'progressive annual decline'.[4] The nation's crude birth rate fell from 34.1 per 1,000 living in 1870–2 to 24.5 in 1910–12.[5] Huddersfield followed the national pattern, with the birth rate per 1,000 falling from a high of 32.9 between 1877 and 1881 to its lowest rate of 19.8 between 1910 and 1914. The widespread decrease in the birth rate and high abortion rate showed in practice that increasingly more couples were limiting their families and that women were anxious to control their own fertility.[6]

When examining the actual pattern of birth rates in Huddersfield, Graph 4.1 depicts the fluctuations in births throughout the period. It is clear that birth rates fell throughout our period but most spectacularly until 1890, where the rate fell from 35.1 per 1,000 to 22.7 in 1890 (the only exceptional year being 1887 when birth rates rose slightly to 27.7). Thereafter rates fluctuated between 1891 and 1897, only to rise again to 23.4 in 1897. From 1898 until 1910, the birth rate in Huddersfield did remain stable with the average rate for the 13-year period being 23.6. The last years 1911–14 saw the birth rate decline by 21 per cent to a low of 18.1 by 1914.

Graph 4.1. Birth Rate per 1,000 Living in the Huddersfield Borough, 1877–1914

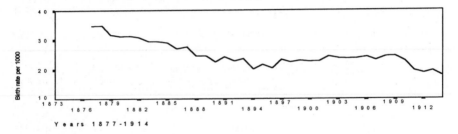

Source: Huddersfield MOH, *Annual Reports*

The decline in birth rates was not uniform across Huddersfield and corresponded closely to district and class. The reason for this difference was that decades after the middle classes and upper working classes had begun to limit the size of their families, the poor working classes too were deciding to reduce the number of their children.[7] In recent years there has been an ongoing debate among historians surrounding the decline in birth rates witnessed nationally, and as a consequence there have been many explanations as to why the birth rates declined so dramatically in the late Victorian and Edwardian period.

The well-advocated reason for the decline in births, supported by writers such as C. Chinn and J. Lewis, was fertility and the popular role of birth control among many working-class women. As Chinn argues, the decline in the number of births per 1,000 was 'mainly due to the causes over which the individual had control'. In the euphemisms of the era, this meant couples using means of birth control to limit the size of their families.[8] However, it must be remembered that methods of birth control were not always affordable to the working classes, and that on the whole working-class women were often forced to rely on abstinence and abortion. There are numerous examples of women taking hot mustard baths and large quantities of Epsom salts which were commonly used to induce abortion.[9] Also birth control was not always seen as acceptable and attitudes remained antiquated until 'Marie Stopes provided a more respectable justification for the use of contraceptives during the 1920s'.[10]

Another explanation, particularly relevant to Huddersfield, is the importance of female employment in the decline of birth rates, especially the attraction of work in mills, particularly in the West Riding. This may have encouraged many working-class women to practise birth control and therefore brought down the birth rate.[11] Birth control both allowed women the opportunity to work continuously without having a break to have children and to gain independence in the form of a weekly wage.

It is clear that factors such as women marrying at an older age and the decrease in illegitimate births, made possible by the 1906 Huddersfield Corporation Act which made the notification of births to the Medical Officer of Health (MOH) compulsory within 48 hours of the birth, had little relevance in the fall in birth rates. It was the introduction of some crude methods of birth control into the lives of working-class women and the higher percentage of women employed in industry in the late nineteenth and early twentieth centuries that had a crucial effect on the pattern of declining birth rates. If these factors are coupled with the nationwide improvement in living standards after 1890 then it is clear why the birth rate in Huddersfield between 1877 and 1914 fell from 34.9 per 1,000 population to 18.08 as families were deciding to limit their family size and spend their new 'disposable income' on the range of consumer durables which were emerging.

Mortality Rate

The decline of mortality in Huddersfield in the period 1870–1914 was unprecedented, again following the national pattern. Death rates fell from a peak of 22.3 per 1,000 persons living in 1877 to a low of 13.8 in 1912. J.M. Winter gauges this fall in terms of life expectancy, arguing that in England and Wales in 1861 life expectancy stood at 40.5 years for men and 43 years for women, whereas in 1918 the 50-year mark was passed by women and nearly by men.[12]

Looking at the data for the borough demonstrated in Graph 4.2 it is clear that the mortality rate fell uninterrupted in the first five years from 22.3 per 1,000 living in 1877 to 20.4 in 1881. In 1882 and 1883 the figures peaked again with the rate reaching 22.4 and 21.4 respectively. The figures then continued to fall between 1884 and 1894 from 19.5 to 15.9 (this decline was interrupted twice in 1887 and 1891). Thereafter from 1894 until 1912 the figures fluctuated and steadily decreased from 17.1 in 1895 to a low of 13.8 in 1912, only to rise again in the last two years of the period to 14.8 and 14.7 in 1913 and 1914 respectively.

Graph 4.2. Mortality Rate per 1,000 Living in the Borough of Huddersfield, 1877–1914

Source: Huddersfield MOH, *Annual Reports*

The main reasons for the fall in mortality rate depicted in Graph 4.2 will be investigated in more detail in Part II of this chapter. Environmental explanations for the improvement in health in Huddersfield in the late Victorian and Edwardian period figure largely in this section.

Infant Mortality

In recent years there have been a number of national studies on infant mortality in the late Victorian and Edwardian period. The most useful are papers published in the late 1980s by R.I. Woods, P.A. Watterson and J.H. Woodward.[13] Writers have also acknowledged that the Borough of Huddersfield between 1870 and 1914 made much effort in reducing the rate of infant mortality.[14] H. Marland recognizes the need to examine infant mortality programmes and initiatives at a local level.

She admits that 'Huddersfield is recognised as a pioneer of infant welfare provision, having initiated a comprehensive system of notification of births and health visiting in the first decade of this century.'[15]

Throughout the period, the number of infant deaths in Huddersfield fell consistently and was well below the national average. For example, in 1893, Huddersfield had the joint lowest infant mortality rate of the 33 large English towns, sharing a rate of 141 per 1,000 living with Bristol, as opposed to the mean rate for the 33 towns of 191.3. Even in 1910, in the latter part of our period, Huddersfield's infant mortality rate in children under one per 1,000 living was just 99 compared to the mean rate for the now 77 English towns which was 115. The fall in the numbers of infant deaths is reflected in Graph 4.3.

Graph 4.3. Number of Deaths in Infants under the Age of One Year in Huddersfield, 1877–1914

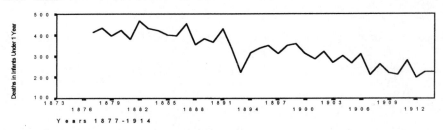

Source: Huddersfield MOH, *Annual Reports*

With regard to infant mortality, specifically under the age of one, the number of cases declined steadily. At the start of the period the number of deaths fluctuated erratically from 414 in 1877, dropping to 382 in 1881, and increased to a peak of 468 in 1882. Thereafter from 1883 to 1887 the rate fell consistently although 1887 witnessed an increase in the number of deaths by 12.5 per cent due mainly to the increased number of deaths from the childhood killers of measles and whooping cough.[16] From the late 1880s until the early 1890s, the number of infant deaths fell relatively uninterrupted to a low level of 225 in 1893. This level was achieved due to a small number of deaths from measles, whooping cough and diphtheria in the year 1893 of 25, 13 and 3 respectively. From the mid-1890s until 1905, the number of deaths remained relatively consistent, with the mean number of deaths in the period being 316. Between 1907 and 1914, the number of deaths fell dramatically to just 199 in 1912. The number of deaths rose in the last two years. However, the number was still almost 52 per cent lower than the highest figure of 468 for the year 1882.

The main reason for this staggering fall in infant mortality in Huddersfield is the work of two men – Alderman Benjamin Broadbent, chairman of the Health Committee and Dr S.G.H. Moore, the town's MOH. It was Broadbent's initiatives that set up the Infantile Mortality Sub-committee in Huddersfield in 1903 and, more importantly, on his becoming mayor in 1904, he gave 20s to every child born in the Longwood district during his term in office, with the presentation being made when the child reached one year of age.[17] Although the Longwood scheme was small-scale, this study disagrees with Marland's comment that 'its results were not very conclusive'.[18] On the contrary, the effects of Broadbent's scheme were astonishing, as Graph 4.4 illustrates, with the number of infant deaths in the Longwood district falling from an average of 27 for the years 1887–91 to just 7 for the years 1912–14.

Graph 4.4. Number of Deaths in Infants under the Age of One Year in the Longwood District of Huddersfield, 1891–1914

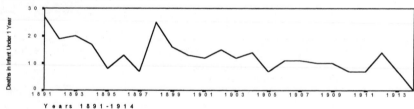

Source: Huddersfield MOH, *Annual Reports*

Huddersfield historian R. Brook agrees with the success of Broadbent's policy, arguing that after the scheme ended, in 1906, child mortality in Huddersfield was less than half the national average.[19] Broadbent was also responsible for the implementation of Part XI of the 1906 Huddersfield Corporation Act which made the notification of births to the town's MOH compulsory within 48 hours.[20] This part of the scheme was successful as by March 1907, 92 per cent of births were being notified,[21] due largely to the incentive of giving parents one shilling if the birth was notified. Another benefit derived from the scheme was that all parents of children born in Huddersfield between 1904 and 1906 were visited by members of a ladies' committee who were able to use their influence and advise parents in the best interests of the young children.

Another local Act in 1876, requiring doctors and parents to notify the MOH immediately of any outbreak of an infectious disease, also contributed to reducing the number of infant deaths in Huddersfield. The Act resulted in the provision of an isolation hospital for zymotic disease patients being set up in Birkby, and later at Mill Hill. This measure clearly reduced infant mortality as infectious diseases, the biggest childhood killer, were in part isolated and thus restricted from spreading, and only in 1889 were similar provisions applied to the country as a whole.

An explanation advocated by some historians is the eugenics argument that it was the low nutritional standards and poor diet of working-class mothers which increased the risk of miscarrying, of premature birth and more importantly the risks associated with childbirth. Wohl agrees with this interpretation, stating that 'the nutritional inadequacies of the Victorian working-class diet often led to rickets which could cause contracted pelvises, making childbirth difficult'.[22]

Recent studies support the eugenics theory, showing that working-class women were considerably more underweight than their middle-class counterparts. Wohl uses the example of pre-1914 Manchester where 13-year-old girls from a working-class background were more than three inches shorter and eight pounds lighter than girls of a 'good class'. Hence, this blatant malnutrition endured by working-class women contributed significantly to the high levels of infant mortality that existed, especially in the early half of the period in question. The information collected by M. Llewelyn Davies supports the eugenics argument. Most of the women interviewed were habitually too poor to seek medical advice during pregnancy and frequently forced through poverty to go out to 'char' to earn a living. They often went without food to feed their husband and children. As one woman wrote, 'I can assure you I have told my husband many times that I had had my dinner before he came in, so as there should be plenty to go around for the children and himself.'[23]

However, more optimistic writers like J. Burnett dismiss the eugenics theory and the issue of poor diet in connection with high infant mortality rates, arguing that infant mortality did decline somewhat in the early twentieth century as overall living standards increased for the majority of the working class, and this is reflected in the rise of the levels and quality of food consumed by the working classes after 1900.[24]

Another alleged cause of infant mortality, favoured by contemporary writers, was the widespread ineptitude of parents to care adequately for their children. John Benson Pritchett, the first MOH in Huddersfield (1873–7), drew attention to this, condemning mothers in Huddersfield for taking their children to places of entertainment, and argued that the levels of infant mortality would have been greatly reduced 'if the guardians of these victims had not exposed them to such perils as maternal instinct should have shielded them from; if the love of excitement and company had not drawn them away to such public places as the theatre and the circus, to which they had to take their infants or stay at home.'[25] This criticism is fairly common among middle-class commentators and is unjust given the fact that they were not leading the impoverished lives that many working-class families suffered in Huddersfield.

The most serious fault of many working-class parents was the widespread practice of giving infants opium to quieten them. Opium was a cheap, effective and widely available cure given to relieve pain, consumption, cholera and diarrhoea. However, its effects on small children when used in excessive amounts were lethal, as it starved them. Opium was used liberally throughout England, with Wohl estimating in late nineteenth-century Manchester that five out of six working-class families used it habitually.[26] Many infants died as a result of opium intake, either from starvation or from an overdose.

Huddersfield was not exempt from the use of narcotics with children. One local contemporary, N. Porritt, writing in the 1880s, wrote in his work *Cornered* of an unqualified nurse treating local children with opium.[27] The point Porritt was making was that the commonplace use of opium and other narcotics among the working classes was lethal to their children's health, as it led to either narcotic poisoning or starvation, and was a contributory factor in the infant mortality of the period.

Particular concern has traditionally been expressed by contemporaries that working mothers in full-time employment might contribute to the high rates of infant mortality. MOHs throughout the country reported that employment drew mothers back to work before their babies were completely weaned, which increased the likelihood of a variety of childhood diseases. For example, Preston's MOH reporting in 1902 on the causes of infant mortality, noted that 'first among these causes is the employment of female labour in the mills . . . the return of the mother to her work within a short period after confinement, thus depriving the infant of a mother's care and of the sustenance which nature intended for it, constitutes even a still greater evil.'[28]

Pritchett follows this traditional contemporary consensus, believing that infant mortality is related to the large number of mothers who go out to work as 'millhands, charwomen and servants' and have to leave their offspring in the care of others.[29] Arguments from modern historians, however, reveal the immense complexity of the infant mortality debate. E. Roberts argues that there is no definite correlation between high rates of infant mortality and a high percentage of married women in full-time employment.[30] For example, Manchester in 1901 had a massive infant mortality rate of 211 per 1,000 births, but a mere 19 per cent of married women in employment, while Haslingden (Lancashire) had 28.7 per cent of women in work but a lower infant mortality rate of 163.[31]

Most recent writers have abandoned the contemporary explanation of high infant mortality rates and argue that full-time working mothers did not neglect their children. Relatives and neighbours provided an adequate child-minding network and the fact that working-class women worked actually improved their child's chances of survival by raising the family's standard of living.

Another reason for the enormous national rates of infant mortality was the fatality of the infectious diseases, particularly whooping cough and diarrhoea.[32] Both diseases thrived in hot weather and insanitary conditions, so to combat the latter, the local councils set up slum clearance programmes and enacted new sanitation laws. The Borough of Huddersfield was a very forward-thinking and progressive town when it came to combating the diseases. As already stated, a local Act in 1876 set up the hospital in Birkby and later Mill Hill for infectious disease victims, and made it compulsory for every suspected outbreak of a disease to be notified. This initiative in part explains Huddersfield's persistently low levels of zymotic death rate and consequently low infant mortality rate.

PART II

With regard to the influence of environmental factors on the health and well-being of the people of Huddersfield, this second section attempts to measure the relationship between sanitary conditions and health, particularly mortality rates.

The state of housing in Huddersfield, particularly in areas of overcrowding, is clearly a crucial determinant to healthy living in an industrial society. Overcrowding is traditionally associated with air-borne infectious diseases such as measles and whooping cough. The occupancy rate expressed by number of people per room or people per house has traditionally been used as the classic measure of housing living conditions. The criterion for the measuring of overcrowding is usually defined 'as a person/room ratio in excess of a certain arbitrary limit'.[33] In the late Victorian and Edwardian context the limit was that of two people per room, and anything exceeding that limit constituted overcrowding.

Table 4.5 highlights the number of overcrowded tenements and the percentage and number of the population of Huddersfield who lived in these overcrowded conditions. The statistics below are founded on the contemporary definition that overcrowding was the situation where there were more than two people per room.[34]

Table 4.1. Overcrowding Rates in Huddersfield, 1891–1911

	No. of Overcrowded Tenements	No. of Overcrowded Population	Percentage of the Population in Overcrowded Conditions
1891	4,183	18,966	19.9
1901	2,891	12,245	12.9
1911	2,020	12,866	11.9

Source: County of York Censuses, 1891–1911

Table 4.1 illustrates that the town of Huddersfield followed the national pattern, with the proportion of those living in overcrowded accommodation in relation to the population falling from 19.9 per cent in 1891 to 11.9 per cent by 1911, with the most significant reduction being between 1891 and 1901. Despite the fact that Huddersfield's overcrowding problems were easing towards the end of our period, the experiences there were worse when compared to the country as a whole. One writer estimates that in 1891 only 'eleven per cent of the population of England and Wales were housed at densities of more than two persons per room',[35] although it must be pointed out that this estimate was only based on one to four-roomed tenements and is therefore an underestimate. Nevertheless, despite the fact that in the regional context Huddersfield had higher levels of overcrowding than the country as a whole, this higher rate did not have an overtly adverse effect on the town's infectious disease rate. For example, after 1900 the number of deaths from measles had fallen to 0 in 1903 and 5 in 1905, compared to levels of 80 in 1882 and 125 in 1887.

As well as housing achievements, Huddersfield Borough Council was attempting to improve the town's quality of life and health record by modernizing sanitary facilities. Water supply was the first major task attempted by the new council and had a direct consequence in reducing the mortality rates from typhus and typhoid fever. The first Corporation Waterworks Committee (1869–71) met in 1869 under the chairmanship of Charles Henry Jones.[36] It was Jones's experience and dynamism which led to the passing of the Huddersfield Waterworks Act in July 1869, as he recognized the need for 'an adequate water supply for both domestic and trade purposes, and to develop the scheme already planned by the Waterworks Commissioners'.[37] As a result of the Act, the Commissioners for the Huddersfield Waterworks were transferred to Huddersfield Corporation, and consequently, between 1872 and 1892, Deerhill, Blackmoorfoot and Wessenden Head reservoirs were completed, and Wessenden Old reservoir was purchased from the Wessenden Commissioners. Deerhill reservoir was the first reservoir constructed between 1870 and 1875 and had a capacity of 160 million gallons. It was the second Huddersfield Waterworks and Improvement Act in 1876 and a further Act in 1890 which authorized a second phase of extensive construction of reservoirs. The combined water supply yielded from these new reservoirs was over 6.5 million gallons per day by 1918.

Although typhus and typhoid fever were never major killers in Huddersfield, the increased pure water supply was partly responsible for reducing the numbers of deaths from fever from a mean of 29.8 deaths between 1877 and 1881 to 6 deaths between 1910 and 1914. A.S. Wohl agrees with the success of an increased water supply nationally when he wrote that 'improvements in water supply and sewerage did succeed in reducing its [typhoid's] virulence. [So much that] The death rate from typhoid in the decade 1891–1900 was almost half that of 1871–1880 and by 1904 the death rate was well under one-third the rate that had prevailed throughout the 1870s.'[38]

Between 1878 and 1908 not only did the number of gallons per head of population per day increase by over 50 per cent from 18.1 gallons to 27.2 gallons, but the number of the population suffering from fever or 'fever'-related symptoms like diarrhoea was being steadily reduced.

Improvements in domestic sanitation, particularly sewage disposal, was also a major contributory factor to the fall in Huddersfield's mortality rate. In Huddersfield, sewerage construction began extensively in 1869 and the success of the town's sewerage system in coping with its rapid population growth is reflected by the town's chief sanitary inspector in his 1879 *Annual Report* when he stated that 'improvements for the general health and comfort of the inhabitants of the Borough have been many and important'.[39] The streets of the town had been provided with sewers and paved, and the main sewers had been extended to meet the growing requirements which arose from both the erection of new dwellings and the growing population. Unwholesome wells were being closed and water was being supplied from the corporation's waterworks.

The most important achievement was the introduction of new methods employed in removing household excrement and waste in Huddersfield between 1870 and 1914. Before 1870, antiquated methods of excrement disposal, particularly the privy midden system, were in use in Huddersfield.[40] However, despite the existence of the privy midden system in Huddersfield throughout the period 1870–1914, efforts were being made by the corporation to convert the privies from the old sunken midden system to the pail and water carriage system. For example, in 1878 just 3,700 pails were in use, whereas by the close of our period in 1914 there were 15,457 pails in use.[41] It was especially the years 1890 and 1891 that proved the most significant in terms of excrement and waste disposal. First, under the powers of the 1875 Public Health Act and the 1871 Huddersfield Improvement Act, the corporation constructed large intercepting sewers for the main drainage of the borough and extended the borough's sewers by 4.4 miles in 1890. Secondly, in 1891 a refuse destructor was installed at a depot in Hillhouse in connection with the scavenging of the town's streets.

The scavenging system of collecting the pails was particularly popular in the outlying districts where the sewerage system had not been laid, and thus the water carriage system had not yet been introduced, with the number of pails brought to the depot rising almost uninterruptedly from 508,448 in 1898 to 810,531 in 1913. These figures represent the fact that more people in Huddersfield were using the pail system as opposed to the privy midden system. The number of loads of excrement taken to the tip and buried rose gradually after 1896 from 1,518 loads in 1896 to its highest figure of 7,527 loads in 1912, and the number of tonnes of excrement made into manure and sold by the corporation which proved to be a valuable source of revenue for the council stayed consistent throughout the 1896–1914 period.

Although expensive, the borough's sewerage works were completed in 1910 and the system adopted its sedimentation and the application of the sewage by means of revolving troughs to large beds of coarse clinker, which purified the sewage biologically and chemically. This extension of the sewerage system led the MOH in 1913 to remark that 'where a sufficient sewer and water supply is available, all closets were on the water carriage system and were flushed with clean water'.[42] Between the years 1910 and 1914, the number of fresh water closets in use increased by 25 per cent, but they only accounted for half the total provision and were concentrated in the town's centre. Nevertheless, the chief sanitary inspector justified this lack of provision in his 1910 *Annual Report* when he stated that 'owing to the great area of the Borough, in relation to the number of inhabitants (the density of the population is eight persons per acre) the sewerage of the district is very expensive, and in certain districts, notably the agricultural parts of the Borough, is still incomplete and defective, but . . . considerable sums of money are [being] spent on improvements.'[43]

Even so, the very existence of this cleaner system in Huddersfield did have effects on health, especially the incidence of mortality from scarlet fever, other fevers and diarrhoea. For example, the high density housing that existed in districts like Fartown, Dalton, Central and Lockwood coupled with the close proximity of the midden privies to large numbers of houses, did contribute to the higher than average mortality rates in these districts. The reason for this is that the dangers posed by inadequate sanitary arrangements were more serious in houses with high densities, and because it was the working classes in the lower income bracket who were forced to occupy this type of dwelling.

Pollution is an area where there were also health improvements. The area of pollution has been a recurrent topic of debate from the 1840s onwards among contemporaries, especially in the late Victorian and Edwardian period. According to local contemporary sources, pollution existed in two forms – water and air pollution. As mentioned earlier in this chapter, an essential requirement for a healthy life, especially among the more vulnerable working classes, was a pure, clean and uncontaminated supply of fresh water. The water also needed to be abundant as water was used in a number of domestic roles, ranging from drinking, cooking and sewage disposal.

Throughout the period 1870–1914, Huddersfield was supplied with water from the rivers Colne and Holme, and pollution did not seem to have been seen to be a major problem in the area judging from the lack of reference to river pollution by the Rivers Board in the chief sanitary inspector's *Annual Reports*.[44] The only two notable mentions of water pollution were in 1873, when a stream in the Fartown district, which was being used as a source of water supply, was polluted by refuse and excrement from a stable and farmyard,[45] and in 1894 when the River Holme was polluted by the emission of logwood chips.[46] However, these problems were quickly and effectively resolved by the intervention of the Rivers Board. It is clear from Huddersfield's relatively clean health record of water-related diseases, particularly its low number of deaths from enteric fever, that the town did not have a major problem with river pollution.[47]

The second area of pollution which has traditionally been associated with respiratory illnesses is atmospheric pollution. Although several contemporary accounts refer to this area of contamination existing within the borough, contemporary medical and sanitary authorities made little attempt to tackle the problem of smoke nuisances. An example reflecting this lack of action in dealing with the problem is made by the MOH in his 1892 *Annual Report* that 'the pressure of work has rendered us unable to prosecute the nuisance more vigorously'.[48] Another problem, apart from the non-active pursuit of the problem by the authorities, which faces those attempting to analyse the incidence and extremity of smoke pollution, was the primitive techniques used by contemporaries to assess smoke pollution.[49] From 1900 onwards, however, there was a drive to measure the number of smoke nuisances and to caution the offending manufacturers. From 355 observations and 0 manufacturers cautioned in 1900, the number rose to 919 observations and 27 manufacturers cautioned in 1913.[50] However, the effect of these cautions was minimal, as very few of those who were cautioned and reoffended were actually prosecuted.

With regard to the effects of air pollution and the relationship of that to health, there is little evidence to suggest a strong correlation between the two, as Huddersfield had a relatively low rate of mortality from respiratory diseases. For example, the number of deaths from the chief respiratory diseases of pneumonia, pleurisy and bronchitis fell by over 25 per cent from a mean of 359.8 per year between 1891 and 1895 to a mean of 266.6 between 1910 and 1914. Nevertheless, given the high levels of black smoke recorded after 1898, it would be fair to suggest that it was likely to have been at least a minor factor in the later formation of respiratory diseases. The non-immediacy of death from respiratory diseases may well be connected directly to the polluted and impure air that the populace of Huddersfield were forced to breathe in.

CONCLUSION

Sanitary improvements, the advance of medical science and the steady improvements in working-class life, especially after the period of increasing real wages from 1891, were all factors which ensured that the Borough of Huddersfield was one of the most progressive and healthiest in the country between 1870 and 1914. Birth rates for all classes fell steadily between 1877 and 1914. However, it was in the predominantly working-class districts of Central Huddersfield, Dalton and Lockwood where the levels fell most dramatically by 30.2, 42.8 and 42.8 per cent respectively. The improvement in the quality of town life resulted in the decline of mortality rates; the death rate in the borough fell by over 34 per cent, with the main reasons for this decrease being Huddersfield's persistently low level of infant mortality followed by its low case-fatality rate from the seven zymotic diseases compared to England and Wales as a whole.

Environmental considerations were important in the decline of mortality rates in Huddersfield in the late Victorian and Edwardian period, particularly in relation to Huddersfield's infectious disease mortality rate which continued to be among the lowest in the country, with the mean mortality falling by 70 per cent in the period. Sanitary developments including the 1869, 1876 and 1890 Waterworks acts, which increased the quality of water and the water supply, the overhaul of domestic sanitation and improvements in housing, all helped reduce the incidence of case-fatality from the infectious diseases.

Overall, then, it is clear that as Huddersfield entered the twentieth century its inhabitants were a great deal fitter and healthier than in 1870, and it was ranked as one of the healthiest boroughs in the country. However, as Wohl argues, huge differentials between classes still existed and 'it became a matter of common knowledge that the poor had not shared equally in the sanitary improvements and advances in public health and that, whatever the fears of the social Darwinians, their hold on life was still far more precarious than that of the more comfortable classes.'[51]

THE 1908 OLD AGE PENSIONS ACT:

THE POOR LAW IN NEW DISGUISE?

MARGARET JONES

The 1908 Old Age Pensions Act introduced a non-contributory pension of 5s a week to British citizens over 70 years of age. It was means-tested – only those with an income of less than £21 per year received the full amount. Section 3 of the Act also imposed character tests on recipients. Initially, those who had received poor relief, or been convicted of drunkenness, or imprisoned or failed to work were disqualified from receiving a pension. From 1911 onwards the poor relief exclusion was dropped. In the period up to 1920 more than two million elderly citizens received the pension.[1]

Both contemporaries and historians have seen this Act as a milestone in social legislation, offering a new type of benefit to the aged poor which lacked the disciplinary element and stigma of the Poor Law. Francis Stead, secretary of the National Committee of Organised Labour on Old Age Pensions, who saw the hand of the Almighty in the passing of the Act, viewed it as a first step in a social revolution. 'Not with the bursting of bombs, not with the click of the guillotine, but with the quiet handing over in innumerable post-offices of a weekly couple of half-crowns has the English Revolution of the Twentieth Century begun.'[2] Some historians have been equally as positive. Derek Fraser described the new pension as a 'remarkable breakthrough: to the grateful recipient . . . it was a new birthright of an Englishman, a part of his citizenship, not a deprivation of it'.[3]

Maurice Bruce, while acknowledging the deficiencies of the Act, still terms it 'a new chapter in the history of the community's care for its less fortunate members'. As it did not carry the penalty of disenfranchisement the 'moral obloquy so long attaching to poverty was at last beginning to give way to social concern'.[4] David Vincent also takes a positive view, claiming that the behavioural clauses in the Old Age Pensions Act 'proved unworkable' and that the only 'test of eligibility apart from poverty was the very substantial hurdle of living long enough'. For those who survived, 'the new benefit made a significant contribution not only to their immediate well-being but also to their burden of anxiety which weighed down their declining years'.[5] Only Pat Thane partially dissents from this view, seeing the Pension Act as very much a compromise. It was 'an *ad-hoc* response to pressure' and in no way 'part of a grand design of state welfare, or the result of the government's conscious recognition of a new welfare role', though it did reflect a 'general shift in attitudes towards the poor'.[6]

In this chapter I will argue that while the passing of the Act did indeed indicate a desire to provide a state benefit for the deserving aged poor which carried no stigma, in its operation the similarities to the Poor Law become obvious. This analysis will be based mainly on the activities of the Pension Committees for Wakefield Town Council and Salisbury City Council in the period 1908–19. The sources used are the minutes of the two committees, the Clerk's Letter Book and the Register of Claims for Salisbury Council. I have also used A.J. Hoare's account of the workings of the Act published in 1915 under the title, *Old Age Pensions; Their Actual Working and Ascertained Results in the United Kingdom*. Hoare was clerk to the local pension sub-committee for Camberwell and Lewisham. To examine the take-up of the pension I have compiled tables using national and local figures. The reports of the Inland Revenue and Customs and Excise provide the national statistics and the Register of Claims the local figures.

H.H. Asquith, in attempting to put the 1908 Old Age Pensions Act in its most positive light, claimed that the administration of the old age pension was to be 'once and for all outside the machinery and the associations of our Poor Law system'.[7] Claims were made by filling in a form at the post office at which the claimant wanted to collect the pension. The claim was then investigated by the pension officer who was initially an appointee of the Inland Revenue Board and then after

April 1909 the Customs and Excise Board. The officer visited the homes of all claimants, checked the proofs offered of financial circumstances, age and so on and then submitted a report to the local pension committee advising on the claimant's suitability for a pension.

The Pension Committee was appointed by the local councils. It met monthly to review pension claims based on the pension officer's report. If they were uncertain the practice was to defer the decision until the following meeting when the claimant was advised to appear in person to present his/her case. Evidence from the Salisbury minutes suggests that in the event of a problematic claim it helped to come to the committee meeting. Both the claimant and the pension officer had the right to appeal against the decision of the committee, a right which the officer in the two areas studied used more frequently than the claimant. In Wakefield and Salisbury the pension committees were sub-committees of the councils. Hoare notes that committees could be composed of 'members of Friendly Societies, Boards of Guardians, of Trade Unions and Ministers of Religion, as well as members of the appointing council; in many cases women members have been appointed'[8]; and the Local Government Board recommended that representatives from the 'Trade Unions, Friendly Societies and similar bodies' were co-opted on to committees.[9] Representatives of the friendly societies were co-opted on to Salisbury Pension Committee after they had protested at their omission, and Salisbury Council also made a point of appointing 'ladies'.

So the administration of the pension at the local level was a dual one. The pension officer was responsible to the Inland Revenue (later the Customs and Excise Board) while the Pension Committee received its instructions from the Local Government Board. This reflected the twofold concerns of the government: the need to control expenditure and the relief functions of the pension. The latter naturally fell to the Local Government Board as the authority in charge of the Poor Law. There was the 'minimum of co-operation between the central departments. Each issued separate regulations to its local representatives – the excise officers and pension committees – without apparent consultation with the other.'[10] It could be argued that these two bodies had conflicting interests; however, there is no evidence in either set of sources that this caused any friction and there are examples of extra information being passed by the Clerk of Salisbury Committee to Mr Hopkinson, the pension officer.[11]

Table 5.1 shows the national pattern derived from the Inland Revenue and Customs and Excise Board's figures for the years 1909–19.[12] They show that in the first year there were more than 800,000 claims for the new pension, of which 12 per cent were rejected. This testifies to the numbers of the aged poor who had managed somehow to survive without recourse to the Poor Law. The table also shows the dramatic increase in new claims in 1911 as a result of the dropping of the pauper disqualification at the end of 1910. There is a noticeable decrease in claims in the wartime years of 1916–18 with a big rise in 1919 reflecting opportunities for work available during the war. The table, following Customs and Excise practice, breaks down the reasons for the refusal of a pension into age, poor relief and means; all other reasons come under the heading of 'other causes'. 'Other causes' encompasses the disqualifications for failure to work, drunkenness, lunacy and imprisonment, so there is no way of finding out the exact numbers for these exclusions. However, as the table shows, they together form only a small percentage of all those refused a pension.

Inadequate proof of age, receipt of poor relief and excessive means were the three primary reasons for disqualification. It is not clear what the figures for disqualification for poor relief mean in these national figures. As receipt of poor relief in itself was not a disqualification for receipt of the pension after 31 December 1910 it must mean either that these claimants were rejected because they were receiving poor relief at the time of their claim and were not in a position to give up that benefit in order to receive a pension, or that their pensions were discontinued because of their receipt of poor relief. For these claimants then the benefit from poor relief must have been greater than the benefit from the pension, whether it was outdoor relief or care in a workhouse.

Table 5.2 presents equivalent figures for Salisbury City Council taken from the Register of Claims for the years 1908–1919.[13] The general pattern is the same; age and income are the main reasons for disqualification. In this table, however, I have been able to show specifically the numbers of pensioners who were rejected because they already had poor relief and those who had their pensions discontinued because of receipt of poor relief. There were two claimants in 1911 whose pensions were disallowed for receipt of poor relief and two whose pensions were discontinued because of receipt of poor relief. From 1912 to 1919 there were no first time claimants who were

Table 5.1. Old Age Pensions: National Data 1908–1920

	1908/09	1909/10	1910/11	1911/12	1912/13	1913/14	1914/15	1915/16	1916/17	1917/18	1918/19	1919/20	1908–20
Total claims('000)	837.8	173.3	385.8	187	175	171.9	160.4	0	144	141	142.1	213.3	2731.6
Questions raised			9.2	31	29.3	28.4	29.1	0	34.2	30.5	31.2	35.5	258.4
Claims rejected/revoked	102.1	67.7	49.3	49.4	43.3	40.1	41.9	0	56.4	48.5	47.7	52.6	599
Due to:													
Age	29.1	33.3	22.6	24.5	20.5	18.9	17.9	0	12.4	13.4	10.3	12.5	215.4
Poor relief	27.1	10.4	11.8	10.1	8.7	9.3	10.6	0	13.1	11.3	11.2	14.5	138.1
Means	27.2	14.2	10.1	11.7	12	10	11.7	0	16.7	22.5	25.1	24.2	185.4
Other causes	7.6	3.2	4.8	3.1	2.1	1.9	1.7	0	1.3	1.3	1.1	1.4	29.5
Death or withdrawal	11.1	6.4		7.4	6	5.4	5.1	0	5.2	5.7	6.6	8	66.9
Payments:													
Full pension	582.6	638.1	847.6	839.8	915.8	931.3	934.4	0	891.7	881.9	855.3	910.5	9229
Less than full	64.9	61.3	59.6	72.3	51.2	52.8	52.8	0	56.1	61.2	64.9	47.5	644.6
Total	647.5	699.4	907.2	912.1	967	984.1	987.2	0	947.8	943.1	920.2	957.9	9873.5
Men			333	351.4	363.8	369.4	369.4	0	343.7	336.6	322.1	337.6	3127
Women			574.4	590.7	604.1	614.8	617.8	0	604.1	606.5	597.2	620.3	5429.9
Total claims rejected (%)	12.19	39.07	12.78	26.42	24.74	23.33	26.12		39.17	34.40	33.57	24.66	21.93
Due to:													
Age	3.47	19.22	5.86	13.10	11.71	10.99	11.16		8.61	9.50	7.25	5.86	7.89
Poor relief	3.23	6.00	3.06	5.40	4.97	5.41	6.61		9.10	8.01	7.88	6.80	5.06
Means	3.25	8.19	2.62	6.26	6.86	5.82	7.29		11.60	15.96	17.66	11.35	6.79
Other causes	0.91	1.85	1.24	1.66	1.20	1.11	1.06		0.90	0.92	0.77	0.66	1.08
Death or withdrawal	1.32	3.69	0.00	3.96	3.43	3.14	3.18		3.61	4.04	4.64	3.75	2.45
% payments full	89.98	91.24	93.43	92.07	94.71	94.63	94.65		94.08	93.51	92.95	95.05	93.47
% men	0.00	0.00	36.71	38.53	37.62	37.54	37.42		36.26	35.69	35.00	35.24	31.67

refused a pension for receipt of poor relief. Claimants were granted a pension when they ceased to receive poor relief and as far as it is possible to ascertain that is what happened. But there were a number of pensioners who had their pensions discontinued because they opted for poor relief instead of the pension. It is likely that entry into a workhouse was not an entirely free choice but a result of necessity. The national data does not make this distinction explicit. However, both the national and local data in these tables show that the pension and poor relief were in some senses interchangeable benefits depending on circumstances.

A gender breakdown of the Salisbury figures shows, as one might expect given life expectancy differences, that more women than men received the pension, but interestingly they also show that more men than women were refused a pension – 21.9 per cent of men to 13.6 per cent of women. The difference lies first in the numbers refused on the basis of poor relief – 6.4 per cent of men to 4.6 per cent of women. This could be explained by women's capacity to look after themselves; families were more likely to take in the aged female parent than the male because of their greater usefulness. Men were, therefore, more likely to need care in the workhouse. A second difference is in the numbers refused for excess income – 9.5 per cent of men to 4.6 per cent of women. This could be explained by men's greater earning power at any age (see Table 5.2).

In their study, published during the Second World War, Wilson and MacKay divide the conditions for receiving the pension into three categories: the political, the economic and the moral.[14] Let me look at each of these conditions in turn.

As a political qualification, the recipient of a pension was to be a British subject, resident in the country for at least 20 years prior to receipt of a pension. This looks straightforward enough, but even this in practice posed problems. As Hoare pointed out, a foreigner married to a British subject was entitled to a pension. Yet a British woman who married a foreigner lost her nationality, and therefore could not receive a pension.[15] This was the case even if she had subsequently been separated, divorced or widowed.[16] The Act of 1911 dealt with this by allowing for a pension providing the other conditions were met if the marriage had been dissolved, annulled or ended by death.[17] Questions as to nationality did arise subsequent to the 1911 Act. The case of John Barnes posed problems for both the Salisbury committee and the Local Government Board as he had been born in the Channel Islands. In the event the Local Government Board decided in his favour.[18]

Table 5.2. Old Age Pensions in Salisbury, 1908–1919

	1908	1909	1910	1911	1912	1913	1914	1915	1916	1917	1918	1919	1908–19
Numbers													
Claims registered	294	127	151	112	96	80	70	82	75	88	77	96	1348
Pensions allowed	267	111	141	89	88	69	57	61	52	63	48	72	1118
Total pensions disallowed	27	16	10	23	8	11	13	21	23	25	29	24	230
Due to													
1. Poor relief	6	4	1	4	0	0	0	0	0	0	0	0	15
2. Discont. due to poor relief	0	0	0	4	0	2	8	3	9	12	8	11	57
3. Excess income	16	8	3	2	3	2	1	8	7	10	19	10	89
4. Age	1	2	4	11	2	5	2	4	6	1	2	2	42
5. Other	4	2	2	2	3	2	2	6	1	2	0	1	27
Percentages													
Total disallowed	9.18	12.60	6.62	20.54	8.33	13.75	18.57	25.61	30.67	28.41	37.66	25.00	17.06
Disallowed due to:													
1. + 2. Poor relief	2.04	3.15	0.66	7.14	0.00	2.50	11.43	3.66	12.00	13.64	10.39	11.46	5.34
3. Excess income	5.44	6.30	1.99	1.79	3.13	2.50	1.43	9.76	9.33	11.36	24.68	10.42	6.60
4. Age	0.34	1.57	2.65	9.82	2.08	6.25	2.86	4.88	8.00	1.14	2.60	2.08	3.12
5. Other	1.36	1.57	1.32	1.79	3.13	2.50	2.86	7.32	1.33	2.27	0.00	1.04	2.00

Residency crops up infrequently in the local minutes. There was one case of disputed residency in Wakefield and only six in Salisbury, among whom were a Robert Southey and a Catherine Wilkins residing at the same address who were refused a pension because they had 'not resided in the United Kingdom for the qualifying period'.[19]

The third qualification in this category was age. Claimants had to show that they were 70 years of age to qualify for a pension. Table 5.1 shows that for most years for which figures are available age was the predominant reason for rejection. Why is this so? The major problem for claimants rejected, it seems, was producing sufficient and acceptable proof of age. Various documents, according to Hoare, were acceptable as proof apart from birth certificates. Although registration of births began in 1837 it was not made compulsory until 1875. Insurance policies, apprenticeship indentures, records of service in the armed forces, birth certificate of the eldest child, marriage certificate of parents and baptismal certificates are examples Hoare gives of possible documentation. Census records could also be used by the pension officer and the family bible with lists of births could be acceptable.[20]

However, all these proofs presented problems. The family bible might list births but could the dates therein be relied upon? The entry in Anna Lane's bible was accepted but then she was also known to committee members – 'judging from the family Bible produced by the Pension officer and the personal knowledge of some committee members' the claimant was agreed to be over 70.[21] Julie Shergold was not so lucky. The Registrar General gave the date of birth as 1843, the family bible as 1842. The bible entry was obviously scrutinized thoroughly: 'the entry was of necessity as late as 1850 because the entries therein were all in the same handwriting and written at the same time, the last appearing in 1850'. Thus, with the help of their powers of detection the committee was able to conclude that the Registrar General's date was the correct one.[22]

Marriage certificates were produced as evidence of age and accepted. Mrs March's marriage certificate showed her to have been 19 when she was married on 19 August 1865.[23] The only evidence Mary Howard had was her copy of the register of 'her father and mother's marriage which took place a year before she was born', and this was not enough. Mary Martin was successful with her own marriage certificate,[24] while Caroline Rogers was not.[25] Marriage certificates were frequently not helpful as in the majority of cases the age was given as only 'Full' or 'Minor'.[26] This was indeed the case with Mary Denner's certificate which only stated that she was 'of full age'.[27] She was granted her pension on the basis of her appearance but this was overturned on the pension officer's appeal.

Appearance was on many occasions taken by the committees in this study as proof of age where no other evidence was available. Hoare confirms that this was common practice but one that was frowned upon by the Local Government Board as unsatisfactory. 'The Local Government Board . . . has expressed the view that a judgement of age, based on appearance and entirely unsupported by other evidence, should not as a rule, be accepted.'[28] This advice seems to have been ignored by the Wakefield and Salisbury committees though not by the pension officers concerned who usually appealed against such decisions with some success. Patience Bruton appeared before the Salisbury committee in support of herself: the pension was allowed 'as from the knowledge of the claimant by some of the members and judging from the appearance of the claimant' the sub-committee considered her 'not less than 70 years of age'. Jane Elizabeth Major's pension was also allowed on the basis of her appearance.[29] A lifetime of hard work and struggle at last had its reward; you looked your age or even older!

Baptismal certificates were acceptable proof as in the case of Elizabeth Blake in Salisbury,[30] but they could raise questions. Hoare cites the example of a claimant whose name was Mary but whose baptismal certificate when she produced it was in the name of Elizabeth. Was she who she said she was? There was an explanation. When she had entered domestic service her employer had decided to call her 'Mary' and she had used the name ever since, a not uncommon practice according to Hoare and an interesting insight into the anonymity of domestic servants to the Victorian propertied classes. Sadly, although the committee accepted that she was in good faith, the Local Government Board reversed their decision. So Mary was deprived of her pension possibly because of the whim of an employer many years before.

Another aspect which testifies to the thoroughness of this age test was in the use of census returns – the relevant years being 1841 and 1851. As Hoare pointed out, they only show the year of birth, not the actual date. He suggested that additional useful proof would be birthday cards which established that a claimant always celebrated his or her birthday on a particular day.[31] It obviously helped to be popular and a hoarder of useless memorabilia. Lastly, one other factor sometimes inhibited claimants from producing valid evidence of age and that was the cost of getting copies of birth certificates. In a letter to the Board on 10 July 1911 Francis Hodding (Clerk to Salisbury Pension Committee) stated that the claimant Mrs Hogg had 'no means to enable her to go to any expense' in the pursuit of certificates.[32] Pension officers were empowered to apply to the Registrar General's Office to obtain copies of birth certificates at no expense to the claimant but any other expense would have to be undertaken by them.[33]

Given the rigour of these tests it is not at all surprising that a steady percentage of claimants failed to pass (see Table 5.1). Hoare claimed that an analysis of one London sub-committee shows a small 17.5 per cent disallowed because of lack of evidence; the majority were disallowed because the claimant was not 70.[34] The Salisbury minutes and Register of Claims provide some evidence but the results are sketchy. However, some tentative conclusions can be posited as follows:

Claims rejected

Not yet 70	12
Insufficient proof	7
Granted on appearance	13
Overturned on appeal	7

What this suggests is that it was a considerable disadvantage not to have indisputable proof of age and that if the Salisbury Committee had not followed the practice of granting a pension on appearance many more pensioners would have been deprived of their 5s a week.

The national data shows excess income, the economic qualification, to be the second overall most common reason for disqualification, running second in the years 1909–15 and then in first place for the years 1916 to 1920 (see Table 5.1). The Salisbury figures show an almost identical pattern (see Table 5.2). How do we explain this? The pressures of cost and the desire not to discourage thrift meant that the pension was aimed at a particular group of the elderly. Anyone completely destitute and thus dependent on the Poor Law did not qualify; likewise those who could not demonstrate sufficient need. This meant that many at the top of the scale who thought they might be eligible were, as a result of the stringent means testing, excluded. The variation in the national pattern over the years looked at could be explained by opportunities for work which arose during the war which pulled people above the statutory level. George Slade visited Francis

Hodding in November 1918 to tell him that 'in consequence of the shortage of labour the City Surveyor had asked him to resume work for a short time'. His pension was thence withdrawn.[35] By January 1918 4,000 pensioners admitted to weekly earnings of 30s a week and it must be assumed that others concealed such earnings.[36] Alternatively it could reflect the fact that the rising cost of living was putting pressure on people's income and encouraging more around the crucial cut-off point to apply for a pension.

The pension was a means-tested benefit. However, assessing claimants' means was a far from simple task and it is not surprising that the pension officer was an appointee of the Inland Revenue. The Inland Revenue Commissioners displayed undue optimism about the ease with which means could be assessed. As the 1909 Report stated, 'the determination of the "means" of claimants has been fairly simple and straightforward as regards the great bulk of the claims received'. Any difficulties experienced by pension officers in finding out means were put down by the Commissioners to the 'dulled senses of old age'. However, that 'the personal investigations of Pension Officers have been persistent and searching' could have been due to the natural reluctance of an alert and independent septuagenarian to government prying into his or her affairs.[37]

Means were calculated on the basis of the income received in the preceding year but if there were changes in the current year then the pension officer could be asked to review the pension. There are numerous examples in the committees' minutes of pensions being raised or lowered according to circumstances. William Ricketts, for example, had his pension discontinued from 13 January 1913 because, as he stated in a letter to the pension officer, 'he has had some work offered him'.[38] What, however, constituted income for the basis of assessment? Obviously any earnings or benefits from friendly societies were included. It is apparent that many over-70s worked when they could. Thomas Elkins appeared before the Salisbury Committee in January 1919 but explained that 'on account of his failing health and age he has not been able to do *a full week's* [my italics] work for some time' and under the circumstances his average weekly earnings were 15s.[39]

Monetary income was only part of the assessment. Account had to be taken of the yearly advantage which came from property owned and occupied or leased and sub-let by the claimant. This value was taken from the rateable value of the property less costs such as fire insurance, and other 'management expenses'.[40] Richard Clerk failed to declare his costs 'for loss and repair on his property' in time and lost a proportion of his pension as a result.[41] A familiar ruse was used to reduce income. A Richard Clerk (the same Mr Clerk?) produced for the committee a 'deed showing the conveyance of some of his property to one of his daughters' and successfully thereby got his full pension.[42] This caused more problems in Ireland where it was common practice to make the farm over to the oldest son when the father became too old to work.[43] Some calculation also had to be made as to the value of living with relatives, especially those who were 'in circumstances of considerable comfort and comparative luxury'. Here the yearly value of the benefit enjoyed had to be estimated as if the claimant was paying for it.[44] It was just this situation which prompted Frances Judd to visit Francis Hodding in June 1913 to explain her circumstances: 'she and her two sisters live together so that it is incorrect that she should be stated to be receiving anything for free lodging'. This was accepted and she received the full pension.[45]

The value of furniture and effects had to be taken into account: before the 1911 Act only if the value exceeded £30 and then only for the amount exceeding £30; subsequent to this Act the value of all effects if they were worth more than £50 was added in. All such value along with any other property which was not used profitably was assessed for its potential income at the rate of 4 per cent per annum.[46] This was amended in 1911 to 5 per cent.[47] This was so that claimants with capital sums of a few hundred who had invested at a low rate of return became ineligible for a pension. The influence of Poor Law assessments and the pattern for future means-tested benefits are clearly evident in these calculations.

One other important source of income had to be disclosed by the claimant, and that was gifts in kind or cash from children. Pension officers from the start included them in their calculations and when this was questioned the Local Government Board in a circular on 11 December 1908 affirmed their actions. This followed 300 years of Poor Law practice where family responsibility of parents to children, husbands to wives, and children to parents had been enshrined in laws of maintenance 'virtually intact since 1601'.[48] The new Pensions Act, like the Poor Law expected children to contribute to the maintenance of their parents. Only gifts which were assumed to be regular were counted[49] but there could be misunderstandings or worse with regard to income of this kind, and it was an offence for children to withhold help in the hope of acquiring a pension for their parent. The daughter and son-in-law of William Symes told the committee that his income was only £13 'received from St Cross Hospital Winchester', whereas the claimant told the pension officer that he received £52 from his children and gave him 'a written list of the names of the children and the amount contributed by each intimating . . . it would in the future be £42 only'. Francis Hodding had his suspicions that there was an attempt here to manipulate the system.[50] Albert King received £26 per annum from his daughter in Silver Street and between 25s and 30s per annum from a daughter in King's Lynn, who also 'at the same time supplies him with ties and socks which would bring the annual receipts up to £28'.[51]

Attempting to thwart the system could have serious consequences. The 1909 Inland Revenue Report draws attention to the number of complaints of fraudulent claims, chiefly in relation to falsification of evidence of age and suppression of income. It gives no indication of figures but states that when adequate evidence of fraud was obtained by the pension officer then the offender was prosecuted 'without hesitation' and convictions obtained. It was hoped that this would act as a deterrent.[52] Mrs Carter almost fell foul of this fate. She had informed the committee that her husband's wages 'were 8/- whereas his Employer stated that for the last 12 months his wages have been 18/- per week till September, from then until March 1st and since that time 25/-'. This provoked a stern rebuke from the committee 'that she had rendered herself liable for prosecution and warned her as to being more careful in the future'.[53]

As with the age question, less tangible evidence sometimes carried weight. The impression a claimant gave as to his means had a part to play in the decision if it was not clear cut, as Hodding's letters reveal. William Symes's daughters who appeared before the committee for him were 'very well dressed and in quite a superior position'.[54] Albert King 'apparently does nothing' yet 'he lives in a house which is rented at 6/6d per week and he always has the appearance of being well clothed and fed . . . from the general behaviour and bearing of the claimant the Committee feel that there must be some other income'. The claimant admitted to an income of only £28 per annum and no evidence of any other income could be found, thus casting suspicion on his evidence.[55] Sidney Coombs's claim was deferred for further consideration because the committee 'thought the claimant earns more money than that mentioned in the statement'.[56] None of these claimants got their pension.

In calculating the pension level of couples there were injustices which were remedied by the 1911 Act, at least for married couples. The 1908 Act did not divide means equally which meant that in many cases the partner who had the income failed to receive a pension because the expense of having a dependent partner was not taken into account. The 1911 Act remedied this by dividing means equally between the couple, thus ensuring that both received a pension. But this only applied to married couples, not cohabiting ones. 'The effect of this alteration in the law was a large increase in the number of pensions at the full rate.'[57]

Despite the complications of this means testing Table 5.1 shows that if the claimant was deemed eligible at all for a pension it was likely that this would be a full one. The figures show that the percentage of those receiving a full pension in every one year was over 90 per cent and the average for the whole period was 93.47 per cent. This suggests that the sliding scale imposed for the pension, while being an administrative inconvenience, did not save the exchequer very much money, whereas it is clear given the level of disqualifications on the basis of income that the means-testing system did help Treasury accounts.

There was considerable debate about the moral tests. They were not nearly as stringent as many would have liked. How significant were they for those applying for a pension? Section 3 of the Act delineated what might be termed the undeserving poor – those elderly who had forfeited their right to a pension by their conduct and lifestyle. Before looking at the link between the pension and the Poor Law, which is by far the most important and complex aspect of these clauses, it is worth looking at the other exclusions.

The first of these was the habitual failure to work clause, the second was detention in a lunatic asylum, the third was imprisonment and the fourth was conviction under the Inebriates Act of 1898. It has been suggested that these clauses may not have been implemented. Thane has noted that 'some of the intended disqualifications from the Old Age Pension were not implemented or were quickly repealed'.[58] It is impossible to test this using the national data, as no separate category was given for these particular clauses.

In this first moral test Hoare claims that the disqualification for 'idleness has been enforced only in the most flagrant cases', so the fears of many that this clause, because it was so vague, would be interpreted harshly had not materialized.[59] The test of industry was to be 10 years' contribution to a friendly society, but no reference to 'drinking propensities and other undesirable qualities was to be made'.[60] According to Hoare there were 366 appeals in England and Wales against decisions of this character between the institution of the Act and March 1913. Hoare assumes that almost everyone would appeal against such a disqualification and that therefore the number of appeals indicates the number of disqualifications. This would give an annual figure of such disqualifications of just over 70.[61] There are just two cases cited in Salisbury: one in the minutes of 14 December 1910 when the pension officer's report informed the committee that Michael Shears, the claimant, had 'habitually failed to work according to his ability, opportunity and need for the maintenance of himself and is therefore not entitled to an old age pension'.[62] He did not appear, his claim was disallowed and there is no evidence that he appealed. Much later in April 1914 James Oliver was refused a pension on this same basis.[63] There is also no record of his appealing against this decision. This does show that although rarely invoked the clause was still in operation some five years after the Act came into force. There is no record of any such case in the Wakefield minutes. The fact that neither of these two claimants appealed against the decisions must cast doubt on Hoare's estimated figures above.

The second disqualification was detention in a lunatic asylum, probably the least controversial within this category. Hoare makes no comment on this subject and no national figures are available. There are three cases in the Salisbury minutes of pensions being discontinued because of 'admission to the County Asylum'.[64]

The third test disqualified claimants who had been convicted of an offence for the duration of the sentence and for 10 years afterwards. This was considered harsh; it meant that convicted claimants were punished twice and also ensured their destitution for a long period after they had completed the sentence. Given that they would be over 70 anyway their chance of ever collecting a pension was remote, and dependence on the Poor Law then became an extra punishment for transgression. The 1911 Act relaxed the rules: provided the period of sentence did not exceed six weeks the disqualification period was reduced to two years.[65] The effect of this more generous concession would still be to leave the moral message intact. There is only one example in the local minutes studied of a disqualification on these grounds. The pension officer's report on 16 November 1910 for Michael Thomas stated that he had 'within the last 10 years been in prison under sentence of imprisonment'. His pension was disallowed and his appeal to the Local Government Board turned down.[66] There are no local examples of the fourth disqualification – a conviction under the Inebriates Act.

Hoare notes that suggestions were made for an additional disqualification and one with which he had some sympathy. That is that the aged should not be entitled to a pension if they failed to keep themselves 'in a satisfactory condition of domestic and bodily cleanliness. . . . It seems contrary to public policy that persons receiving State aid should live below a reasonable standard of domestic and bodily cleanliness'.[67] This discussion could be set against the examples cited of claimants whose *good* appearance counted against them when assessments of their income were being made. The matter was apparently discussed at length by the London local pension committee but it was decided that it would be too difficult to agree on a uniform standard of cleanliness and would entail the appointment of additional staff. If nothing else this does give some insight into the very paternalistic nature of one pension committee at least and lends weight to the view that if, in theory, the Old Age Pension Act was to be a departure from the Poor Law, in practice those who administered it still had the remnants of the traditional attitude that state help should only be given without stigma to those who deserved it through their conformity to the values of their 'betters'.

Numerically these four 'moral' disqualifications were not found to be significant but the fact that they were in existence and used to disqualify claimants on occasion is.[68] After the removal of the pauper disqualification 'the criminal, the drunkard and . . . the malingerer were doubly stigmatised'.[69]

By far the most interesting area to explore is the relationship of the old age pension to the Poor Law. This relationship varied over the period as the legal position changed. Section 3 of the Act disqualified a claimant from entitlement to a pension if she or he was in receipt of poor law relief, apart from medical relief, in any part of the period from January 1908 to 31 December 1910. This was clearly intended to be a punitive clause directed against the 'undeserving poor', as it acted retrospectively. Both nationally and locally the data show this to be an important cause of disqualification (see Tables 5.1 and 5.2). The Wakefield minutes also show that in the first year of the Act, of the 508 claims made, 75 were disallowed and a staggering 51 of those were disallowed because of receipt of poor law relief. The most telling set of figures on this, however, comes from the Customs and Excise Report for 1911 which looks at the new pensions given as a result of the partial lapse of the poor law relief disqualification.[70]

New Pension Payable

	To Men	To Women	Total
England and Wales	40,707	91,678	132,385
Scotland	2,311	8,133	10,444
Wales	5,698	11,608	17,306
Total	48,716	111,419	160,135

Thus 160,135 aged poor were punished for receiving one form of state help by being refused another. This backlog of the over 70s, formerly deprived of a pension because at any time in the proscribed period they had had poor relief, created an immense amount of extra work in the last four months of 1910 for those involved.[71]

It can only be imagined how those refused a pension on this basis felt, especially as it was a blanket exclusion which took no account of the amount of aid received from the Poor Law. Hoare cites a number of cases where this clause operated extremely harshly. There was the claimant who had been in an infirmary in December 1908 but had been moved to the workhouse by the doctor, until she was cured, to make room for urgent cases. The Local Government Board felt this probably came under the heading of allowable medical relief; the local Guardians thought otherwise and their opinion held sway. Another claimant had been in hospital for three weeks in December 1908 and while there his wife had been forced to obtain some outdoor relief. As a result of this he was deprived of the pension.[72] A woman had received 2 lb of tea from a Guardian, another on two occasions had received 1s 6d when destitute; both were disqualified.[73]

The Wakefield and Salisbury minutes, although giving numerous examples of claimants being refused a pension because of poor relief, are sadly lacking in any details of the circumstances of the claimants except in the entry of Elizabeth Howell in the Register of Claims for Salisbury. Her claim was considered by the Salisbury Committee on 18 November 1908 and was disallowed because she had been in receipt of poor relief at the rate of 3s 6d a week since 1 January 1908.[74] Anybody who was surviving on that level of relief surely could not be accused of wastefulness and profligacy.

The Inland Revenue Report of 1909 highlights the difficulty that pension officers had in interpreting this clause. One of the problems was if an individual married man or woman received poor relief, did this disqualify the other partner? In the case of a married couple any relief given to either husband or wife disqualified both from receiving the pension unless it could be shown that the relief given was solely for the husband's support, in which case the wife was not disqualified. This applied whether the couple lived together or not.[75] Not unexpectedly the husband was expected to take responsibility for his wife, a view which Beveridge still subscribed to in his National Insurance Scheme 35 years later.[76] Edwin Tucker was forced to admit to the Salisbury Committee when he appeared before it on 2 January 1911 that his wife was in 'receipt of relief' and hence his pension was refused.[77]

The Customs and Excise Board opened its 1911 Report with the statement: 'The outstanding feature of the Old Age Pension work during the year 1910–1911 was the partial lapse of the Poor Relief disqualification at the end of 1910. On the 1st January 1911, the past receipt of Poor Relief at any time since the 1st January 1908, automatically ceased to operate as a disqualification for the grant of an Old Age Pension.'[78] This certainly removed the most iniquitous of these 'moral' tests. However, the link between the Poor Law and the pension did not end there. The end of the most obvious moral disqualification did not mean that the Poor Law ceased to play a part in the pension administration. The two kinds of benefit could not be given concurrently – the formula in use in both Wakefield and Salisbury was that 'the claimant on ceasing to be in receipt of poor law relief will be entitled to a pension of 5/- a week'.[79] Table 5.2 shows the numbers in Salisbury who lost their pension because they were in receipt of poor law relief. The figures show an increase in the numbers from 1916 onwards, arguably reflecting the wartime inflation which made it a struggle for pensioners to manage even with the increased allowance.

In some cases it is clearly stated in the minutes that the reason a pension was discontinued was because a claimant had entered the workhouse. Elizabeth Maenad, for example, 'entered the body of the Salisbury Union Workhouse on Saturday ult. and is therefore disqualified from receiving a pension'.[80] Despite writing to the clerk that this was temporary and that she hoped 'to leave the workhouse in a few days time', her pension was discontinued, thus depriving her presumably of any chance of leaving the workhouse.[81] Other examples state that the pensioner had entered the 'workhouse infirmary . . . and is not likely to leave'; in those circumstances the pension was discontinued as this was not temporary medical relief.[82] In other cases it is not so clear what kind of relief had been granted. The pension officer's report on Henry Scuse simply notes that 'he was disqualified because he had been in receipt of poor relief since January 1st'.[83] This seems to imply that it was outdoor relief so he would then have to reapply for his pension. Of the twelve people in Salisbury who lost their pension in 1917 (the highest recorded figure – see Table 5.2), five lost it because of entry to the workhouse and were disqualified from continuing to receive pensions 'by receipt of Poor Law Relief'. Thus the elderly could only receive one form or the other of state aid. They could not use poor relief to top up an inadequate pension, as they can today with the supplementary pension, although it is clear that some tried.

After the relaxation of the poor relief disqualification the Customs and Excise officials in their 1912 Report noted that a certain number of the new pensioners 'were reverting to poor relief. Generally no doubt the reason was they found it impossible to support themselves on 5/- a week.'[84] Those who had been on poor relief before receipt of a pension were those most likely to have no other source of income and therefore would find 5s a week inadequate.

The Board was concerned that some people were trying to play the system and 'combine the advantages of pension and poor relief by systematically returning to the workhouse after drawing a week's pension, and coming out again, when another week's pension was due'. To prevent this abuse the 1911 Act gave the pension officer the power 'to stop a pension as soon as he received information that it was infringing the rules and once that was done a fresh claim had to be made'. This presupposes communication between Poor Law officials and the Pension Office. No general instructions were issued by the Local Government Board according to Hoare but in the case of London at least 'in practice in many instances a poor law official notified the pension officer when a pensioner was admitted to a poor law institution'.[85] There is no direct evidence of this link in the sources available beyond the recording of a visit from the master of Salisbury workhouse to the clerk concerning a Jane Seth,[86] but of course it would be the pension officer who would be contacted. The information of entry to the workhouse almost invariably appears at the next monthly committee meeting, as in the example of Albert Swift who was admitted to the workhouse on 18 January 1913 and had his pension discontinued at the 12 February meeting. The news then travelled quite quickly, which suggests a channel of information and does again blur somewhat the distinction between pension and poor relief.

For some the pension was very much a transitional benefit, their source of sustenance going from poor relief to pension and back to poor relief again. It could represent a substantial period of time away from the stigma of poor relief. George Conduit was refused a pension twice, on 18 December 1908 and 24 April 1909, because he had had poor relief. With the relaxation of the rules in 1911 he was granted one. However, on 27 March 1918 he lost it again on entering the Salisbury workhouse. It gave him seven years of independent living but hardly removed the spectre of the workhouse altogether. Michael Thomas, refused a pension because of a term of imprisonment in November 1910, eventually gained one after the relaxation of the rules but had it discontinued in August 1917 because he was receiving poor relief.[87] What the pension did was to entitle some of the elderly to survive without having to resort to the Poor Law authorities at least for part of their old age, but without other substantial sources of income and help this was a struggle which many lost and they still ended their days in the workhouse. This problem was foreseen by Haldane, Secretary of War in the Liberal government, on the first day of the parliamentary debate on the Pensions Bill in 1908. He pointed out that the Act did not help very much if it removed the aged from the Poor Law only to leave them with no alternative when they needed care but to go into the workhouse.[88] Although it seems some of the elderly preferred poor law relief because 'they could not exist without the kindly supervision and personal assistance of the Inspector of the Poor',[89] the Ryland Adkins Committee in 1919 found that the stigma of the Poor Law had not lessened among the aged.[90] It could be argued then that the pension was of dubious long-term benefit to the aged poor and for many did not provide a permanent escape from the disgrace of the workhouse.

How far then did the Old Age Pensions Act of 1908 mark a complete break with the Poor Law? There is no doubt that the Act was, in part, a breakthrough in social policy. It granted state help as a right to a needy section of the population which did not deprive the recipient of citizenship. It established a central machinery which was intended to provide uniformity and thus fairness. It involved an acknowledgement of the economic and social causes of poverty and the duty of the state to intervene and redistribute wealth from the better off to those struggling to survive.

However, it was a small step towards a modern bureaucratic model of social security. The machinery which the Act set up, which remained virtually unchanged even with the introduction of contributory pensions in 1925, still owed much to the 'face to face' relationships of 'Victorian social welfare provision'.[91] In its need to limit costs and to uphold the accepted principle of self-help the government established a system which was reminiscent of the paternalistic, family-based and personal system of nineteenth-century welfare as exemplified by the Poor Law. The government was anxious to present the pension as a right and not charity but claimants remained supplicants who had to prove their fitness to receive it through a series of personal encounters and moral restrictions. A.V. Dicey, the jurist, anticipated this when he described the pension in 1908 as a 'new form of outdoor relief for the poor'.[92] This continuity with the Poor Law does not derive solely from the moral tests but from the whole apparatus set up by the Act.

The moral disqualifications simply add to the impression that the Act was as much backward as forward looking. The exclusions for drunkenness, idleness and imprisonment were numerically not significant, though they were certainly invoked on occasions, as the local sources reveal. However, their symbolic importance and their influence on the operation of the Act was significant. They suggested that the new pension like the old Poor Law was using social assistance as part of a disciplinary process. The pauper disqualification which lasted until 31 December 1910 was of more than just symbolic importance. In the first two years an estimated 160,000 of the aged poor were deprived of a pension because they had received poor law relief.[93] This represented a considerable moral judgement as well as economic hardship on many of the aged poor. Additionally, the pension did not remove the spectre of the Poor Law from their lives. They often had to choose between poor relief or pension; they could not have both, so many had no choice but to end their days in the workhouse.

Thus while the *introduction* of the Act was and still is regarded by some as a major break with the past, I argue that in its *operation* the continuities were as significant. These continuities can be explained in two ways.

On the one hand, D. Ashford stresses the inherited ideas and institutions. First, there is the 'moralizing tone' of much of collectivist liberal thinking on social reform: 'the individualistic assumptions prevailing in the British debate over new liberalism, were later manifested in the organization of new social legislation, the design and extension of social benefits, and, most dramatically in the persistence of the Poor Laws'. The same could be said of the exclusion clauses and administration of the 1908 Act. Second, and equally significant for Ashford, is the policy-making process: 'the principles of social progress and social change had to pass the hurdle of the policy process'. This meant that the new legislation could not escape the institutional and historical precedents; it had to blend 'with the pre-existing institutional norms and practices to permit the state to engage in entirely new endeavours'.[94] Hence the makers of the Old Age Pensions Act (and it was designed in secrecy by a few close advisers to Asquith and Treasury civil servants) naturally drew upon the closest example they had – the Poor Law. The new pension was social policy on the hoof; it could not be expected totally to break new ground and indeed its resemblance to the Poor Law should perhaps be expected.

On the other hand, my findings lend support to the Marxist view that such social legislation is an essential feature by which the capitalist class organizes its social power. Corrigan and Sayer argue that moral regulation is fundamental to state power and this is achieved through 'the continuous and more or less violent suppression of alternatives coupled with active encouragement by state agencies . . . of preferred forms'.[95] The continuities between the Poor Law and the 1908 Act were not fortuitous – both were centralized forms of administration designed to discipline the lower orders in a time of heightening class tensions. I. Gough recognizes this but interprets the Edwardian social reforms in a more contradictory light. The provision of a new benefit outside the Poor Law was in the objective interests of the aged poor and did mitigate some hardship, but at the same time it furthered the interests of the state in 'integrating and controlling' the working class. This contradiction takes the form of 'a potential conflict over who controls the social services': it is in the administration of such legislation that the 'apparent harmony of interests . . . breaks down'.[96] The strength of the rising working class was at this time insufficient to force a break with the administrative legacy of the Poor Law.

POLICING AND THE COMMUNITY:

LATE TWENTIETH-CENTURY MYTHS AND LATE NINETEENTH-CENTURY REALITIES[1]

DAVID TAYLOR

The last quarter of the twentieth century has seen a crisis in policing. The disturbances of the 1980s in particular, in which hitherto unsuspected depths of anti-police feeling manifested themselves, led to a widespread questioning not just of police tactics but of the basic philosophy of policing. In the search for solutions to the problems of today, attention was paid to the experiences of yesterday. Appeals were made, explicitly and implicitly, to the principles of Colonel Charles Rowan and Sir Richard Mayne, the 'founding fathers' of modern policing. Community policing became an oft-quoted, if ill-defined, phrase that appealed to a deep-seated belief that there had been an earlier, better way which brought together the police and the overwhelming majority of law-abiding citizens in a common purpose to maintain order and combat criminality.

This thinking has struck a chord with a large number of people for whom such a view of the bobby in the community was part of an inherited culture, dating back at least to the early twentieth century when *The Times* praised the London bobby for his contribution to the well-being of society:

> The policeman, in London, is not merely the guardian of its peace, he is an integral part of its social life. In many a back street and

slum he not merely stands for law and order; he is the true handyman of our streets, the best friend of a mass of people who have no other counsellor or protector.[2]

Such an image was given visual form in the Raphael Tuck 'Real Photograph' postcard series of the 1930s. For example, *The Benevolent Policeman*, with its suitable picture to accompany the printed message, proclaims that 'To pilot children over crowded roads is daily proof of the policeman's kind and efficient service.'[3] Reassuring images such as this have been recreated in popular culture in a variety of dramatic fiction on the police in postwar Britain. Although television representation of the police is complex, there is a recurring (and recurrently popular) image, running from *Dixon of Dock Green*, through *The Bill*, *The Chief* and, perhaps most intriguingly, to *Heartbeat*, with its fond look back to an idealized 1960s but with an implied message for the 1990s, that portrays society in terms of an organic community (*gemeinschaft*) in which the local bobby is an integral and esteemed member of the community who both embodies and defends widely shared moral values against the intrigues of local petty criminals and the threat of outside villains. The successful bobby is the man who knows his community and its inhabitants, who knows when to turn a blind eye and when to take firm but fair action. Moral persuasion more than physical force characterizes his approach to policing. Success is brought about by 'policing by consent', predicated on a shared set of values and a common sense of purpose. Known and respected by the community, he has their positive support in his task of maintaining order and fighting crime. All this stands in stark contrast to the images of policing in the inner cities in the 1980s where an alien figure, the para-military policeman, complete with riot shield and helmet, faced an alienated community all too ready to take up stones and petrol bombs in a fight in which there were no winners.

Nor are such ideas restricted to the world of television and its fictional policemen. In his recent study of chief constables, Robert Reiner includes some telling quotations on the subject of community policing. One, not totally sympathetic, chief constable recognized the friendly image of the community policeman as 'the guy who is the avuncular bobby with his size 12 boots, [who] smiles at everybody, and pats little kids on the head'.[4] The idea of the policeman in the community was stated clearly and sympathetically by another respondent who praised the community policing approach because it 'puts value on having a policeman who can stay a minute, can be flexible, get to know the community. . . . It's the business of getting close and staying close to the community that's being policed.'[5] This approach was firmly rooted in a vision of policing in the past. The ideal figure was

> the village policeman . . . a man related to the village and its surrounds, who was part of them and yet had to stand apart from them in a sense. He had an understanding of what that village was about, the need for that tranquillity, and to sort of ensure that strangers coming into the ground were clocked and identified.[6]

In this brief quotation we can see the key elements of the myth of policing in times past: the rural setting, the intrinsically tranquil community, a policeman, detached but still part of the community, who understood its needs, and the implicit link between outsiders and the threat to law and order.

It is not surprising, therefore, to find commentators advocating changes in policing which would re-create the conditions in which policing by consent and minimal force once again became the order of the day. In addition, it is no surprise to find demands for a return to moral certainties and a sense of civic responsibility as part of the solution to the troubles of the present. The issues raised by the reappraisal of policing in the late twentieth century are too complex to discuss adequately in the span of a chapter. The purpose here is to take one aspect, the notion of the effective bobby in the community in times past, and to see if the historical evidence is strong enough to bear the weight of this interpretation. It is my contention that the realities of policing in the late nineteenth and early twentieth centuries were more complex and less successful than is commonly supposed. There is a considerable body of evidence to suggest that the bobby, in town and country, was a figure set apart and distanced from the community he policed, often viewed with suspicion and not uncommonly treated with violence.[7] Turning a blind eye was not a sign of wisdom and discretion deriving from the strength of his position, but a recognition of the limitations of the support he enjoyed and the restrictions that this imposed on his authority. Insofar as levels of criminality had declined in the last quarter of the nineteenth century, this reflects less the success of the police and more the restraint of the policed. Put another way, the apparent success of late Victorian and Edwardian policing was the product rather than the cause of a wider sense and practice of law-abidingness.

Before examining the evidence of late Victorian and Edwardian England, it is important to say a word about the evolution of modern policing and the central principles that the 'founding fathers' sought to inculcate. Despite, or perhaps precisely because of, the significance of the changes associated with police reform after 1829, great stress was placed on continuity. In particular, the choice of the term constable was a conscious decision to emphasize the fact that the new policeman was part of a time-honoured tradition of the responsible civilian serving the community. Thus the constable was seen to be responsible, not simply to the law, but to the community he served. Although the advent of modern policing coincided with large-scale urbanization, the dominant model of policing that underpinned such crucial legislation as the 1856 County and Borough Police Act was a rural one. Although the Act spelt the end of parochial control, it was a defeat for the boroughs as 'the provincial vision of the rural police', with all that that implied, triumphed.[8] This view of a rural force, hierarchical and deferential, akin to a soldiery, watching over and protecting an equally hierarchical and deferential community, was of a piece with much contemporary thinking on the nature and causes of rural disturbances and crime.[9]

In the development of practical policing, from the early days of Rowan and Mayne in charge of the Metropolitan Police onwards, great emphasis was also placed on the positive relationship between the police and the policed community. Policing was to be by consent and with minimum force. The first police handbook, the *General Instructions* drawn up by Rowan and Mayne, makes clear the need to 'be civil and attentive to all persons, of every rank and class' and the crucial importance of 'a perfect command of temper' to ensure that duty is done in 'a quiet and determined manner'.[10] The message was reinforced via the General Orders issued in the early days of the Metropolitan Police which stressed the need 'to execute their duty with good temper and discretion' and to avoid 'unnecessary violence'.[11] Thus the police were to be non-partisan and accountable. At an individual level, policemen were encouraged to develop a service role, both formally as inspectors of weights and measures, for example, or informally as 'knockers-up' and the like. Although it could be argued that such thinking was motivated by more pragmatic considerations, it would be wrong to deny the importance of idealism. The realism of having to police by consent coexisted with the idealism of wishing to have a force that policed by consent. However, intention and outcome are not necessarily the same and it is important to see the extent to which the practice of policing lived up to the ideals outlined above.

In view of the importance attached to the experience of rural policing in the past, we will begin with a consideration of the situation in the late Victorian and Edwardian English countryside. Flora Thompson, often accused of seeing the late nineteenth century through rose-coloured spectacles, did not see the constable in Candleford Green as being part of the tight-knit community. She noted that:

> he was a kindly and good-tempered man; yet nobody seemed to like him, and he and his wife led a somewhat isolated life, in the village but not entirely of the village. Law-abiding as most country people were in those days, and few as were those who had any personal reason for fearing the police, the village constable was still regarded as a potential enemy, set to spy upon them by the authorities.[12]

Billy Dixon, a Norfolk labourer interviewed by Alun Howkins, made a similar point in a more forceful manner. 'Course the police were against the population then in them days . . . the police was sort of a bit of an enemy. . . .'[13] Such a sense of enmity could lead to open hostility. This was particularly so when the rural police were seen as landowners' lackeys, as in the poaching wars that rumbled on for much of the nineteenth century. In extreme cases, such as the Hungerford murders of 1877, they could be killed.[14]

A less spectacular but still striking case of communal hostility took place in Stebbing, Essex, where the inhabitants of the village were so incensed with the activities of PC Enoch Raison that they threatened to run him out of the village. On 5 November 1888 he was burnt in effigy in a display of communal protest that was recorded on camera. An attempt by the police authorities to smuggle the unfortunate Raison from the village was bungled and he left to an ignominious shower of catcalls and missiles.[15]

More common were individual assaults incurred during the course of duty. Interference in popular customs, such as the celebration of Guy Fawkes' night, could be particularly sensitive but probably the commonest location for conflict was in or around the public house. It was an extremely fortunate constable who was not attacked at least once in his career. Others were less lucky. Richard Hann, in a career that took him to many parts of Dorset, was assaulted on at least seven occasions by a variety of men and women, including a retired, but hardly retiring, sailor with a wooden leg. In one spectacular case which finally appeared before the Wimborne Petty Sessions in 1871, six men were tried for assaulting Hann and a fellow officer. It had taken the police three-quarters of an hour to bring their prisoners, kicking and biting, the 100 yards to the gaol.[16]

The incidence of acts of hostility should not be overstated. More often than not, police and policed viewed each other with mutual suspicion and continued their separate lives, observing public courtesies but little more. Non-cooperation with the police was the most likely outcome of such suspicion. With manpower limited, the rural police had little option but to watch over the districts in which they were stationed and to tolerate much of what happened.[17] The chances of overcoming the barrier of suspicion were further reduced by the numerous postings that many constables experienced. Alfred Jewitt of the East Riding Constabulary moved station nine times in a career that spanned 28 years while Richard Hann, whose career lasted 27 years, served in thirteen different places. His longest stay, four and a half years in Sixpenny Handley, was his tenth posting.[18]

The policing of the late Victorian countryside remains an under-researched area but it is clear from the evidence cited above that there is little support for the belief in a golden age of community-based policing there. More importantly, rural policing was becoming relatively less important as England became an increasingly urban society. Moreover, as many historians have noted, the late nineteenth century saw the growth of powerful working-class communities in the burgeoning towns and cities. But what was happening in these districts? Was *The Times* correct in describing the London 'bobby' as the 'handyman of the street'? And was this typical of the country at large?

The policing of London had been characterized by violent conflict from the outset. The disturbances at Cold Bath Fields in 1833, which saw the celebrated 'justifiable homicide' of PC Culley, the Hyde Park Sunday Trading riots of 1855 and the electoral reform riots of 1866/7, during which Commissioner Mayne suffered a bloodied head and found himself condemned by *Fun*, a satirical weekly, as 'the leader of an organised gang of ruffians' responsible 'for assaulting the Public in the execution of its duty',[19] were among the more spectacular examples of an ongoing and turbulent relationship between the police and various sections of the working-class population. However, contrary to traditional interpretations, it is by no means clear that these problems had been overcome by the late nineteenth or early twentieth century. Indeed, with the increase in police responsibilities, especially in enforcing morals, and the increased tensions brought about by the growth of organized labour, in its various guises, tension between the police and the overwhelmingly working-class policed increased and, as a consequence, conflict continued at higher levels than might have been expected in view of the general decline in violent behaviour in late Victorian and Edwardian England.[20]

The events of 'Bloody Sunday', 13 November 1887, offer a spectacular example of conflict. Protests against the government's failure to deal with the problems of the unemployed became violent when an attempt was made to ban a meeting called by the Metropolitan Radical Association to take place in Trafalgar Square. Over 400 arrests took place and there were some 200 casualties, including three fatalities. Trouble continued at the funeral of one of the victims, Alfred Linnell. Although, in retrospect, the role of the police is less clear-cut than contemporary critics, including *The Times*, suggested, the myth of 'Bloody Sunday' merely confirmed the belief, in some quarters of working-class society at least, that the police were the unequivocal defenders of the propertied against the unjustly treated and suffering propertyless.

The twentieth-century myth of communal policing does not allow for political conflict and industrial divisions but they were important, not only in separating the propertied and the propertyless and employers and employees but also the police and the policed. Public demonstrations and political rallies, however, were exceptional and confined to a minority of working-class Londoners. None the less, the Metropolitan Police impinged upon the daily lives of Londoners in an ever-increasing number of ways. The concern with order and decorum on the streets led to interventions in the work and leisure habits of far greater numbers than participated in overtly political activity. Street recreations and the street economy had come under increasing attack for many years. The police were an important component in the conflict between 'respectable' and 'rough' cultures during the nineteenth century. By the early twentieth century, according to Archibald's *Metropolitan Police Guide*, there were just under 650 statutes relating to police work, most of which referred either to economic or recreational activities in the streets.[21] In the last quarter of the nineteenth century there was a more focused attack on specific problem cases. The prostitute, the habitual drunkard, the habitual vagrant, the habitual criminal, the juvenile delinquent, the gambler and the alien were identified as specific components of a wider social problem that required state action. The police were also under pressure to act from reformist groups, though this could add to the problems of the former by exposing divisions within the wider community. In 1883, under pressure from parish vestries and vigilance societies, Sir Edmund Henderson started a campaign against street prostitution which lasted four years.

However, the campaign and the response it engendered was a near disaster in terms of publicity for the Metropolitan Police. Allegations of the blackmailing of poor prostitutes and of indiscriminate arrests came to a climax with the celebrated Cass case of 1887.[22] Questions were asked in parliament and a more general condemnation of excessive police powers forced the new commissioner, Sir Charles Warren, to back down. A further campaign after the turn of the century reached a similar conclusion with the d'Angely case of 1906. Once again, the Metropolitan Police appeared to be guilty of arresting respectable women, and of harassing them afterwards, while known prostitutes paid the police to ensure they plied their trade undisturbed.[23] Nor was such payment of bribes confined to the pre-war years. In a notorious case involving George Goddard, a sergeant at Vine Street station, it became clear that there was extensive, and lucrative, collaboration between some members of the force and those, such as Kate 'Ma' Meyrick, involved in the vice trade of the West End. The spectacular cases should not obscure the more routine attacks on street prostitution which, like earlier campaigns against prostitution in casinos and music halls, alienated certain sectors of the populace.[24]

The same applied to the campaign against the habitual criminal which was an important factor in the development of the detective force. The growth of this branch of police activity was fraught with difficulties. The Turf Fraud case of 1877 spectacularly highlighted the problem of corruption, but there were other less prominent cases of malpractice which helped to confirm popular fears. While the campaign against the habitual criminal touched on a relatively small section of the population, the attempts to curb drinking and gambling, through such legislation as the 1869 Wine and Beerhouses Act, the 1872 Licensing Act, the 1873 Betting Houses Act and especially the 1906 Street Betting Act, brought the police into contact, and conflict, with a wider body of people. It is a measure of community pressure on the police that they were reluctant to arrest drunkards unless under pressure from temperance and purity reformers.

The precise impact of the changes in police activity in the late nineteenth century is almost impossible to measure. Gatrell's recent general calculations give some indication of the impact of the greater regulation of society at this time. Between 1861 and 1891, a period in which serious crime rates were falling, the ratio of arrests and summons to the total population rose from 1 in 29 to 1 in 24 for men. In fact, the law fell most heavily on the poor and the young. The unskilled young man of London's East End probably had a 1 in 6 chance (or less) of falling foul of the law. The 'rozzers' were a constant and threatening presence for many working-class people. The popular cry of 'Give it to the copper' does not sit comfortably with the notion of the policeman being seen as the 'handyman of our street', and neither do the statistics for assaults on the police.

While it is true that the level of recorded assaults on the police declined in the late nineteenth century, in part the product of a change to less intrusive and less confrontational police tactics, the problem remained a serious one for the Met. Despite Charles Booth's claim that 'nearly everyone speaks well of the police' and 'relations were noticeably friendly',[25] it remained the case that a London constable was more likely than not to be attacked while on duty. Between 1903 and 1906 some 2,500 men, or roughly one in every four constables in the Met, were assaulted. Mass assaults to rescue prisoners remained a feature of certain working-class districts well into the twentieth century. The notorious Campbell Bunk, in Islington, where flower pots were kept to throw at the police, retained its popular name of 'Kill Copper Row' until the 1920s, while gangs of youths in many parts of Edwardian London attacked the police as a means of resisting the criminalization of traditional street activities.[26] Such evidence suggests little tolerance and less affection for the police. Even in less violent districts the decline in assaults upon the police did not necessarily mean greater acceptance or affection. Acquiescence was more the order of the day, and often sullen acquiescence at that.

One further point needs to be stressed. Given the constraints of numbers, the police had to make certain assumptions about likely trouble spots and likely troublemakers in determining the thrust of their day-to-day policing. Areas believed to be inhabited by criminals were subjected to closer scrutiny. The greater police presence led to more arrests which in turn 'confirmed' the initial judgement and justified continuing police activity. But what appeared as common sense to the police could appear as victimization to the policed. The voices of the latter are rarely recorded but it is not difficult to see how and why suspicion and mistrust of the police persisted into the twentieth century. Indeed, for some feelings went beyond mistrust to outright hostility. One Londoner had no doubts about 'the hired enforcers of authority headed by the hated, yes really hated, bullying fat cozpots who strutted arrogantly upon our turf'.[27]

However, the experience of slums like Campbell Bunk reveals a more complex picture of the relationship between working-class communities and the police. Many people took an instrumentalist view of the police. The law in general and the police in particular had a role to play in these districts. Protection of person and property led many Londoners to make use of the forces of law and order. It was also the case that a few policemen 'took pains to enter into the spirit' of these areas and became 'honorary members of the community'. There were, however, clear limits to such relationships. Being on good terms with some of the locals was not sufficient to save a policeman from abuse and assault if the circumstances were not right.[28]

It might be objected that London was *sui generis*. To some extent the sheer size and complexity of the city brought with it certain problems that were not to be found elsewhere, but it would be misleading to suggest that the tensions and conflicts between police and policed in the capital were unique to that city. True, by the end of the nineteenth century there was none of the large-scale and spectacular opposition that had seen the police driven out of Colne in 1840 or attacked for three days in Leeds in 1844. It is also the case that there was a decline in the number of recorded assaults upon the police, though this does not necessarily mean that there was greater love for them. Indeed, there was a continuing suspicion and hostility that persisted well into the twentieth century. Writing in 1911, Reynolds and Wooley summed up the situation succinctly:

> The police are charged not only with the prevention and detection of crime among them [the working classes], as among other people, but with the enforcement of a whole mass of petty enactments, which are little more than social regulations bearing almost entirely on working-class life. At the bidding of one class, they attempt to impose a certain social discipline on another. In

every direction, inside his own house as well as out, the working man's habits and convenience are interfered with, or his poverty is penalised by the police.[29]

The situation was made worse by the fact that by the turn of the twentieth century the police forces of England were larger, almost certainly more efficient and were charged with the responsibility for the supervision of a wider range of activities than had been the case with their mid-Victorian predecessors. As a consequence, 'Whether or not he [a working-class man] comes into collision with them [the police] is more a matter of good fortune than of law-abidingness, and he is a lucky man who does not find himself in their hands at one time or another in his life.'[30] The police were clearly identified as being the agents of another class, imposing alien values that led to working-class people being punished for actions that they did not see as wrong. 'For that reason alone, there is hardly a man who cannot, from the working-class point of view, bring up instances of gross injustices on the part of the police towards himself or his friends or relations. . . .'[31]

Juveniles could easily find themselves on the receiving end of heavy-handed policing. Street games, especially football, were a recurring source of friction. In certain areas, as Stephen Humphries has noted, gang attacks on the police were a form of resistance to the criminalization of street leisure.[32] Robert Roberts took a very similar view in his recollections of Edwardian Salford. The violent dispersal of strikers that had left at least one neighbour 'knocked silly' meant that 'among the lower working class the actions of the police had left them no better loved than before'. As in London the young, especially if indulging in gambling, could expect heavy-handed treatment from the local police which left 'a fear and hatred of the police that in some perfectly law-abiding citizens lasted through life'. Summing up the situation as he saw it, and in a way that consciously referred to the claims of *The Times*, Roberts concluded:

Nobody in our Northern slum, to my recollection, ever spoke in fond regard, then, or afterwards of the policeman as 'social worker' and 'handyman of the street'. Like their children, delinquent or not, the poor in general looked upon him with fear and dislike. When one arrived on a 'social' visit they watched his passing with suspicion and his disappearance with relief. . . .[33]

The myth of community policing does not allow for fundamental conflicts within society but such were the deeply structured inequalities in Victorian and Edwardian society that social and industrial conflict was a not uncommon happening. The police could not avoid being drawn into such conflicts. There is little doubt that policing industrial disputes could be difficult and dangerous. The bitter nine-week strike in the north Lancashire cotton district in 1878, for example, led to riots in several towns and widespread hostility directed at the police. At its worst, in Darwen, there was an effective collapse of law and order that lasted for several days. A crowd estimated to be in the region of 2,000 attacked police reinforcements, who had been brought in from Blackburn, Bolton, Burnley, Clitheroe and Manchester, and laid siege to the police station in the town. Some years later, in what became known as 'The Battle of Howe Bridge', police armed with cutlasses fought with striking miners in 1881. However, in contrast, during the 1893 miners' strike in Leigh, the police opened soup kitchens and fed hundreds of people in a gesture that won much local approval.[34]

Some of the worst disturbances took place in the tight-knit mining communities in the South Wales coalfield where the local police chiefs had openly identified themselves with the colliery owners for many years. In the early twentieth century the Chief Constable of Glamorgan, Captain Lionel Lindsay, took a very simple view of matters: there was a threat from socialist subversives that had to be dealt with firmly and forcefully. Tensions were increased by the introduction of the Metropolitan Police but, perhaps a little surprisingly, this led to a different approach to the situation. General Macready, the man in charge of the Metropolitan Police, sought to act impartially. Distancing himself and his men from the employers, he was prepared to negotiate with the strikers and even to permit peaceful picketing. However, Macready's initiative failed. The Metropolitan Police were unpopular and there were several accusations in the local press, coming not simply from strikers but also from shopkeepers and clerics, of indiscriminate baton charges and other police brutalities.[35]

The transport strikes of 1911 also brought major disturbances, most notably Liverpool's 'Bloody Sunday', 13 August 1911. Once again the presence of outside police exacerbated an already tense situation. Police had been brought in from Birmingham and Leeds with the express purpose, approved by Winston Churchill at the Home Office, of clearing the strikers off the streets. A police attack on the largest demonstration precipitated two days of rioting in which two people were killed and many more injured. Not for the first time, an industrial dispute had revealed fundamental divisions within the local economy and the policing of the strike had left the police as unpopular figures on the side of employers against employees.

The hostility engendered during periods of industrial conflict could also affect the families of policemen. Recollecting the Cornish clay strikes of 1911, one policeman's daughter recalled the 'awful life' she had:

> . . . they was all against you. When we did go to school the other children'd chase you and pelt you with stones. . . . I used to say 'twas a wonder I wasn't killed. They used to bully me – 'tisn't all fun being a policeman's child. They used to have a fun time chasing us; we was just 'Bobby's child'. You were outsiders, really, being policemen's children.[36]

However, hostility and violence was not an inevitable outcome. The engineers' lock-out of 1897/8 in Middlesbrough took place with little trouble, and even though the town's Trades and Labour Council complained of police intimidation of strikers in 1900 there were no outbreaks of violence. Likewise, the transport strike in Hull in 1911 passed with relative calm. Despite pressure for strong action from the city's influential shipowners, who also had the backing of Churchill, the local Watch Committee decided to act cautiously and was only prepared to offer police assistance if a breach of the peace seemed imminent. The offer of outside police help was refused in a deliberate attempt to prevent the situation overheating. By paying attention to the varying needs within the town and adopting a more conciliatory line, there was none of the rioting and anti-police incidents that had happened elsewhere.

Community policing could also founder on racial differences. By the late nineteenth century there were well-established Irish communities in the towns and cities of mainland Britain. Religious and other cultural differences combined with a perception in certain quarters that the Irish were peculiarly violent and criminally inclined produced a stereotype which, among other things, influenced the way in which this group and the districts in which they lived were policed. Certain slum areas were identified as particularly problematic and singled out for special policing. One such area, as Jennifer Davis has shown, was Jennings' Buildings, a notorious slum off Kensington High Street inhabited by large numbers of Irish and other poor. The 'lower order of Irish' were, in the opinion of the *West London Observer* in 1860, 'continually creating disturbances, assaulting the police and by their violent and disgraceful habits the inhabitants of Kensington are continually kept in fear of some outrage'.[37]

The police appear to have shared this perception and paid close attention to the inhabitants of the buildings, a policy greatly aided by the fact that the Kensington police station was located directly opposite the entrance! Unsurprisingly, close police attention was reflected in a disproportionate number of Irish men and women appearing in court. Equally unsurprising was the conflict between them and the police. With the threat of abusive words and more solid stones in the air, the police tended to turn a blind eye to some of the less attractive features of social life in the buildings. Fighting and drunkenness were tolerated as long as it took place within the slum. However, the police did have contacts in the area. Lacking the power to suppress trouble within the buildings, they relied upon a local lodging house and beershop keeper, John 'Falstaff' Simpson, who also recruited casual labourers and provided a money-lending service. Clearly a criminal he escaped prosecution in return, or so it would seem, for maintaining a semblance of order in the buildings and also for turning in 'outside' criminals seeking refuge there. Whether one can see this as a precursor of 1980s community policing in the inner-city centres, as Davis claims, is open to debate but the case of Jennings' Buildings highlights the limitations of Victorian police in the face of a community which, however criminal in the eyes of respectable society, was sufficiently large and concentrated to force the authorities either to ignore criminal behaviour or to cooperate with local men of influence to negotiate a level of crime control acceptable to both parties.

In other parts of the country the policing of Irish communities proved difficult, notwithstanding (indeed perhaps because of) the fact that many Irishmen were constables. In Middlesbrough in the 1860s and '70s particularly there were repeated cases of large-scale assaults and crowd rescues as the town police sought to arrest Irish men and women living 'over the border' in the old town centre. Superintendent Saggerson, a canny and pragmatic chief of police not given to exaggeration, felt it necessary to inform the Watch Committee in the autumn of 1864 of the worrying fact of 'an increase of fifty-seven assaults on the police arising out of the opposition (by the lowest class of Irish people) to the Constables when endeavouring in the execution

117

of their duty to check disorderly conduct and preserve the peace'.[38] Assaults continued and early in the new year the local newspaper carried the following reports of incidents involving the police and Irishmen. In one case, PC Stainsby attempted to arrest a labourer, Michael Lougheran,

> who commenced kicking the officer and striking him, [while another] four or five men came up and assisted him in committing a most brutal attack. The officer was knocked down and the men attacked him in the most savage manner kicking him with their feet, striking him with sticks which they carried with them and biting him. Two severe wounds were inflicted on the top of his head and the officer was rendered well-nigh insensible.[39]

In another case during the same month the attempted arrest of Patrick Evans, 'an Emeralder' according to the press account, by PC Wilkinson resulted in a crowd of between 500 and 600 surrounding the officer who was then subject to a vicious assault by Evans and his comrades. The local magistrates finally took a tougher line and imprisoned without option of a fine all arrested for such assaults. There was a drop in the scale of anti-police assaults but the problem rumbled on for many years. In December 1875, Sergeant Raisbeck was attacked by six 'low Irishmen' and, as the *Middlesbrough Weekly News* disapprovingly noted, there was at least one section of the local community for whom the police were seen as enemies.[40]

A similar situation prevailed in Wolverhampton and the Black Country, as David Woods has demonstrated, with violent resistance on the part of individuals and collective attempts to rescue prisoners not uncommon in the 1870s. At times the danger to the police took somewhat comical forms. When PC Purchase tried to persuade the drunk and disorderly Brigit Regan to return to her home on 'Irish Row', off Willenhall Road, Wolverhampton, he could have had little idea of the difficulties and dangers that were to follow. Having failed more than once to persuade the woman to stay indoors, Purchase finally appeared to have succeeded but, after a five-minute break, the door opened once again and Regan reappeared and began assaulting the constable with a poker. Assisted by PC Thompson, Purchase tried to take the woman into custody only for a hostile crowd, estimated at some 1,500 people, to assemble. The two constables were attacked and dragged into Regan's house where they were 'maltreated by the mob' and held for several hours before finally making it to safety.[41] As in other parts of the country, the 1870s were the worst years for vicious assaults. Thereafter, attitudes and actions changed as outright antagonism became a reluctant acquiescence born of a realization that police powers were considerable and long-lasting.

The policing of the Irish, and of the other outcast groups created in the late nineteenth century which were discussed above, raises a number of interesting questions about popular responses to police action. There is a sense in which police popularity was enhanced as a result of the actions that they took, and were very clearly seen to take, against outcast groups which had been identified as threats to the well-being of society. By creating scapegoats, in the form of the habitual criminal, the habitual drunkard, the rough Irish and the corrupting alien, the anxieties of late Victorian and Edwardian society were both displaced and more clearly focused upon what were seen as enemies within. The police, in taking action against such threatening groups, stood to gain in reputation and appear to have done so, particularly in the eyes of the middle classes. The extent to which such actions won them working-class support is less certain. Obviously, there was not a single working-class experience of or response to policing. It is clear that many working-class men and women took an instrumental view of the police while others, a smaller percentage almost certainly, welcomed the attempts to check forms of behaviour that they themselves condemned. None the less, there remained a general belief that the law was made by one group in society and imposed upon another, and that the police were the agents of enforcement. More specifically, there remained the awareness of the ease with which an individual, or a close relative or friend, could end up on the wrong side of the law. Thus, when policing strikes, arresting street gamblers or prosecuting the drunk and disorderly, a constable could easily find himself not simply on the outside of the community he was policing but also facing outright hostility. Commonly coming from a working-class background, the constable was expected to enforce, as well as to conform to, a code of behaviour that distanced him from those around him.

However, it would be misleading to suggest that it was impossible to gain acceptance, even affection, from a community. The hundreds of people who lined the streets of Leicester for the funeral of PC Stephens in 1908 seem to have done so out of a genuine sense of grief at the loss of a respected figure in the community. Other obituaries in the local press reveal a similar sentiment. Reasons for this are not difficult to find. It is not implausible to argue that, particularly with the spread of codes of respectability in working-class as well as middle-class society, there were a growing number of men and women who welcomed the greater safety of the person and security of property that came with the development of efficient police forces. Similarly, the attacks upon 'immorality' in its various guises would not have been universally unpopular throughout working-class society.

In addition, although easily parodied, the police did play a routine 'social service' role which saw lost children reunited with their parents at the local station, old ladies given assistance in crossing busy roads and early-morning workers get a waking knock to ensure that they arrived on time. It is impossible to say to what extent this changed popular perceptions but it is the case that a more benign image of the police existed among certain working-class men and women who grew up in the 1890s and 1900s. Furthermore, the reputation of the police could be enhanced when they were called upon to display courage in dealing with dangerous situations. It is not uncommon to find references in the local Watch Committee minutes to policemen injured when stopping runaway horses or dealing with dangerous dogs. Among a number of men who were praised for such action, PC Summersgill of the Middlesbrough force was highly commended in February 1903 for his 'courageous action' in finally halting a runaway horse which had dragged him for some fifty yards while in full flight.

These and other even braver actions, particularly at fires, added to the perception of the police as servants of the public, prepared to put considerations of the public good above those of personal safety. PC Barnes, also of Middlesbrough, was both highly commended and promoted for his 'heroic conduct' at the Hippodrome disaster in the town in April 1911 which saw two people killed and several more injured as panic ensued when fire broke out in a crowded theatre. The public response in this instance was clear but the extent of public recognition for such actions cannot easily be gauged. Letters of thanks sent to the police or the local Watch Committee and references in local press reports give a tantalizing but incomplete glimpse into public attitudes. Thus, for example, during the Norfolk floods of August 1912, there were a number of brave rescue actions, one of which involved a policeman and a local boatman bringing some 100 people to safety. The local press was fulsome in its praise of the police:

Day and night they have been at their posts, and have cheerfully undertaken tasks that lie beyond the scope of their recognised duties. . . . At the height of the flood [they] rendered yeoman service in rescuing, pacifying and removing to places of shelter numberless wretched, half-drowned men, women, and children and all this was done with a gentleness and solicitude for their welfare and comfort that won the gratitude of the affected ones.[42]

It is also the case that the relationship between the police and 'petty' criminals could become more positive, with something approaching an element of mutual respect in some cases. Arthur Harding, hardly a friend of the police, none the less struck up working relationships with certain officers, some of whom became friends. More generally, the police and the policed could develop their own rules of behaviour to minimize conflict. Such legislation as the 1906 Street Betting Act, which was perceived to have a clear class bias, was not enforced with the utmost rigour in many parts of the country. In Middlesbrough and Stockton street gambling schools were given ample advance warning as the local bobbies made their way steadily towards the offenders.[43] Young 'hooligans' likewise appear to have accepted that they were playing a game which involved being caught and punished at times but which did not bring any particular animosity towards the policemen who were responsible for bringing them to justice. A similar situation obtained in Salford. Successful action against street gamblers appears to have owed more to good fortune and was often achieved in the face of community support for the pitch-and-toss or crown-and-anchor players. Police action against street bookmakers was often 'sporadic'. Indeed, collusion, including staged arrests, between them seems to have been commonplace.[44]

The historical record of policing late Victorian and Edwardian society reveals a complex situation, determined by accidents of personality, place and circumstances. One thing, however, is clear. There was never a 'golden age' of policing in which the local officer, in town or country, was the unquestioned and respected guardian and enforcer of a commonly accepted code of law and order. Society was too complex and too structurally riven for this. The police (through choice or not is immaterial) could not escape from being drawn into the various conflicts that characterized the period. However, one should not replace a simplistic consensus model with an equally simplistic conflict interpretation. It is essential to the understanding of policing, both in the past and in the present, to recognize the complex and contradictory nature of the tasks that the policeman is asked to do as part of the job and, similarly, the complexities and contradictions of the expectations that surround him (and now her) in the execution of those tasks. The late Victorian or Edwardian policeman could appear in many guises. In one circumstance he was a genial figure, returning a lost child; in another, a welcome defender against petty thieves. But equally he could appear at other times, *to the same person*, let alone to different members of society, as a heavy-handed and insensitive figure, brusquely enforcing laws and even exacting punishments for actions and activities that appeared neither sinful nor threatening. Worse still, he could appear as a brutal threat to rights as he escorted scab labour to work during a strike or broke up groups of political demonstrators, male and female, protesting for the vote. The multi-faceted nature of police work as it had developed by the early twentieth century, let alone the immense variability of the police as a body of men, makes a nonsense of the nostalgic and uncritical late twentieth century appeals to a lost golden age of community policing. The crisis of present-day policing would have a familiar ring to the worried chief constables of a century ago for whom community and the police were often seen to be in conflict rather than harmony. The last word rests with a neglected fictional policeman, commenting on the harsh realities of policing in the 1960s:

> The story is all coppers are just civilians like anyone else . . . but you and I know that's just a legend for mugs. We are cut off; we're not like everyone else. Some civilians fear us and play up to us, some dislike us and keep out of our way but no one – well, very few indeed – accepts us as just ordinary like them. In one sense, dear, we're just like hostile troops occupying an enemy country.[45]

'ONE COULD LITERALLY HAVE WALKED ON THE HEADS OF THE PEOPLE CONGREGATED THERE.'

SPORT, THE TOWN AND IDENTITY

JACK WILLIAMS

Recent writings about the nature of English culture in the late nineteenth and early twentieth centuries have stressed the importance of the pastoral tradition. Alun Howkins has shown how perceptions of England and Englishness between 1880 and the 1920s emphasized rusticity as an essential component of England and Englishness.[1] Georgina Boyes has demonstrated in *The Imagined Village* how both the political left and the right came to see the town as embodying spiritual and physical decay, and that the revival of folk song and dance was in part an attempt to restore to English culture the moral worth of rural values.[2] Yet while there is no denying the unedifying aspects of town life, especially in the northern industrial towns, it can be argued that the town was a symbol of pride to many of its inhabitants in the late nineteenth century and that town identities figured prominently in how many people imagined themselves. Sport had a key role in the formation and expression of town identities.[3]

SPORT IN URBAN POPULAR CULTURE

The watching of sport brought a new dimension to the calendar of popular culture in the last two decades of the nineteenth century.

Traditional sports such as rough football, prize-fighting and horse racing had attracted large crowds but in most localities this was only for a few days each year. In the 1880s large numbers began to watch team sports each week. Association Football drew most paying spectators. The average attendance at a Football League match in 1888/9, the first season of the Football League, had been over 4,600. By 1899/1900 the average attendance at a match in the First Division of the Football League was 9,500 and nearly 22,000 by 1913/14. In 1892/3, the average attendance at matches in the Second Division of the Football League was just over 2,700 and more than 10,700 in 1913/14.[4] This increase in attendance at Football League matches was not due entirely to the higher proportion of clubs from big cities. Spectator numbers for most clubs increased over the same time. The average number of spectators attending a home league match of Blackburn Rovers, for instance, had been 5,505 in 1888/9, 6,725 in 1899/1900 and 22,295 in 1913/14. Barnsley played in the Second Division from 1898/9 until the First World War. Its seasonal attendances were usually below the average for the Second Division, but the average number of spectators at the home matches of Barnsley rose from 2,650 in 1898/9 to 7,800 in 1913/14. Cup ties usually attracted bigger crowds than league matches.

Before 1914 the Football League was predominantly a league of clubs from the north and Midlands. Less material is available about attendances in other leagues but Bristol City, when playing in the Southern League, had average home attendances of 4,500 in 1897/8 and 15,500 in 1906/7,[5] which were above the average for First Division Football League clubs in those seasons. High numbers watched other team sports. Yorkshire County Cricket Club had 185,000 paying spectators in 1904 but fewer than 100,000 in 1914. Yorkshire was always among the best supported counties. Essex, less well supported, had around 50,000 spectators in 1904 and about 60,000 in 1914.[6] These are numbers of paying spectators alone and do not include club members who were admitted to matches free. It is very likely that on most Saturdays after 1900 more watched league rather than county cricket in Lancashire and Yorkshire. In the Lancashire League, arguably the most prestigious of all cricket leagues but whose fourteen clubs were concentrated within 20 miles of each other, a few matches each season attracted over 5,000 spectators. Like county clubs, league clubs allowed members into matches free of charge.

In some Lancashire and Yorkshire towns, rugby league, or Northern

Union rugby football as rugby league was called until 1922, was the main spectator sport, but precise details of match attendances are scarce and not sufficient to show whether or not the general trend of attendances was rising. Match attendances averaged over 5,000 in the opening weeks of the first Northern Union season in 1895. Towards the close of the Edwardian period average crowds for the first round of the Northern Union Cup were around 6,000 but about 15,000 for the third round.[7] In 1904/5 a crowd of 4,000 was described as 'an average attendance' for a Warrington home match, but the first three matches played in 1913 attracted crowds of 5,000, 1,000 (played in a blizzard) and 6,000, which may mean that attendances for Warrington had risen slightly since 1904/5.[8] In both seasons the Warrington team was playing well enough to reach the Northern Union Cup final. Numbers of spectators for the two Northern Union clubs in Bradford – Bradford Park Avenue and Manningham – were around 4,000 in 1903 compared with 13,000 a few years earlier.[9] Twenty-one clubs from England dropped out of the senior level of the Northern Union before 1914,[10] almost certainly because they failed to attract sufficient spectators, though some were from small towns such as Liversedge and Tyldesley.

Lincoln Allison and Richard Holt have shown that watching football became part of the urban way of life in the late nineteenth century.[11] In some towns this was equally true of league cricket and northern rugby union football. Without the population base provided by towns large numbers could not have watched sport week after week. Except for county cricket with its connotations of the historic shires and English pastoralism, the teams which spectators watched were town teams, and even county cricket clubs played their matches on grounds in towns. Professional football clubs, Northern Union clubs and league cricket clubs were town clubs, or the teams of clubs based on large industrialized villages.

Supporting a town club was an expression of a town identity, an association with others from the town that asserted a collective geographical allegiance. Town identities reflected assumptions about the otherness of those not from the town. James Walvin has shown that rivalries between towns was nothing new.[12] In the early nineteenth century folk festivals such as rushbearing had been occasions of town rivalries in Lancashire,[13] but in the later nineteenth century the rise of team spectator sports created new forms of town identity when other social and economic forces were producing greater homogeneity in urban culture. The expansion of mass schooling, much improved communications, mass circulation newspapers, the greater centralization of politics and the rise of cinema can be seen as encouraging standardization in urban life. The development of sport can be seen as part of this process towards cultural uniformity. Even in the early nineteenth century practically all cricket had become played in accordance with the laws of the MCC. Local forms of football all but disappeared following the formation of the Football Association in 1863 and the Rugby Union in 1871, and the introduction of national and regional cup and league competitions added a further dimension of uniformity to football. While not national forms of sports organization, the regionalized extent of Northern Union rugby and league cricket means that they can be regarded as consistent with the trend towards greater cultural uniformity. Yet when sports were coming to be played in accordance with the same rules and organized on similar lines in different localities, supporting a town team reinvigorated town identities and expressed a source of social differentiation between towns.

CLUBS AND TOWN ALLEGIANCES

Clubs were very much town institutions. Almost all Football League clubs and a high proportion of Northern Union clubs became limited companies before 1914. Usually more than 90 per cent of their shareholdings were held locally, with practically all the small shareholders living within the town.[14] When Bradford Park Avenue football club became a limited company in 1909, a husband, wife and son who lived in Harrogate but with business interests in Bradford held 3,000 of the 3,562 shares. The other fifty-seven shareholders all lived in Bradford.[15] Hardly any league cricket clubs became limited companies, but addresses of club committee members show that usually they lived in the same town as their club. Where football spectators lived is unclear, but Saturday morning work probably meant that most spectators of a club must have lived in the town or close to it. The reporting of sport by local newspapers shows that interest in sport was concerned very much with the town team. In the early 1880s weekly or bi-weekly newspapers usually devoted only one or two columns to sport. By 1914 there would often be at least one page of sport reports, but most of these were about the local town team. Little space was given to matches between leading clubs in other areas. The frequent criticisms made by those from the public schools of the partisanship of football crowds in particular shows that most spectators were very much committed to one team.

Those who controlled clubs dependent on attracting paying spectators encouraged perceptions of clubs as town institutions. Attempts were made to foster recreational sport and so suggest that the town club was at the apex of a sporting pyramid with an organic relationship between the professional club and teams playing for recreation. In 1903 Nelson CC included the winners of the local Sunday school cricket league in the league championship celebrations.[16] Just before the First World War Blackburn Rovers paid a subscription to the local recreational football leagues and to the leading amateur clubs, but in return expected to be informed about players with an exceptional aptitude for the game. The role of a club as a town institution with an interest in sport in general was well illustrated by the debates concerning proposals to convert Blackburn Rovers' club into a limited company in 1897. There was much discussion about whether there should be an agreement that the ground would be handed over to the town council if the club ever collapsed.[17] Football, rugby and league cricket clubs organized medal competitions for recreational, workshop and scratch sides. Teams paid an entry fee and matches were played on the ground of the town team, with medals being awarded to the winners. These competitions allowed a town club to pose as the sponsor of local recreational sport, but also helped to discover talented players and brought in a little extra gate receipt income. In 1897 sixteen local clubs entered Blackburn Rovers' medal competition. Many clubs also held sports days or allowed other organizations such as the police or hospital charities to hold them on their grounds. Press reports of these sports days show that they were great events in the local sporting calendar and further emphasized the club as a patron of local sport. They included running and cycle races for local and national competitors and could attract large crowds. In 1903, 5,000 attended the fourteenth annual sports day of Nelson CC, and this was when there was disappointment that some big name competitors had not appeared.[18]

Town teams began to be a source of town pride in the 1880s. Local dignitaries were quick to proclaim that the success of a town team in national or regional competitions boosted the reputation of a town. In 1883, when Blackburn Olympic became the first northern team to win the FA Cup, the two MPs for Blackburn – Coddington, a Conservative, and Briggs, a Liberal, both industrialists – entertained the team to dinner, and Coddington declared that the 'honour of representing Blackburn had been increased by the distinguished position in which it had been placed that day'.[19] After Warrington won the Northern Union Cup in 1905, one alderman declared that 'the victory was an honour to Warrington. The team had done yeoman service to the dear old town of Warrington.'[20] When Burnley reached the FA Cup Final in 1914 Philip Morrell, the Burnley MP, said that the team 'had made the name of the town famous throughout the country'.[21]

The most intense effusions of support for town teams occurred when they won national or regional competitions. Enormous crowds turned out to welcome the teams home. These occurred spontaneously in the early 1880s but soon became a ritualized festivity and a vibrant form of street theatre. The first such demonstration may have been that in Blackburn in 1882 when Blackburn Rovers became the first northern team to reach the final of the FA Cup. When the team returned from winning the semi-final, all approaches to the station were 'densely packed', fog signals were exploded on the railway line and the players were escorted home shoulder high.[22] Even though the team lost in the final, several thousand still turned out to welcome it home. Two players, the team captain and his brother, did not return to Blackburn, but left the train in Manchester where they worked, which indicates the novelty of such celebrations. Even bigger crowds turned out the following year when Blackburn Olympic won the Cup.[23] In 1890 between 30,000 and 40,000 were thought to be in the centre of Blackburn to welcome the Rovers team after it had won the FA Cup for the fourth time in seven seasons.[24] Blackburn's population was 120,000. Press reports often commented that the crowds on such occasions were the biggest seen in towns. Similar displays of enthusiasm occurred when league cricket and Northern Union clubs won trophies. *The Nelson Leader* commented that when the Nelson team returned to the town after winning the Lancashire Cricket League in 1903 'The journey was one wild, triumphant march, and nothing like the same enthusiasm has been seen in Nelson before . . . no-one who took part in it will ever live to forget it. . . . In the centre of the town was one huge mass of humanity, and one could literally have walked on the heads of the people congregated there.'[25] In 1905 when the Warrington team returned home at 11 p.m. with the Northern Union Cup, the streets were 'well-nigh impassable'. When the team toured the town a week later in an illuminated tram, the crowds were compared to those on Mafeking night.[26]

Watching matches is one measure of allegiance to a town club. A wealth of descriptive writing shows that the overwhelming majority of spectators at professional football were working-class males, but evidence about their occupational background or whether this varied between towns or changed over time is tantalizingly rare. Scraps of data suggest, but do no more than suggest, a sizeable presence and perhaps a majority of skilled workers. Whether match admission costs of 6d were affordable would have depended on other commitments and the strength of the desire to see a particular match. League cricket is thought to have had a working-class ambience before 1914 and it is possible that a fair proportion of the 562 members of Nelson CC in 1896 and of the 685 members in 1908 who paid subscriptions of 5s or 2s 6d could have been working class.[27] Four of the twelve representatives of the First Division clubs on the executive committee of the Bolton and District Cricket Association had blue-collar jobs and two who could not be traced in local directories were probably manual workers.[28] This could mean that those with blue-collar jobs watched the matches of these leading clubs. In 1905 when Warrington was playing in the final of the Northern Union Cup, most large works in the town paid their employees a day earlier, which suggests a high level of working-class interest. The *Warrington Guardian* described some who went to the final as 'the rougher fraternity',[29] which indicates that supporters were found among the poorest sections of the working class but says nothing about what groups within the working class provided most spectators.

The town identities based on sport were a form of solidarity among working men. Richard Holt has argued that watching football was 'a periodic affirmation of collective identity', 'so many people were anxious emotionally to identify themselves with a team of players, hired to represent a club, which in turn represented a town'. Football created identities which 'gave recognition to the sheer scale of urban life. . . . By supporting a club and assembling with thousands of others like himself a man could assert a kind of membership of the city, the heart of which was physically and emotionally his for the afternoon.'[30] This also seems to have been true for Northern Union rugby and league cricket. Most Edwardian towns must have been, as Robert Roberts described Salford, a collection of adjoining industrial villages whose inhabitants had little regular contact with each other.[31] While those who lived in different parts of a town may have remained very conscious of the district where they lived, sport helped to create a town identity which existed alongside such district identities. Criticism of a town team by those from other towns could consolidate town identities. The complaints that the Barnsley players had been especially brutal in the FA Cup semi-final of 1912 led Barnsley supporters to glory in the hard physicality of their team.[32]

Enthusiasm for town teams was at its peak, of course, when teams did well. A long series of defeats did not stimulate celebrations in the streets, but support for many football clubs remained buoyant even during seasons of poor results. Match attendances for most Football League clubs rose up to the First World War. Spectator numbers did not usually fall if results were poor. Gates tended to drop only when clubs were relegated to the Second Division.[33] Unfortunately, there are not the materials to establish whether match attendances for Northern Union and league cricket fell when teams played badly.

Sport did not always encourage fiercely held town loyalties. At some clubs poor results caused a drift of support to a more successful team in a neighbouring town. In 1896 the Accrington club collapsed partly because it had lost supporters to the Burnley and Blackburn clubs.[34] Although there had been fierce rivalry between the Blackburn clubs and Darwen in the 1880s, the withdrawal of Darwen from the Second Division in 1899 was seen by the Darwen chairman as a result of Blackburn Rovers moving to Ewood Park, which was on the Darwen side of Blackburn, in 1890.[35] In 1899 the Darwen club had finished at the bottom of the Second Division and had conceded a record number of goals. Because of financial difficulties the club was disbanded, but there was sufficient local feeling that the town should have a football club and a new one was formed to play in the Lancashire League. In 1911/12 Blackburn won the Football League championship while Darwen was near the bottom of the Second Division of the Lancashire Combination. The Darwen chairman argued that 'it had been becoming quite evident that there was no room for a club in Darwen. The interest of the Darwen people was becoming more and more taken up with the Blackburn Rovers club.'[36] The Darwen club had become a weak symbol of town identity and pride.

Sport teams created new foci for town loyalties and helped working people to become included in new ways within the civic life of towns. Civic pride was strong in Victorian towns. The building of architecturally flamboyant town halls, public libraries, museums and art galleries, often using local building materials, especially in the industrial towns of the north and Midlands, was an expression of municipal self-esteem. So too was the erection of statues to local civic worthies. Such physical manifestations of town pride involved imitation and competition between towns. James Vernon has argued that:

> civic landscapes can be read as cultural texts in themselves, texts of equal significance to the ceremonies and other symbolic practices that were staged upon them. Then as now, the civic landscape represented the town to itself . . . it articulated not only the competing narratives of the community's historical purpose and identity, but also the roles of different individuals and groups within these narratives.[37]

Grandiose public buildings tended to be erected while the public life of towns was still dominated by the local economic elite and in Vernon's phraseology were used to 'articulate a highly selective version of the town's official identity'.[38] It is not clear whether the mass of working people shared such narratives of town pride, though large numbers watched the opening ceremonies of major public buildings. Town identities based on sport can be interpreted as cultural texts through which working people created a narrative for themselves which eventually drew them into the civic life of towns in a new way.

The extent to which political worthies and town councils became involved with sports clubs varied between towns. It has been mentioned earlier that the Blackburn MPs associated themselves with the Rovers and the Olympic when they reached the FA Cup Finals of 1882 and 1883, but the town council took no part in the celebrations of these successes. The festivities organized for Queen Victoria's Diamond Jubilee in 1897 show that the town fathers did not consider sporting success a very important source of civic honour. The council's congratulatory address stressed the population growth of Blackburn and particularly the growth of its cotton industry during Victoria's reign, but did not mention the town's footballing achievements which had probably brought more national fame to the town than any other activity. The processions organized by the council to mark the jubilee included the police, fire service, the local yeomanry, bands, schools and the Oddfellows but no sports organizations. The council decided that an extension to the hospital would be its official recognition of the jubilee. It rejected a proposal to provide a municipal playing field.[39] The celebrations of the Diamond Jubilee in the neighbouring towns of Burnley and Darwen also excluded sports organizations.

Municipal dignitaries in other towns began to be associated with town teams in the Edwardian period. This indicated the strength of clubs as a source of town pride and may have owed something to more lower-middle-class and working men serving on town councils. In 1903 when Bury FC won the FA Cup the mayor met the team, but an editorial in the *Bury Times* commented, 'It is no part of the duty of a Chief Magistrate to welcome home a successful football team.'[40] That day had been declared a public holiday in Bury, not because of the success of the football team, but because a local industrialist was being invested as the High Sheriff of Lancashire. When the Warrington team returned with the Northern Union Cup in 1905, they were greeted at the town hall by three aldermen who each made congratulatory speeches linking the success of the team with the reputation of the town. The scale of the celebrations may have surprised the mayor as he arranged an official reception for the team and the club officials at the town hall a few days later: he said that he was atoning for his absence when the team arrived in Warrington after the Cup Final.[41]

Two or more teams from one town may have been a cause of division among supporters. Football matches between the clubs from the same town or city attracted very high attendances but it is not clear whether support for one local club enjoined bitter hostility to the other team, as is the case so often today. Press reports suggest that a greater sense of hostility was found in the 1880s at matches between Darwen and Blackburn Rovers or Blackburn Olympic than at matches between the two Blackburn clubs. On the day that Blackburn Olympic won the FA Cup in 1883, Blackburn Rovers played Darwen in the final of the Lancashire Cup. The preview of the Lancashire Cup Final in the *Blackburn Standard* was six times longer than that of the FA Cup Final and the newspaper commented: 'The meeting of the Blackburn Rovers and Darwen was an event of greater excitement than even the meeting of Olympic and Old Etonians.'[42] The *Blackburn Times* felt, however, that some of the Rovers' followers would 'grudge the Olympic what they had fairly worked for'.[43]

According to popular tradition Manchester United and Everton were football clubs with strong Catholic support while Manchester City and Liverpool had Protestant connections, but in no English town did clubs perpetuate sectarian rivalries on a scale similar to that between Rangers and Celtic in Glasgow. An equally strong case, however, can be made for seeing two rival teams in a town as an expression of a town identity and of town pride. Richard Holt has argued that in football 'competing so fiercely for the sporting dominance of a particular city, derby games paradoxically strengthened rather than weakened civic pride'.[44] Where cricket leagues of the highest quality were based upon towns and their immediate surroundings, such as the Bradford League or the Bolton Association, matches were highly combative, but the leagues themselves were seen as emphasizing the importance of these towns in the cricket world and were a source of town pride.

Different sports created different geographical identities. Farnworth, for instance, a small town bordering on Bolton county borough, had two clubs which played in the First Division of the Bolton and District Cricket Association, one of the more prestigious cricket leagues in northern England. Great local pride was taken in these two clubs, which drew attention to the distinctive identity of Farnworth as a place separate from Bolton. Having two senior league clubs celebrated the importance of the town of Farnworth in the world of league cricket. Yet in winter those from Farnworth with an interest in football supported Bolton Wanderers and showed that a footballing loyalty to Bolton did not stop at the boundary of the county borough. Alan Metcalfe has shown that recreational football stimulated rivalry between the mining villages of Northumberland but that these village rivalries could be subsumed under a broader loyalty to Newcastle United.[45]

Although sport encouraged town allegiances, it also fomented regional loyalties which, in the north, often evinced hostility to the south and to London in particular. The decision of the rugby clubs which broke away from the Rugby Union to call themselves the Northern Union was an expression of a northern identity which emphasized the otherness of the south. In 1882 the *Blackburn Times* described the Blackburn Rovers team which played in the FA Cup Final as 'the team who went to London to represent the town, the county and the provinces, against "Metropolitan" protection and "Metropolitan" monopoly'.[46] In 1890, when Blackburn Rovers had won the FA Cup for the fourth time in seven seasons and by a record score for a Cup Final, the *Northern Telegraph* complained that the England team selected to play Scotland

will strike all Northerners with astonishment. What is to be thought of the deliberate selection of a national team which does not include a single member of the Blackburn Rovers or Preston North End or Everton? Half an hour before the committee had seen eleven men carry off their proudest trophy by the unprecedented score of six goals to one, and yet not one of the eight English members is voted a place in the team to represent their country. . . . There may be reasons for such an outrageous selection which are unknown to the general body of supporters of football, but at present the feeling is that the Southern clique have carried their hatred of Northerners to an insane extent, and inflicted a gratuitous insult upon the strongest supporters of the Association.[47]

Within cricket, support for a league club often went hand in hand with support for a county. Having a local player selected for the county was a source of pride in the locality and in the county.

SPORT, TOWN IDENTITIES AND SOCIAL HARMONY

The town identities based on sport were a demonstration of solidarity among working men, but they were more an expression of harmony with than of antagonism towards other groups. Interest in sport was not restricted to working-class men. Supporting a town club was very much an expression of male social power. The greater numbers of male to female spectators show that within many families money and leisure time were budgeted in favour of male interests, but this was not necessarily a source of conflict between the sexes. Doubtless some women objected to the involvement of their menfolk with sport and some men may have stopped watching sport because of such objections, but there is no method for establishing how often this occurred or whether it increased over time. Oral evidence from the interwar period reveals that wives often felt that their husbands could have done much worse than watch or play sport. 'Doing much worse' for wives meant leisure pursuits which could have harmed family welfare. It is likely that many women would have viewed male involvement with sport in a similar light before 1914. Male support for sport may have relied upon the exploitation of women, but it was not necessarily viewed in this light by many women and male interest in sport may well have been encouraged by women.

Some women watched sport, though they were far outnumbered by men. In 1885 2,000 women attended a Preston North End match, but photographs of spectators standing at football matches in the Edwardian period show few women and Taylor has suggested that as crowds became more numerous, the proportion of women spectators fell.[48] In 1911/12 and 1912/13 nearly 20 per cent of Blackburn Rovers' grandstand season tickets were taken by women, which suggests a degree of interest in football among middle-class women.[49] Evidence about the number of women at rugby matches is very patchy. In 1897 1,000 'ladies' were thought to have watched Swinton play Salford, but this was described as 'an unusually large number of ladies'.[50] The fear that poor children could suffer because their parents had gone to the Northern Union Cup Final in 1905 shows that some women had watched this particular game.[51]

The involvement of women with the festivities to welcome home teams which had won trophies shows that women shared the town identities centred upon sport. In 1905 when the Warrington team arrived home after winning the Northern Union Cup for the first time, the *Warrington Guardian* mentioned that two of the players had tried to escape the demonstration by slipping into a railway station waiting room, 'evidently not anxious – or too modest to show their anxiety – to receive the osculatory salutations of some designing damsels whose desire to kiss them for luck was greater than the fear of the publicity thereof'.[52] In 1912 when the Barnsley team returned home after winning the FA Cup, the streets were

a solid mass . . . The women folk were as excited as, and almost as numerous, as the men, and their familiarity with the names of the members of the team was astonishing. They called for a sight of their favourite players, and talked of the prowess of 'Dicky Downs' and the other heroes with amazing glibness.[53]

Town identities based on sport crossed class boundaries. Crowds included middle-class supporters. Taylor argues that the proportion of middle-class spectators fell as football crowds became larger,[54] though the total number of middle-class spectators could have remained constant or even risen. By 1914 covered grandstands had been built at almost all Football League and Northern Union grounds. Seats in grandstands are thought to have been occupied mainly by the middle classes. The grandstands of the Everton and Liverpool clubs each had more than 3,000 seats by the mid-1890s. Blackburn Rovers' ground had 7,000 stand seats in 1914.[55] In the late 1890s the average attendance at the home matches of Everton and Liverpool had been around 15,000 and in 1913/14 that of Blackburn was over 22,000. If only half the stand seats had been occupied at the matches of these clubs and if they are assumed to be typical of other clubs, it would seem that at least 10 per cent of spectators could have been middle class. The highest levels of subscriptions at league cricket clubs were probably aimed at the local middle class. In 1896 and 1908 the 20 per cent of the members of Nelson CC who paid subscriptions of one or two guineas could have been middle class.[56]

It is not easy to establish the sections of the middle class to which spectators belonged. No doubt those imbued with the public school ethos of amateurism which the Rugby Union espoused boycotted Northern Union matches. The disparaging comments made by those with public school backgrounds about the partisanship of spectators at Football League matches suggests that few of them watched league football regularly. Cricket clubs for the social elite rarely played in league competitions, which could mean that watching league cricket was not common among the wealthier sections of the middle class, but many of the prominent league clubs in Lancashire had patrons who were wealthy industrialists. Many middle-class supporters of town teams may have been lower-middle-class or local businessmen who had not been educated at public schools. Those involved with the drink trade figured prominently among the shareholders of football and rugby clubs which became limited companies, but so too did proprietors of businesses and managers. Members of the *haute bourgeoisie*, such as wealthy industrialists, became directors of football clubs and on occasion even landed aristocrats were prepared to act as patrons of football clubs. In 1892 Lord Londonderry opened Sunderland's new ground. In 1900 Lord Derby opened the bazaar of Bury FC and in 1922 gave to the club his half share of its ground.[57] Wealthy industrialists were among the directors of Blackburn Rovers. Lawrence Cotton, chairman of the club from 1905 until 1919, was an industrialist who owned 6,000 cotton looms and 70,000 spindles.[58] His brother, one of his business partners, succeeded him as chairman of the football club. Both had been educated locally. When the club had held a four-day bazaar in 1895 to pay off debts resulting from the purchase of its ground, not one cotton firm was among the fifty-two businesses which had full-page advertisements in the bazaar brochure. Most of these were taken by businesses which traded directly with the public, such as the larger town centre shops, though the local breweries took one-page advertisements.[59]

Class differences were apparent in sport. The segregation of working men on the terraces and the better-off in the grandstands emphasized economic and cultural differences. Contemporary reports often mentioned that the standing spectators were noisier, rowdier and more openly partisan than those in the stands. When there were disturbances in the stands it was often stated that such behaviour was unusual and more often associated with the terraces. Yet there were also important common elements among both middle- and working-class supporters. Both were sufficiently interested in the team to watch matches. Both wanted the local team to win. Grandstand season tickets which were probably beyond the pockets of most working men would not have been provided by clubs had there not been a sufficient number from the wealthier classes wanting to support a club on a regular basis.

The growth of spectator interest in team sports more or less coincided with the rise of support for socialism. Between 1892 and 1914 trade union membership increased from one and a half to four million. The number of Labour MPs rose from two in 1900 to forty-two in 1910, though Labour was still only the fourth largest party in the House of Commons. Support for socialism can be seen as evidence that more working people were becoming convinced that the interests of labour and capital were inevitably opposed, but not all trade unionists, of course, were committed socialists, and the reformist outlook of so many Labour MPs means that the growing electoral support for Labour as a sign of class conflict should not be exaggerated. Sporting rivalries between towns may have discouraged a political mass solidarity among working people by creating new perceptions of division between those from different towns, but at the same time sport could have divided the wealthier classes. Socialist organizations condemned spectator sports as a distraction from social and economic issues only occasionally. Between 1899 and 1909, the *Blackburn Labour Journal*, a monthly publication owned by 'a number of representative Socialists, Trade Unionists and Co-operators, who style themselves the Labour Education League', never discussed spectator sport. It mentioned recreational sport only twice. The breakaway of the Northern Union clubs from the Rugby Union might have been seen by some working people as proof of class antagonism, but Northern Union clubs were not entirely working-class institutions and the split of 1895 might have been viewed more as a north–south divide rather than a class issue. It seems unlikely that members of the bourgeoisie would have become associated with professional football clubs, Northern Union or league cricket clubs had they expected that such sports were challenging the capitalist order. What spectator sports do reveal is that any awareness of class conflict cannot have so deeply ingrained as to prevent the forms of cross-class collaboration expressed through support for town teams.

Most of this chapter has been concerned with sport and town identities in the north of England and more particularly the north-west. Because of its size alone, geographical loyalties in London may have been different from those elsewhere. In recent years supporters of rugby league clubs from Yorkshire have chanted 'Yorkshire, Yorkshire' at matches, but supporters of clubs from the other side of the Pennines do not chant 'Lancashire, Lancashire'. Further research will be required to determine whether sport-based county identities were more intense in some counties than others before 1914. In *Town, City and Nation. England 1850–1914*, P.J. Waller showed how an increasing proportion of England's population became urban dwellers in the second half of the nineteenth century and assessed the trials and consolations of urban life. He pointed out the nebulous nature of town identities and argued that 'Consciousness of place, then, is a peculiar phenomenon; but it is evident from the conurbations and other urban areas that, though physically and economically interlocked, a common mood was frequently elusive.'[60] What sporting loyalties show is that sport did represent such 'a common mood'. Supporting a town team was important, especially for men. In Blackburn, for instance, by 1914 about one in every three males living there would have been present at a Rovers' home match.

Higher numbers perhaps attended church or visited the cinema each week, but no single cinema or church had so many patrons for one performance or service as did a football match. Furthermore, churches and cinemas did not express town loyalties to the same extent as sports clubs. Support for town teams was a narrative through which groups and individuals could define themselves and articulate a shared geographical identity. Sporting allegiances could fade and may not have had a great impact on other aspects of social existence or on the way economic inequalities were perceived, but at their most intense town-based sporting identities reveal much about what people felt mattered to them. The town figured highly in how they saw themselves. An appreciation of the complexities of social consciousness in England before 1914 has to pay due regard to the interconnected allegiances based on towns and sport.

8

MASCULINE STATUS AND WORKING-CLASS CULTURE IN THE CLEVELAND IRONSTONE MINING COMMUNITIES, 1850–1881

TONY NICHOLSON

On Christmas Eve 1873, a vagrant called Mary Ward stumbled into the ragged, half-finished margins of 'Abyssinia', the local nickname applied to Carlin-How, a small industrial settlement which had begun to gather untidily beside railway sidings, mines and ironworks within the heart of the new ironstone mining field of Cleveland. Over the previous 25 years, a landscape of similar industrial settlements, some of them appearing in open fields, others attaching themselves to existing agricultural communities, had been created by a dramatic spurt of economic and social energy, transforming a once secluded corner of Britain into a major industrial centre. During this period, over ten thousand workers were recruited to the new district, many of them tramping into Cleveland from the agricultural counties of East Anglia, some being shipped from the docklands of east London, others staying behind after the itinerant navvy gangs had completed their contracts on local railway networks. Most of these raw recruits had no previous experience of mining, but within this rough and bedraggled tide of poor, unskilled migrants there was a small nucleus of experienced and skilled men who were drawn to the new industry, partly to train the rest of the new workforce and partly to act in supervisory capacities. Predictably, most of these skilled miners were drawn to Cleveland from the north-eastern mining districts of Durham and Northumberland but others were recruited from further afield, including the West Yorkshire coalfield and the tin-mining centres of Devon and Cornwall.[1]

Viewed through the abstractions of nineteenth-century Ordnance Survey maps, the new industrial colonies appear as incongruous shapes on the ground: many remain just straight lines scratched across an empty tract of land; others drawn into slightly more elaborate rectangles and squares; a few squeezed into improbable triangular shapes. Yet into the dull geometry of this new industrial landscape flowed the full anarchy of a migrant population, creating working-class settlements which were both the best and worst of worlds for a vagrant woman like Mary Ward. The best, because here was a predominantly male population in which a casual prostitute like Mary might hope to make some money; the worst, because the kind of rough masculine culture which predominated during these early pioneering years created a world in which hard drinking and violence were endemic, and where the skeleton police forces of the new mining area were hard pressed to maintain social order, particularly after dark.[2]

It was already getting dark when Mary entered the settlement in the late afternoon of that Christmas Eve. She immediately gravitated towards the dim lights coming from the oil lamps in the Maynard Arms, the only social facility in the place. The tap room was already filling up, and Mary began to circulate among tables, singing carols in order to raise money or obtain free drinks. In the process, she was spotted by a group of young unmarried miners – 'Punch' Carter, 'Jud' Bowler, 'Sweedy' Jem and Billy Knight. To all intents and purposes, the members of this small gang were typical of many other youths and young men who had found their way into Cleveland during this period of rapid expansion. Some had migrated into the area with their families or friends but many appeared as complete strangers, gaining temporary credit with local shopkeepers and publicans, renting lodgings with other mining families, securing a job in one of the local mines and beginning to spend their new earnings once the first pay day came around, usually at the end of a fortnight. Indeed, these kinds of migrants had been some of the first newcomers to penetrate the new mining district. In the spring of 1851, for example, only a few months after the first major mine in Cleveland had been opened near the village of Eston, a diligent census enumerator recorded what he described as a 'stranger in the hayshed', sleeping rough at one of the farms on the outskirts of the village.[3] The enumerator assumed quite naturally that this stranger was an iron miner, but what he could not possibly know was that here was a harbinger of the rough masculine culture which was about to spread itself right across the district, reaching Carlin-How and other east Cleveland areas in the late 1860s and early 1870s. The young miners who gathered round Mary Ward in the stone-flagged passageway of the Maynard Arms were the product of this rough culture and about to demonstrate some of its most disturbing aspects.

They began by tipping a pail of cold water over her. 'You can do no worse to me if you kill me', Mary was heard to cry. But they could. Next, they decided to march her out of the pub, and parade her soaking wet around the ill-finished streets of the settlement. As it happened, a group of young children were playing in the pool of warmth and light which leaked from the main doors of the Maynard Arms. They had found a piece of old rotted rope and had engaged in a piece of mild mischief, tying the handles of the doors together. As the young miners frog-marched Mary out into the street, they burst through these childish knots, grabbed the fallen piece of rope, and headed off into the darkness. The children, sensing that something exciting was about to happen, tagged on behind, occasionally drawing too close to the miners, only to be whipped back to a more discreet distance.

To begin with, the miners contented themselves with marching Mary around the streets, sometimes tripping her up or knocking her into the gutter. Finally, they tired of this jesting and took her out to the very edge of the settlement, to a place where a small solitary row of railway cottages stood on one side of the road and open fields stretched away into the darkness on the other. As they pushed her through one of the field gates, she began to resist. During this struggle, the wife of a railway platelayer who was returning to one of the cottages from the pub happened to encounter the group and confronted them, asking what they were doing with Mary and suggesting that they should let her alone or perhaps allow the police to deal with her. 'Are you her mother, old girl?', asked one of the miners menacingly. The woman recoiled. After more struggling, the miners bundled Mary into the field where she was taken to a point away from the road and subjected to a multiple rape and beating. The platelayer's wife, who had run to her own house in order to enlist help, later testified that she and her husband heard a single scream but nothing more; the clatter of a mineral train thundering by in the darkness drowned out any further sound.

After the attack, the gang of young miners returned to one of their lodgings; more beer was ordered from the pub; 'Jud' Bowler dug out his accordion and they all launched into a sing-song. For her part, Mary managed to struggle back into the settlement and began knocking on doors asking for shelter. Witnesses recollected her doing this shortly before midnight, the time when the young miners re-emerged on the streets and when everyone else, including the children, went home to their beds. Next morning – Christmas morning – the first shift of miners who entered the nearby Cragg Hall mine found Mary's body 'fearfully mangled' at the bottom of the mine shaft.

News of Mary's rape and murder caused a sensation throughout the mining district. Crowds gathered at Middlesbrough railway station, eager to catch a glimpse of the arrested miners as they were brought to court from Northallerton gaol; a street ballad was run off fulminating against the barbarism of Mary's oppressors and extolling the simplicity and improbable virtues of her poverty-stricken lifestyle; local newspapers covered the story in the fullest possible fashion and were subsequently criticized by the local magistracy for the levels of sexual detail which they included. However, for all the demonic details which emerged relating to the assault itself, it was the wider picture of social conditions within the Cleveland mining communities which created the most fundamental level of anxiety among contemporary observers.

Here it seemed was a working-class culture – essentially a *masculine* working-class culture – which threatened the core values of civilized society. Traditional images of miners as a race apart, complete with their own tribal loyalties and codes were re-invoked, sometimes consciously, sometimes unwittingly. The street ballad represented the miners as 'monsters, not men',[4] and local newspaper reporters who were despatched to the scene of the crime conjured the macabre atmosphere which they supposed existed in the world through which these barbaric young miners roamed unfettered. Indeed, the inclusion of their nicknames in newspaper accounts – 'Punch' Carter, 'Sweedy' Jem and 'Jud' Bowler – while offering an accurate enough picture (almost all adult male miners did indeed have nicknames of this sort) imparted its own special sense of masculine menace and pugnacity. This was all very worrying, but terrible as the circumstances of that

Christmas Eve undoubtedly were, the coverage of Mary's murder would not have registered the same levels of anxiety among contemporary observers had it remained an isolated and uncharacteristic episode. However, most local commentators who claimed to be familiar with the new mining settlements argued that the rough masculine culture which found such terrible expression in the particular events of that Christmas Eve was present throughout the district. Evidence of such brutality was plentiful, particularly in the weekly newspaper reports of local petty sessional courts.[5] A litany of drunk and disorderly cases was always capable of filling the dense columns of newsprint, providing a deep well from which middle-class anxieties could draw. 'Shebeens' (miners' houses where beer and spirits could be purchased and consumed illegally) proliferated during the early years and were raided on a regular but apparently ineffective basis by the police;[6] growing numbers of casual prostitutes were prosecuted for soliciting in the busier streets of the new mining towns.[7] A number of police constables were attacked by large crowds when they attempted to arrest local working people judged to be the worse for drink;[8] elopements and sexual improprieties took place in the overcrowded housing conditions of the mining terraces where lodgers and families shared a limited domestic space;[9] male violence was endemic – in some cases directed against wives and families (wife beating was given particular prominence in the press during the 1870s)[10] and in other cases among themselves.[11] Large 'pitch-and-toss' gangs (betting rings), made up for the most part of ironstone miners, gathered at various remote locations within the surrounding countryside and could often erupt into violent clashes with the police;[12] some of the rougher public houses organized a range of dubious pleasures – rabbit coursing, dog-fights, cock-fights, prize-fights and the earthy rowdyism of early music halls.[13] Gangs of miners lounged on the street corners of mining settlements or intimidated the more respectable members of local society as they passed by on their way to church; on summer weekends, these 'dog-men' of mining society would often appear on the beaches of local seaside resorts to organize races and to swim naked in the sea, offering the genteel sections of Cleveland society an uncomfortable physical reminder that such 'roughness' or 'ruffianism' was (quite literally) only a stone's throw away.[14]

The principal concern was that a new working-class community was emerging in which traditional mechanisms of social control were absent. The social leadership of the landed classes, while by no means disappearing in the face of these changes, was none the less circumscribed. Some of the new mineowners and ironmasters lived within the boundaries of the mining district, but usually confined themselves to the discreet isolation of country estates. Almost invariably they relied on mine managers and other company officials to exercise a limited social leadership of the new mining populations.[15] Familial and apprenticeship codes which once would have exerted a measure of control over the behaviour of young people, especially young men, were also disappearing. In keeping with most mining areas, there was no formal system of apprenticeship in operation within the Cleveland ironstone mines, certainly nothing approaching the traditional arrangement whereby apprentices lived alongside their masters and mistresses, reliant on their protection and subject to their authority. Moreover, in many cases, young men were not simply free of these traditional apprenticeship constraints but had moved beyond the guidance of their own family networks. Many of the migrants into Cleveland were single men who secured lodgings with other mining families, an arrangement which may have offered a limited measure of restraint on behaviour, but one which was predicated on monetary rather than moral values. As long as the lodger paid his rental and observed the basic rules of the house, he was free to do as he wished beyond its walls.

Responses to these new social conditions varied. At the structural level, local landowners and mineowners engaged in a number of initiatives. Three 'model' mining communities were created by the Quaker mineowning family of the Peases which sought to encourage the pleasures of domesticity and 'rational recreations' in contrast to a rougher cultural lifestyle centred on the public house.[16] Landowners and their agents played an active role in establishing a new local government structure which struggled to impose a greater degree of control over building standards, overcrowding, sanitation and the provision of medical facilities.[17] New police forces were funded and organized; new schools built and staffed. Support was also given to a number of respectable 'societies' and movements which operated within local mining culture; the temperance movement was an obvious example, but other initiatives included support for chapels, brass bands, allotment and flower societies, building societies, mutual improvement clubs, friendly societies and, in the fullness of time, even trade unions.

Evidence of middle- and upper-class attempts to influence working-class values and behaviour is therefore not difficult to find in the

Cleveland of this era, but this is not to say that such attempts were always successful. Structural initiatives did not necessarily lead to a significant change in values and behaviour. Many of the miners living in the model mining community of New Marske, for example, did not abstain from alcohol simply because there were no public houses in the settlement; instead, they reacted as one would predict they might in the circumstances, by walking out of the 'model' environment to the pubs of surrounding towns, drinking their fill and leaving a trail of uprooted flowers and unhinged garden gates in their wake as they returned home.[18] Similarly, support of societies and movements which sought to foster a more respectable lifestyle were never likely to achieve a significant impact unless they were rooted in the core cultural values of working-class society; values which were ultimately authorized and sanctioned by working people themselves.

Each working-class community had its own unique character, but a common, deeply held set of codes which can be found everywhere clustered around the concept of masculine identity. This is not to say that working-class masculinity was monolithic and unchanging, but whatever forms emerged in particular places at particular times, there was always a powerful masculine presence at the very centre of working-class culture. Indeed, it is hard to think of a more influential lever by which to change working-class behaviour than a redefinition of masculinity or 'manliness'. Attempts to persuade a man to forsake the demon drink, for example, might take many forms – he might be told that such a course would improve his living standards, that he might enjoy better health or walk closer to his God – but what good were any of these if this new spirit of abstinence 'unmanned' him, leaving him exposed to the daily ridicule and contempt of his fellow males, particularly in the intense male culture of the workplace? Similarly, there was little point in exhorting a working man to privilege moral over physical force if this kind of radical change in values and behaviour was not underpinned by a new concept of manliness and strength, a concept moreover which could command, if only begrudgingly, a certain level of respect among other males. Many social factors played a part in establishing a working man's status within his local community, but his manliness was certainly not least among them. Robbed of that, what level of satisfaction could he derive from the charms of a cosy, well-furnished home, a superior education, membership of his trade union or a mahogany wardrobe full of Sunday suits and flat caps?

To illustrate the point, let us consider a brief and very typical example. During the early 1890s, at a time when most Cleveland miners had joined the union and the values of a 'respectable' masculinity had assumed a moral ascendancy within local mining culture, one of the union lodges sent printed circulars to the few remaining non-unionists who were living and working within the community. The tone of the circular veered between entreaty and threat. In its early sections, it talked the language of respectable moderation, expressing a 'wish' that the non-unionists should recognize their moral responsibilities and join the union, but towards the close, a more forceful mood emerged which warned that the time for argument had passed and that 'trouble' might ensue if the men did not fall into line. Significantly, the key middle sentence of the letter, which acted as its turning point, branded the non-unionists as 'cowardly and unmanly', pitching their status in the most abject terms possible, representing them as outsiders, beyond the normal tolerance and protection of the local community. It is significant that the lodge should choose to phrase things in this fashion. Instead of accusing the non-unionists of simply being traitors to their class, they portrayed them as traitors to their gender. To stand outside the union was 'unmanly'. Now, while one recognizes that such language was part of a familiar rhetoric designed, in every sense of the term, to hit blacklegs below the belt, it is precisely the power of this rhetoric, employed whenever appeals to class (and indeed national) loyalties were in danger of flagging, which alerts us to the central importance of 'manliness' or masculine identity within working-class culture.[19]

However, as many cultural theorists have observed, the most potent cultural values and assumptions in any social group are those which run so deep that they appear natural, universal, beyond questioning.[20] Working-class masculine values are no exception to this rule. Both in terms of the way in which male working-class cultures organized and represented themselves, as well as the way in which (predominantly male) labour historians have subsequently sought to overlay their own interpretative representations, masculinity has always been seen (if seen at all) as a cultural given, something which seems so normal and unexceptionable as to be almost invisible. Unlike class consciousness or patriotism, both of which required considerable levels of explicit and sophisticated advocacy before they could gain any purchase among working men, the importance of manliness seemed wholly natural, something which needed no apparent advocacy, no painstaking process of construction. None the less, working-class masculinity, for all its deeply embedded nature, was subject to a continual process of construction and deconstruction and it is only when this is recognized that we are able to see how a Victorian working-class sense of 'manliness' was being shaped during this period, and how new forms of manliness helped to shape new forms of working-class community.

As far as the Cleveland mining district was concerned, the transition from a predominantly rough to a predominantly respectable masculine culture can be observed in the period between *c.* 1850 and 1880. This was a subtle and complex process, and one which has been thinly documented. This chapter seeks to explore two main areas which help to illuminate such a transition. First, it argues that there was at least one major structural factor which contributed to the equation; the way in which Cleveland mineowners organized their new workforces along rigid gender lines had a profound impact on the style of masculinity which subsequently emerged. Secondly, it seeks to explore the cultural values and life-cycle associated with the concept of the 'adult male breadwinner', particularly with a view to exploring how the cultures of workplace, home and wider community were linked through the values and experience of this particular masculine configuration.

It is only in recent years that attention has been paid to the role of changing gender values in the stabilization of mid-Victorian society.[21] Indeed, as far as the Cleveland ironstone mining district was concerned, it could be argued that the most influential structural change to affect working-class cultural patterns was not associated with the provision of better quality housing or rational recreations but a radical change in the prevailing patterns of employment among men and women. Some interesting work has been produced on the geographical and occupational backgrounds of the new mining workforce, as well as the working methods and techniques required to 'win' the Cleveland stone,[22] but nothing has been done to analyse what is arguably the most significant feature of the new mining workforce – the complete exclusion of women. In one sense, this exclusion is hardly surprising. The new mining district was developed after the key legislative changes of the 1840s prohibiting women from underground mining work, so one would not expect a large female labour force working underground in defiance of the new legislation.[23] However, their complete exclusion from surface work is more surprising and significant, especially when this is set against the chronic shortage of labour which typified the first 25 years of Cleveland's development. Mining companies went to great lengths in their efforts to attract workers. Recruiting agents were employed in various parts of the country where large pools of cheap unskilled labour were most concentrated.[24] Some companies offered better quality housing and allotments, not simply to improve the moral lifestyle of the new mining populations but also to attract and hold miners, particularly skilled men. Higher wages or other perquisites were often offered by new mining enterprises in order to poach these skilled miners from their competitors.[25] In this kind of context, there must have been enormous pressure on the mineowners to consider employing women in a range of surface jobs, thereby freeing scarce male labour for underground work.

Moreover, adopting this course would not have been difficult in the face of cultural traditions both within the Cleveland area and among the new migrant workers. Traditional employment patterns in Cleveland were by no means hostile to the idea of women's paid employment. The three main areas of work and employment which dominated the economic life of the district prior to the advent of ironstone mining had been in agriculture, fishing and alum making. In the former, it was estimated that about 30 per cent of the adult female population were employed in a range of seasonal tasks which they performed alongside men.[26] In the local fishing communities, women were part of a traditional family economy in which they hunted for bait, made and mended nets, helped to launch and berth fishing cobbles and sometimes sold fish in neighbouring communities.[27] A limited number of women were also employed in the alum works which occupied sites along the Cleveland coastline.[28] It is unlikely therefore that mineowners would have encountered opposition from these more traditional sections of Cleveland society to a policy of female employment within the new mines. Nor is it likely that they would have encountered much opposition from the workers drawn from further afield; most of these recruits came from the most impoverished sections of the Victorian economy where male earnings were low and female employment customary.

Once these economic and cultural factors are taken into account, we begin to see the full significance of women's exclusion from the new mining workforce. Indeed, it is some measure of the way in which the moral climate was changing in the mid-nineteenth century that the employment of women in the Cleveland mines was not simply rejected, but never considered. Within the space of a decade, these new gender values were sufficiently powerful to override economic rationality and to place the ideology of separate spheres at the heart of local mining culture. What is also beyond doubt is that this changing gender ideology was spearheaded by a new middle-class presence in the Cleveland area; a case where middle-class ideology did indeed make a structural impact on working-class culture. The main representatives of this new middle-class presence were the mineowners and ironmasters who were opening out the area to commercial development, but the ideology of separate spheres also found expression in various newspaper editorials and articles. In the mid-1860s, for example, one local editor expressed a mixture of bewilderment and outrage at the kind of rough work which women still performed in the agricultural, fishing and alum communities of Cleveland. Interestingly, he was particularly shocked by the women's carefree attitudes, including their apparent delight in 'usurping men's work, and showing that the prowess of their sex was equal to the most difficult tasks'. Such values and behaviour were represented as primitive and barbaric, relics of an earlier age which needed to be cleared as part of a progressive modernization of local society.[29] And this is precisely what happened in the ironstone mining communities. Mineowners and ironmasters instigated profound changes. In contrast to the prevailing gender pattern of employment in traditional sectors of the local economy, a large mining workforce was recruited and organized along new gender lines, with a typically strong mid-Victorian emphasis on separate spheres. Out of these changes emerged the new masculine ideal of the adult male breadwinner.

During that first generation of Cleveland mining, a particular form of respectable masculine culture, complete with its own values and practices, as well as its own identifiable life-cycle, began to evolve and crystallize around this new, core concept of the adult male breadwinner. A new elite emerged defined in terms of its practical skills and experience within the workplace; its economic power and patriarchal authority within the home and its social leadership of the wider working-class community. Needless to say, the making of this masculine culture could only have been achieved if the earnings of the Cleveland miners were sufficiently high to underpin their new role as breadwinners. During the first 25 years of development, relatively high earnings were maintained among skilled miners by means of a sub-contracting arrangement – the 'hag system' – which paired skilled miners with unskilled labourers or 'breakers-up'. The experienced man took responsibility for the skilled tasks of drilling and firing holes while the unskilled labourer spent most of his time breaking the ironstone into manageable blocks and loading them into tubs. The skilled miner received their joint earnings, taking approximately two-thirds for himself. However, as the unskilled man gradually learnt the techniques of the job, this disparity in earnings levelled out and ultimately he would be deemed 'fit to manage his own working place', a point at which he would repeat the process by taking on an unskilled recruit of his own.[30] It was a working method which helped to train large numbers of raw recruits in the skills of mining and to invest skilled miners with a high degree of status within the local community, measured both in terms of their authority and earnings. By the same token, it was difficult for an unskilled 'breaker-up' to achieve earnings which would allow him to marry, set up a household and begin a family. In most cases, these 'subordinate' workers had to wait until they could acquire their own places in the mines. Indeed, the point at which a miner was deemed 'fit to manage his own working place' underground was a key stage in his progress towards full masculine status. In the very early years, unskilled migrants coming into the Cleveland mines had to undergo this process of training during their adult years, but as the workforce settled into the area, this process became associated with a particular stage in the male life-cycle.

By the early 1870s, the pattern was recognizable. It was standard practice for boys to begin work in the Cleveland mines around the age of 12. Between this point of entry into the mines and their late teens, they went through a 'hardening' process in which they were initiated into the culture of the workplace, developing their physical strength and stamina, their skills and experience, as well as their mental 'toughness' in the face of dangers, hardships, injuries and masculine rivalries.[31] Once they had reached their early to mid-teens – usually around 14 years of age – most boys would be sufficiently strong to become 'drivers', taking responsibility for one of the large horses used in the mines for general haulage work. The driver and his horse would pull empty tubs to the face ('into the stone' was the Cleveland way of describing it) and haul full tubs of ironstone back towards the surface. In effect, here was the first job which gave them a chance to observe the elites of local masculine society – the skilled miners – and to learn something of their working techniques. It also brought them into a troubled alignment with this elite male culture. Miners were paid on a tonnage basis which meant that nothing could be earned until the stone had been blasted from the face, loaded into tubs and carried back to the surface for weighing. Shortage of tubs was commonplace and would lead to situations in which miners could not 'send away' the stone, thereby depriving them of potential earnings.[32] Driver lads were usually subject to the adult authority wielded by these miners, but they none the less enjoyed a measure of control over the distribution of empty tubs. Bargains would often be struck in which informal cash payments were made to the lads for extra deliveries, or unpopular miners might have their supply of tubs reduced.[33]

Not surprisingly, this situation could lead to violent confrontations between miners and lads. Usually, such conflicts led to the beating and bullying of the lads, but in some cases the tables could be turned, and individual miners might be intimidated by gangs of youths, sometimes supported by other miners. In the labyrinthine darkness of the mine, two to three miles underground, these confrontations were unpoliceable by mine management. Within this world, the miners as a body exercised a customary independence and authority, able to establish who would be accepted and who would be driven out. Indeed, gangs of driver lads were sometimes encouraged to impose a rough justice on perceived outsiders, employing tactics which respectable adult miners were often loath to adopt themselves. A non-union miner, Arthur Pettit, for example, working in the Liverton mine in 1873, was harassed and finally attacked by such a gang. A driver lad, William Dale, derailed one of Pettit's full wagons, spilling most of the loaded stone. 'There's a wagon off the road', he taunted Pettit, 'come and get it, blackleg'. As Dale and Pettit began to confront one another, a group of about twenty other driver lads appeared, urging Dale to 'Drive the —— [*sic*] out!' Stones were thrown, Pettit was knocked down and later claimed that he was forced to flee for his life.[34] As one miner who had been driven from another mine observed in a letter to the press:

Many individuals have told me that as the law would have protected me, I ought to have continued work. I knew full well that the law would have protected me when the officers of the law were present, but I knew equally well that there was another law, and an iron-handed one too . . . and therefore I turned coward.[35]

In most situations, the miners exercised a tight social control over the driver lads and breakers-up, but as the case of the Carlin-How rape and murder illustrates, unmarried youths and men, most of them in their late teens and early 20s, were always viewed by both middle-class observers and working-class leaders as a potentially disruptive masculine force within the early mining communities. In rare cases, they mounted their own strikes and demonstrations and were always considered the most militant and hot-headed sections of the labour force when it came to taking industrial action.[36] The 'married men' used different strategies to restrain these more unruly sections. In the early days, the exercise of this kind of authority was the concern of individual miners, but as the mining populations settled down and a new generation of young miners began to mature, the family unit – headed by the adult male breadwinners – reasserted a more effective form of familial control. Increasingly, lads and youths entered the mines under the supervision of family members, and while lodgers always remained a significant element in mining society their numbers fell from the peaks of the 1850–75 period. Indeed, the mid-1870s economic depression played its own part in hastening this process. Many of the 'birds of passage' who had flown into Cleveland during the years of boom, flew out again when the boom turned to bust.[37]

The exercise of authority within the mining workplace was not just a matter of adult miners controlling the behaviour of younger men; it also involved them in a continuous struggle with mine management. The board and pillar system of working the Cleveland mines meant that miners' working places were largely unsupervised by management officials. Apart from periodic safety inspections by deputies (ex-miners who invariably aligned themselves with the men rather than the management), a daily visit from one of the mine overmen and an even less regular appearance from under-managers and managers, the miners were left free to work and 'manage' their places as they saw fit. Indeed, the independence and authority which this arrangement conferred was precisely what made the local phrase – 'fit to manage his own working place' – so pleasing to a miner's ear.

Such an arrangement carried a number of implications. It meant that miners could control the pace and intensity of their work, although this important freedom was also constrained by a piece-work system which ensured that a particular volume of stone must be won before a man could achieve the level of earnings required of a successful breadwinner. The system also invested the miners, rather than the managers of the mine, with control and ownership of key skills and knowledge. Cleveland mine managers were usually recruited from the ranks of north-eastern mining engineers and were accorded their own spheres of influence and expertise by the men, but as far as the actual winning of the stone was concerned, here was a process which was controlled and 'managed' by the skilled miners themselves. It was also a sphere which had to be defended. Sometimes the miners' defence of such independence would be mobilized over serious, district-wide issues such as attempts by owners and managers to impose changed working relationships alongside the introduction of new ratchet drills in the 1890s.[38] Most struggles took place over smaller issues: attempts by mine management to break up well-established working partnerships; the movement of experienced men into poor working places;[39] haggling over 'consideration money' when particular working places were deemed to be too wet or too 'fast' (where the stone was harder than normal and therefore not as easily won).[40] Sometimes the defence could assume a purely symbolic form when miners refused to work while management officials remained in their working places.[41]

In most cases, the relationships between skilled miners and mine managers were conducted on a face-to-face – or a man-to-man – basis, and the tensions implicit in such relationships had to be negotiated through the peculiar codes of male dialogue and banter. Sometimes this would be a battle of wits; sometimes it would be a subtler exchange of masculine pleasantries and compliments which none the less needed to be conducted with considerable tact if the strategy were to succeed. During a pay dispute in 1872, for example, it was reported that the manager of one local mine had complimented local delegates on being 'the noblest set of men amongst the miners of the district'. Needless to say, such gushing sentiment represented a serious error of judgement. 'That was some varnish!' retorted one miner scornfully on hearing a report of this meeting.[42] Indeed, the scarcely concealed contempt which many practical miners had for 'book-learned' mining engineers was often lurking beneath the surface of these face-to-face relationships. Occasionally it was given direct expression. A local trade union leader of the early 1870s, for example, dismissed mining engineers as 'a class that was never respected and never would be loved by working men'.[43] However, when deals were done and problems resolved, both sides tended to indulge in a measure of self-satisfied masculine reflection. At the close of a pay negotiation in the early 1870s, Joe Shepherd, the leader of the Cleveland miners, admitted to the general public that 'there was a bit of hard hitting on both sides, although it was not of much moment'. He might just as well have been a public schoolboy owning up to a fist-fight; his sense of exhilaration barely concealed by an affected air of masculine stoicism and insouciance.[44] For all the important sophisticated analysis which labour history has developed regarding industrial relations, such a statement serves to remind us that a core part of this process involved men engaging in a ritualized form of fighting; winning and losing were undoubtedly important, but whatever the outcome, it was the style in which such combat was conducted which mattered most to a man's sense of self-respect. Developing the physical and moral strength to stand up for one's own interests according to these codes was crucial to a masculine sense of identity, which in turn was a core element in the making of working-class respectability and independence. When Shepherd heralded the formation of a trade union among the Cleveland miners in 1872, he represented this development in gendered, masculine terms. Before the union, he characterized the body of Cleveland men as 'submissive as a common school boy', but once the union had been formed this childish status was sloughed off and they could 'ask, *as men from men* [my italics] that the reign of reason, justice and intelligence be inaugurated . . .'.[45]

Joe Shepherd himself represents a particularly powerful model of working-class masculinity in the context of this period. His rough abrasive style and intense pride in what he described as the skills and status of the 'practical miner' endeared him to the rougher, rank-and-file elements within the new mining population. However, he was also an intelligent and very able union leader who practised many of the values and qualities associated with the new respectable form of masculinity. The two codes were inextricably mixed. 'Mr Shepherd is essentially a man of more force than suavity of character', commented one local editor on Shepherd's re-election to office after a short period in the wilderness

> and it is just to this attribute, and very blunt outspokenness, that he owes his present position. When the union was dissatisfied with him on his former tenure of power, he would brook no cavillings, and went back from his office desk to the mine as though he had a contempt for the distinctions which had separated him from labour. He put-by the Sunday broad cloth and the office tweed and donned the mine fustian with a lack of hesitancy and true manliness which properly described in a book, would become an adornment to the biography of the most illustrious American democrat. It is such qualities which enable Mr Shepherd to be a king amongst the Cleveland miners.[46]

Shepherd's influential form of manliness reminds us that the transition from one dominant style of masculinity to another was not negotiated in the abstract but was experienced at a personal level. Then as now, males found role models or heroes within their own society and these heroes offered new ideals of masculinity which influenced wider shifts in cultural values and behaviour. Shepherd was one such role model. Moreover, his rich and contradictory character illustrates the shifting balance in masculine values which was taking place during this period, and also serves to remind us that the 'rough' and the 'respectable' did not separate out neatly into two distinct camps, but existed in a necessary tension or balance within the masculine psyche of all working men.

That balance was changing unmistakably during the years 1850–80. By the late 1870s and early 1880s, a respectable code of manliness was emerging as the dominant form of masculine behaviour. By this stage, the life-cycle of the 'adult male breadwinner' was beginning to take the kind of shape which it maintained throughout the rest of the nineteenth and most of the twentieth centuries. He would begin work in the local mines as a boy of 12; would develop his strength and aptitude until he was able to become a driver; would continue in this work until his late teens or early 20s when he might expect to be 'taken into the stone' by an experienced miner. For the next two or three years, depending on his personal aptitude for the job, he would work alongside this skilled miner, often a member of his own family, and would learn the special skills required in winning Cleveland stone. Once he had reached the critical point where he was considered able 'to manage his own working place', he would enter into the full dignity of an adult working miner. Not only did this particular rite of passage signify an increased status within the masculine culture of the workplace, it also meant that he was now in a position to make enough money to support a wife and family. This was the point when most miners married, acquired a house (indeed it appears that often only married men were able to get the keys of company houses) and start a family. Furthermore, the acquisition of this full masculine status, rooted in both workplace and the home, laid the necessary foundations for those men who wished to play a part in the social leadership of mining communities.

By the early 1880s, we can see this pattern emerging in the membership records of the Cleveland Miners' Association, and even more so in the social profile of union leaders at both district and lodge levels. Membership records for the 'Hope to Prosper' Lodge based at

North Skelton have survived for 1881, the year in which the national census was taken. By undertaking an exercise in 'nominal record linkage' (i.e. linking names in union membership records with names in the census records) we can analyse the social profiles – particularly the age, household and marital status – of both unionists and non-unionists within this particular mining community.[47]

If we begin by looking at the age structure of unionists and non-unionists, it soon becomes clear that support for the union varied significantly according to a man's place in the life-cycle. Graph 8.1 provides a nice illustration of this point.

Graph 8.1. Age Structure of Trade Unionists

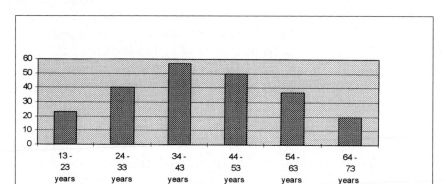

Although we have to interpret such findings with caution, they do suggest that support for the union was strongest among men who can best be described as the adult male breadwinners of local mining society. Admittedly, some trade union members could be as young as 15 years, but the majority of miners appear to have joined the union during their mid to late 20s, to have maintained strongest support during the years when they carried their greatest family responsibilities, and to have fallen away towards the end of their working lives when family members had grown up and themselves started work. The pattern of marital status among unionists and non-unionists lends support to this interpretation. Between two-thirds and three-quarters of all union members were 'married men' and a similar number were also classed as heads of households. Lodgers, by contrast, were the least unionized section of the local male population, a finding which we would expect among a group comprising younger, unmarried, propertyless men who had not attained the full status of adult male breadwinners. Other dependent males, most notably miners' sons living at home, were also unionized at a low level. If we calculate the percentage of union members in each of these three groups we see the pattern very plainly; only 21 per cent of lodgers were union members, compared to 32 per cent of miners' sons and 48 per cent of household heads.

Graph 8.2. Levels of Unionization according to Household Status

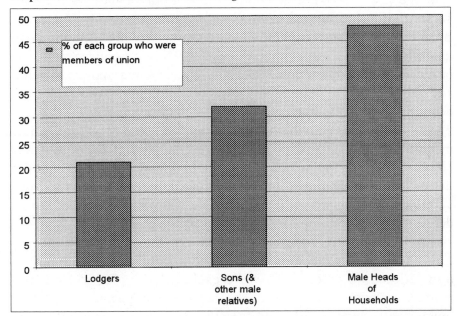

It would therefore appear that masculine status – the type of place which a male had reached in his masculine life-cycle – was a significant contributory factor in accounting for union membership. However, if these social factors were important in determining the profile of rank-and-file members, they were even more significant in determining whether a man would rise to positions of formal leadership within the union structure. Of the twenty-four different lodge officials – presidents, secretaries, treasurers, delegates and committee members – listed in the union records for North Skelton in 1881 and 1882, twenty-one (87.5 per cent) have been located within the census records. Every one of these men was married and the head of a household; all worked in high status jobs within the context of mining communities, with most (86 per cent) described as skilled ironstone miners. Their ages ranged from as young as 25 to as old as 53, but the typical lodge officer of this period was likely to be in his late 30s. Records from the later 1880s suggest that the occasional unmarried man might occupy a position of social leadership within the union and community, but such men were the proverbial exceptions which proved the rule. Adult male breadwinners (skilled miners who were married, the heads of households and aged between 25 and 45) were the most powerful and influential group in local working-class society, particularly in terms of providing formal leadership of such society.

In one sense, of course, this kind of conclusion might appear banal. To say that late nineteenth-century trade unions were male dominated is hardly to say something new. However, what was happening in these union lodges was not just that women were being excluded, but that particular forms of manliness were being celebrated and empowered and other forms of masculinity marginalized. The respectable was being privileged over the rough. As this chapter has shown, the real process of exclusion which underpinned these patterns of union membership and leadership took place at the level of the workplace. Here was a space in which the adult Cleveland ironstone miners defined their masculinity in terms of skill, strength, courage and authority. More than this, it was also a place which allowed them to define themselves in opposition to other major groups in local society. The process operated along three main axes – those of gender, age and class. Adult masculine identity, in other words, was defined first in opposition to women, who were excluded completely from the workplace as part of the new ideology of separate spheres; secondly, in opposition to boys, youths and 'breakers-up' who represented a state out of which the men must progress and who were usually subject to their power and authority; thirdly, in opposition to middle- and upper-class men such as mine managers who lacked the necessary experience and aptitude for the work of a 'practical miner'. The workplace was a key site in this process, but we cannot divide the workplace and the home into the separate spheres of public and private without losing some of the insights gained from this analysis. What happened in the mine, particularly in terms of a man's ability to manage his own working place, affected what he could achieve in the home. Moreover, the achievement of a full masculine status in these supposedly separate spheres underpinned a man's ability to participate in the social leadership of working-class communities, a process which helped to shape the nature of both class and community solidarities.

In the same month – January 1874 – as 'Jud' Bowler and his friends were brought to trial for their treatment of Mary Ward – 'Away,

Muddy!' Jud had shouted to another young miner, as he urged him to share in Mary's rape, 'there's an old woman down here in a field!'[48] – the leaders of the 'Cleveland Miners' Association' were celebrating the anniversary of their new union.

> On Tuesday night, the 'Live and Let Live' lodge . . . held their first anniversary in the Cleveland Hall, Brotton. Tea was provided in the public hall at 4.00 p.m. to which 400 sat down. After tea, a public meeting was held, when the room was crowded, there being present at a rough estimate, between 700 and 800 adult persons. . . .[49]

All of them men. If these two contrasting expressions of masculinity were linked in terms of time, they were also linked in terms of place. The story of Mary's rape and murder was acted out in Carlin-How, less than a mile away from Brotton, the centre of union activity and respectable celebration. Both events were reported in the local press, but the sensational nature of Mary's persecution and death at the hands of Jud Bowler and his friends was bound to capture contemporary attention more forcefully than a description of lodge members sitting down to enjoy the earnest pleasures of an anniversary tea. Yet it was the latter which mattered most. One of the speakers at this union anniversary was recommended to his audience as 'manly, honest and upright' and it is the expression of this particular kind of masculine identity and pride, so characteristic of the radical, respectable culture of this period, which indicates a new and increasingly influential force in local working-class society. Without recognizing the importance of these developments in masculine identity, we miss one of the mainsprings of change in labour history. Much of that history has sought to explain how working-class men organized at a collective and public level, but we also need to recognize that the personal and the subjective aspects of past experience are also there to be explored, not simply because they represent neglected areas which still need to be mapped out, but also because these private and subjective identities played a key role in determining the nature of wider collectivities.

CHAPTER

9

'MEASURING THE DISTANCE':

D.H. LAWRENCE, RAYMOND WILLIAMS AND THE
QUEST FOR 'COMMUNITY'

PETER GURNEY

Communities, like nations, are imagined.[1] This fact needs to be stressed
at the outset for many historians have unfortunately taken the
existence of 'community' (as place and spirit) in the past as axiomatic,
especially among the working class. The 'working-class community', it
has often been assumed, was characterized by warm face-to-face social
relationships between individuals, traditions of solidarity and mutuality
strengthened by scarcity, and was firmly rooted in the local and the
particular. However, if the recent debate over language and class has
taught us anything surely it must be that we need to be much more self-
conscious and critical about the concepts which we employ to pattern
and try to make sense of the past. Thus 'community' can no longer be
used quite so innocently; Joanna Bourke has forcefully argued that the
idea of the 'working-class community' owed much to the (often
idealized) representations found in autobiographical and socialist
writings. Such 'retrospective communities', Bourke maintains, serve
merely to conceal divisions and antagonisms within localities and this
is especially damaging when the history of working-class women is
considered.[2]

In this context, when the very usefulness of 'community' is being
fiercely contested,[3] it might be instructive to look back at a seminal
representation of 'working-class community'. D.H. Lawrence's *Sons*

and Lovers (1913) is arguably the most influential fictional account of such a community produced this century, and it continues to furnish an important point of entry for students of working-class life and labour before the First World War. In this chapter I intend to explore Lawrence's vision of community and how this related to his developing social and political ideology within which the notion of an 'organic community' played a key role. I shall demonstrate and argue for the limitations of the peculiarly depoliticized 'imagined community' found in this work; but rather than jettisoning the keyword totally like Bourke, a contrast will be drawn between Lawrence's representation and Raymond Williams' utopian analysis and projection of community which ought not to be relinquished quite so easily.

Lawrence's social origins and affiliations are well known but no less vital. He was born in the mining village of Eastwood in Nottinghamshire in 1885, his father was a collier, though his mother came originally from a slightly higher social background. At the age of 12 Lawrence won a county council scholarship worth £12 a year and went to Nottingham High School. After leaving school at 16 he became a clerk for a short while until ill-health forced him to quit. At 18 he became a schoolteacher and after, '3 years savage teaching of collier lads', he took his teacher's certificate at Nottingham University. Disappointed with both school and college, he found a job in a new elementary school in Croydon on £100 a year. The girl who had been the chief friend of his youth sent some of his poems to the *English Review*; these were published and William Heinemann subsequently accepted the manuscript of Lawrence's first novel, *The White Peacock*. At the age of 26 he gave up teaching and supported himself for the rest of his short life as an 'author'.[4]

Published in 1913 when he was 28 years old, *Sons and Lovers* presented a particular and highly nuanced representation of familial and social relations in Eastwood (called Bestwood in the novel) during the Edwardian period. Lawrence dramatized and reworked his own past in the novel through the character Paul Morel, and it is important to situate it within the context of a long tradition of working-class autobiographical writing which has been carefully studied by David Vincent and Julia Swindells, among others.[5] Lawrence's text relates to this tradition but departs from it in important ways. Unlike the majority of working-class autobiographers, Lawrence of course was not a labour movement activist, making sense of his life after a prolonged engagement in the world of working-class association. He was young, bent on becoming an 'author' and expressing his experiences and ideas to a different audience, one aware of the latest developments in the world of 'Art' and which supported, nurtured and published what was considered to be intellectually new and challenging: the avant-garde element within the English middle class, typified most clearly by the Bloomsbury group.

Sons and Lovers broke through to this audience because it was presented as 'fiction' rather than autobiography. The fact that most of us know this novel far better than we know other forms of working-class writing, testifies not only to the measure of Lawrence's 'genius' but also to the power of a gender- and class-specific 'selective tradition' which hierarchizes different types of writing and bequeaths to future generations certain texts and representations as *the* tradition.[6] *Sons and Lovers* was, and still is, a story of release, or rather escape; in the book Lawrence retrospectively imagined the place and the people he had left behind as he moved away from the manual working class, and it is to this representation that we must now turn our attention.

In an important study Graham Holderness has discovered at least four different models of community in Lawrence's work. Lawrence variously represented the mining town as 'an organic, homogeneous, rural almost "peasant" community', located in an 'indeterminate historical period'; an anti-community blighted by industrialism; a 'distorted' and partial historical community; and 'a dialectical realisation of the mining community as a social human community, with all its conflicts and traditions, a complex totality of social existence'. According to Holderness, some of the early short stories and *Sons and Lovers* are the best examples of Lawrence's dialectical approach.[7] This is a persuasive argument certainly, though, as we shall see, important qualifications can be suggested.

There are three components of Lawrence's representation of 'community' in *Sons and Lovers* to which I wish to draw attention. First, at the core of the novel there is a sustained critique of capitalist production and the brutalizing effects of capitalist forms of labour. The pit and the local community are interdependent; the colliery provides the work and the wages which make social life possible but on terms which also block its full development. With great subtlety and insight Lawrence shows how harsh, exploitative work deadens the senses and inhibits close, sharing relationships, particularly between men and women. This is well demonstrated by Lawrence's treatment of Paul's father Walter Morel. Based on his own truculent and hard-drinking father, Lawrence's attitude to this character has often been regarded as entirely negative, though his portrayal is far more complex than this. Take Lawrence's description of Paul's birth for example: Morel returns home from work, hardly speaks to the woman who is caring for his wife during childbirth, and is interested only in satisfying his own hunger. Morel's behaviour is coarse and insensitive, motivated purely by selfishness:

> The fact that his wife was ill, that he had another boy, was nothing to him at that moment. He was too tired; he wanted his dinner; he wanted to sit with his arms lying on the board; he did not like having Mrs Bower about. The fire was too small to please him.[8]

This scene is followed by an unsatisfying exchange between husband and wife which serves to underscore their alienation.

Importantly though, this episode was immediately prefaced by a long description of Morel at work down the pit. By the time he returns home we know exactly why he is so tired. Because of insolence to his superiors Morel had been given a bad stall – a section of the coal-face which was particularly difficult to work. His labours are precisely drawn:

> 'Shall ter finish,' cried Barker, his fellow butty.
> 'Finish? Niver while the world stands!' growled Morel.
> And he went on striking. He was tired.
> 'It's a heart-breaking job,' said Barker.
> But Morel was too exasperated, at the end of his tether, to answer. Still he struck and hacked with all his might.
> 'Tha might as well leave it, Walter,' said Barker. 'It'll do tomorrow, without thee hackin' thy guts out.'
> 'I'll lay no bloody finger on this tomorrow, Isr'el!' cried Morel.
> 'Oh, well, if tha wunna, someb'dy else'll ha'e to,' said Israel.
> 'Hey-up there – loose-a!' cried the men, leaving the next stall.
> Morel continued to strike.
> 'Tha'll happen catch me up,' said Barker, departing.
> When he had done, Morel, left alone, felt savage. He had not finished his job. He had overworked himself into a frenzy.[9]

This passage typifies Lawrence at his best, where, as Raymond Williams has noted in his discussion of the early short story, 'Odour of

Chrysanthemums', 'the language of the writer is at one with the language of his characters',[10] a new departure in the English novel. The brutalizing effects of work come through insistently, reinforced through juxtaposition with the subsequent scene. Morel's actions are not excused but they are properly contextualized, and we are given a sense of the structural determinations which thwart social relationships. Walter Morel does not carry all the blame; an avaricious, competitive system which reduces human beings to mere instruments and generalizes 'ugliness' is the root cause.[11]

Secondly, in *Sons and Lovers* Lawrence also showed how a sense of 'community' was constructed by working people around the pit. As he well understood 'community' was more than just a vague feeling but was underpinned by informal caring and sharing networks as well as by the web of formal institutions which structured the lives of the Nottinghamshire miners. The organization of work below ground – the butty system – created divisions between the miners but could also serve to strengthen traditions of independence and collective self-help. Neighbourhood support networks, sick-clubs and Morel's fellow butties tide the family over periods of crisis, especially when Walter Morel is injured below ground.[12] The physical proximity and design of workers' cottages as well as the public house and the local chapel are also defining features of community life. But Lawrence does not idealize a homogeneous working-class community; it is riven with conflict both within the working class and between the genders, and these antagonisms persistently intrude. One of the most striking things about the novel is the separateness of working-class men and women.[13] Morel does not let his wife know how much he earns and enjoys the male company of the pub more than his own home; Mrs Morel inhabits a world peopled by children, neighbours and the Congregational minister. In the novel the miners are 'instinctive', 'spontaneous', closer to and more appreciative of 'nature'; the women are 'rational' and calculating, ruled by the head rather than the heart.[14] I shall unravel this aspect of Lawrence's discourse later.

Lawrence did not idealize his background but mythologized it, and this tendency became more pronounced as he matured. A conversation between Paul and Mrs Morel is symptomatic here:

'You know,' he said to his mother, 'I don't want to belong to the well-to-do middle class. I like my common people best. I belong to the common people.'

'But if anyone else said so, my son, wouldn't you be in a tear. You know you consider yourself equal to any gentleman.'

'In myself,' he answered, 'not in my class or my education or my manners. But in myself I am.'

'Very well, then. Then why talk about the common people?'

'Because – the difference between people isn't in their class, but in themselves. Only from the middle classes one gets ideas, and from the common people – life itself, warmth. You feel their hates and loves.'

'It's all very well, my boy. But, then, why don't you go and talk to your father's pals?'

'But they're rather different.'

'Not at all. They're the common people. After all, whom do you mix with now – among the common people? Those that exchange ideas, like the middle classes. The rest don't interest you.'

'But – there's the life——'[15]

This passage is crucial for an understanding of Lawrence's work. Working-class people are 'instinctive', 'natural', full of life and feeling. The middle class by contrast is dominated by thought and is necessarily 'artificial', cold and 'mechanical'. Lawrence inherited these antinomies from the romantic critique of industrialism (Williams linked him to Carlyle in this respect) and they inform all his adult writing.[16] They gave him a vocabulary with which to attack industrial capitalism and its destructive effects but they also seriously disabled any possibility of a democratic, working-class alternative from below. For if 'intellect' was the property of the bourgeoisie, then calls for worker ownership and control, or any form of socialism, were not only unfeasible but if practised would actually destroy the working-class's most precious quality: spontaneity.

Lawrence kept to this logic and repeatedly voiced the most anti-democratic, proto-fascist sentiments; his correspondence with the Cambridge mathematician Bertrand Russell during the First World War is instructive here. Lawrence had offered to collaborate on a series of lectures Russell was preparing. They had little in common apart from an abhorrence of war and a belief in the necessity of social transformation. By this time Lawrence had married the ex-wife of his modern languages tutor at Nottingham, Frieda von Richthofen, an impoverished German baroness. The couple were living in a cottage in Pulborough owned by Alice Meynell, the upper-class Catholic poetess.

Russell sent Lawrence a proposed draft of the lectures, which he had entitled 'Philosophy of Social Reconstruction', in the summer of 1915. They comprised a scattered and disjointed critique of industrial capitalist society which maintained that the old cohesions of state, property, church, law, morality and marriage were all based on power and required 'fundamental reconstruction'. Russell advocated a form of ethical socialism as the most appropriate solution and in his lecture on 'Industrialism' recommended worker ownership and control along syndicalist lines because, 'Democracy should be economic as well as Political.'

Lawrence violently disagreed and confessed that he was 'terrified' by some of Russell's ideas. He spelt out his opposition in a letter at the end of July:

> I don't believe in democratic control. I think the working man is fit to elect governors or overseers for his immediate circumstances, but for no more. You must utterly revise the electorate. The working man shall elect superiors for the things that shall concern him immediately, no more. From the other classes, as they rise, shall be elected the higher governors. The thing must culminate in one head, as every organic thing must – no foolish republic with foolish presidents, but an elected king, something like Julius Caesar. And as the men elect and govern the industrial side of life, so women must elect and govern the domestic side. And there must be a rising rank of women governors, as of men, culminating in a woman Dictator, of equal authority with the supreme Man. It isn't bosh, but rational sense. The whole thing must be living. Above all there must be no democratic control – that is the worst of all. There must be an elected aristocracy.[17]

A few years later, in similar vein, Lawrence was arguing that 'Democracy and Socialism are dead ideals.'[18] He looked forward to the creation of a living 'organic community', very different to the class-divided modern bourgeois nation state, but equally hierarchical and inequitable. The key word 'community' was often prefixed with 'organic' in Lawrence's discourse, a biological term which likened the 'community' to the human body, similar in that different parts had, necessarily, different functions. The 'body' was controlled and ordered by the 'head', yet the 'head' was simultaneously dependent on the healthy working of the 'body'. Note also how Lawrence in this letter not only divides the 'head' from the 'body' but also separates men and women, absolutely. They are divided by timeless, unalterable and biologically fixed functions, and have duties in and control over clearly defined separate spheres; the men over (public) production, the women over (private) reproduction.

As Francis Mulhern's work has shown, the term 'organic community' was a commonplace in conservative and liberal ideology in England in the inter-war years. Both the conservative Catholic poet T.S. Eliot and the humanist literary and social critic F.R. Leavis wished for the recovery or the reconstitution of such a community.[19] Lawrence offered a critique of 'high' culture by counterposing his own experience of working-class 'community', but, as we have seen, this was a particular representation of 'community', a mythologized version which when projected into the future as a blueprint for an 'organic community' could be anything but progressive or democratic. This notion was also informed by a nostalgic image of a pre-industrial past. In 1929 Lawrence wrote that: 'In the old England, the curious blood-connection held the classes together. The squires might be arrogant, violent, bullying and unjust, yet in some ways they were at one with the people, part of the same blood-stream.'[20] All this points to the problems involved when 'community' is employed as an analytical concept; the fact that the term effaces difference (gender, ethnicity, class and so on) has allowed it to be used in a whole spectrum of contradictory political ideologies. Raymond Williams's early work is marked by an attempt to bend its warm, cosy resonances in a socialist direction, a project which he later regarded as very problematic indeed:

> The term 'community' was very widely used in the thirties and forties in the working class and the labour movement, especially in Wales, where it has also, in the realities of nonconformity, a religious sense. But by the sixties I was constantly hearing of the interest of the community over and against that of a small group of strikers, for example. This caused me to reflect that it is unusable as a term that enables one to make distinctions: one is never certain exactly to which formation the notion is referring. It was when I suddenly realised that no one ever used 'community' in a hostile sense that I saw how dangerous it was.[21]

It was Lawrence's peculiar vision of 'community' which enabled him to depoliticize working-class life, and this is the final aspect to consider.

We learn in the novel, for instance, that Mrs Morel was active in the Women's Co-operative Guild, yet we are not given any details of this organization or what it really meant to her. The history of course is important. The WCG was an autonomous body, part of the British Co-operative movement, and was made up mainly of married women from the 'respectable' strata of the working class. Founded in 1883, it was the largest organization of its kind before or since, with 30,000 active members at the start of the First World War. Members arranged meetings and social events in localities all over the country and gained experience of democratic participation and public speaking, as indeed did Mrs Morel. The Guild organized its own annual congress and campaigned around a variety of so-called 'women's issues' before 1914; divorce and Poor Law reform, maternity benefit, female suffrage and so forth.[22] Lawrence gives us vivid descriptions of the male culture of the pit but largely ignores and trivializes Mrs Morel's social and political activity.

Lawrence's attitude to organized working-class politics was equally dismissive. The Russell correspondence again provides an excellent illustration here. In the summer of 1915 Russell had attacked Lord Northcliffe and the conduct of the war in the Independent Labour Party paper, the *Labour Leader*. Lawrence read this article and responded thus:

> I think Lord Northcliffe wants sinking to the bottom, but you do say rash things, and give yourself away. Let me beg you not to get into trouble now, at this juncture. I do beg you to save yourself for the great attack, later on, when the opportunity comes. We must go much deeper and beyond Lord Northcliffe. Let us wait a little while, till we can assemble the nucleus of a new belief, get a new centre of attack, not using *Labour Leaders* and so on.[23]

A week later Lawrence pointed to the strike in the Welsh coalfield, prophesied a final decisive conflict between labour and capital and warned Russell that:

> It will be a ghastly chaos of destruction, if it is left to Labour to be constructive. The fight must immediately be given a higher aim than the triumph of Labour, or we shall have another French Revolution. The deadly Hydra now is the hydra of Equality. Liberty, Equality and Fraternity is the three-fanged serpent. You must have a government based upon good, better and best.[24]

We may note in passing that the following year, after an irreconcilable break with Lawrence, Russell published a collection of essays on similar themes, entitled *Justice in War Time*. He was immediately dismissed from his post at Cambridge, his library was seized and a passport to America denied. In 1918 he was imprisoned for four and a half months under the Defence of the Realm Act for condemning the use of American troops as strike-breakers.[25]

Lawrence's attitude towards trade unions was similarly negative; there is brief mention of a single dispute in the novel but no consideration of trade union life in general. In part this has to be understood in relation to the particular economic, social and political history of the Nottinghamshire coalfield itself. In his excellent comparative study of mining communities and collective action in South Wales and Nottinghamshire in the nineteenth and early twentieth centuries, David Gilbert has noted that many factors worked against the growth of militant trade unionism in the area where Lawrence grew up. For a start the region had complex economic and social structures (grounded in agricultural production and framework knitting) which pre-dated the development of the mining industry locally. These structures, particularly traditions of employer paternalism, bequeathed a continuing legacy. Employers played a major role in local society, frequently supporting educational and leisure initiatives as well as making generous donations to local churches and chapels. The Barker Walker Company which owned the Eastwood colliery was particularly active in this respect.[26] In fine, employer–worker relations were characterized by conciliation rather than conflict.

Gilbert also emphasizes the persistence of the little butty system in the area, which along with religious divisions (between Congregationalists and Primitive Methodists as well as between Nonconformists and Anglicans) tended to undermine collective action. Finally he argues that the growth of towns in Nottinghamshire, especially Nottingham itself but also Mansfield, exacerbated the fragmentation of the labour force still further; many miners commuted considerable distances to their pits and the diversified economies of the large towns presented a difficult terrain for union and labour organization. The contrast with South Wales comes through clearly; here the miners' lodges functioned as alternative centres of working-class authority and the tightly knit pit villages proved fertile ground for militant ideas and activities.[27] It is not surprising then that Nottinghamshire was the birthplace of Spencerism, the 'non-political' alternative to the Nottinghamshire Miners' Association, after the miners' strike collapsed in the autumn of 1926.[28]

Working-class associations such as trade unions, co-operative societies and political parties were anathema to Lawrence because they threatened the dominance and the principle of the 'head' and would result only in anarchy. Failing to find fulfilment on the 'savage pilgrimage' which took him to Sicily, Ceylon, Australia and New Mexico in the early 1920s, Lawrence went home to Eastwood to visit his family during the miners' strike in 1926. The village was besieged by '"blue bottles", big, big-faced stranger policemen. Every field path, every stile seems to be guarded.'[29] The police were protecting black-legs, trying to break the strike. In an article written soon afterwards, Lawrence described a group of miners' wives who had demonstrated in support of two fellow women as they were being taken to court charged with insulting and obstructing the police. Lawrence was disturbed by what he saw in his old home: 'the women seem to have changed most in this . . . they have no respect for anything.' The women waved red flags and shouted encouragement to Mrs Hufton and Mrs Rowley as they were driven away. Lawrence referred to the 'shouting women' with their 'strange hoarse cheering'. He found the scene threatening because not only were the working class undermining the principle of social hierarchy and authority with their red flags and ambition to take over the system themselves, but it was working-class women who waved the flags, and once 'respectable' women at that: 'There was one, the decent wife of the postman. I had known her and played with her as a girl. But she was waving her red flag, and cheering as the motor-bus rolled up.'[30]

These 'red women' challenged Lawrence's ideas regarding the 'natural' and 'proper' ordering of the sexes and his belief in male authority within the working-class community. His reaction was to rail against this symbolic expression of the desire for real equality with this revealing metaphor: 'We must all rise into the upper classes! Upper! Upper! Upper! Till at last the boots are all uppers, the sole is worn out, and we yell as we walk on stones.'[31]

Williams was considerably off the mark in 1958; the tragedy of Lawrence was not that he 'did not live long enough to come home', but rather that he went home and did not like what he saw.[32] Lawrence's 'imagined community' simply did not correspond with the political community which was being redefined by striking miners and women with red flags in the summer of 1926.[33]

I noted above that Lawrence uncritically described gender divisions within the working-class community and believed that the sexes were separated 'naturally' in biologically determined ways. Kate Millett, in her seminal *Sexual Politics* (1969), has written on this theme; my focus here is more particular. I would suggest that Lawrence's representation or mythologization of working-class 'community', with all its silences and omissions, cannot be understood outside the context of his attitude towards human sexuality and gender relations. At their healthiest, according to Lawrence, 'community' and 'sexuality' should be mutually interdependent; what he referred to as the 'instinct of community' relied upon the 'proper' functioning of the 'sex instinct'. Following Freud (whose work Frieda had introduced him to just before the final draft of *Sons and Lovers*) Lawrence believed that individuals were inserted into the community through their experience of human sexuality, but unlike Freud sexuality and gender were not produced primarily by and through 'culture' in the wider anthropological sense, they were timeless and genetic, transmitted by blood.[34] 'Culture', especially in the narrow and exclusive sense, could deform this process, particularly the bohemian intellectualism of the middle-class elite, producing a weak and degenerate society with a paralysed will. Sodomy (Lawrence's preferred term) and 'strong' public women were the twin and equally pernicious results, omnipresent in the 'sick' modern world.

According to Lawrence E.M. Forster's work was profoundly disabled by his inability to 'take a woman and fight clear to his own basic, primal being'.[35] Love for humanity and social action were founded on this connection, without it the will atrophied. For taking a woman was *the* mysterious journey into the other: 'I go to a woman to know myself, and knowing myself, to go further, to explore into the unknown, which is the woman, venture in upon the coasts of the unknown, and open my discovery to all humanity.'[36] If this natural drive was repressed then sodomy, 'a nearer form of masturbation', was the result.

Feminism presented a related challenge to this 'natural' order. In an article written towards the end of his life, Lawrence admitted that 'perhaps the greatest revolution of modern times is the emancipation of women',[37] but went on to argue that this revolution, like others in the past, had now turned into a tyranny. Woman had won her freedom but continued to fight; why was this so, Lawrence asked? The answer simply was that modern men had lost faith in themselves and their proper roles. This was a defining part of the crisis facing bourgeois democracy.

All through the past, except for brief periods of revolt, woman has played a part of submission to man. Perhaps the inevitable nature of man and woman demands such submission. But it must be an instinctive, unconscious submission, made in unconscious faith. At certain periods this blind faith of woman in man seems to weaken, then break. It always happens at the end of some great phase, before another phase sets in. . . . Today woman is always tense and strung-up, alert, and bare-armed, not for love but for battle. In her shred of a dress and her little helmet of a hat, her cropped hair and her stark bearing she is a sort of soldier, and look at her as one may, one can see nothing else. It is not her fault. It is her doom. It happens when man loses his primary faith in himself and in his very life.[38]

Rationalism, utilitarianism and the acquisitive principle which ruled modern bourgeois society, according to Lawrence, had weakened 'traditional' social and sexual hierarchies which had once structured the 'organic community'. The middle-class intellect or 'head' had dominated the body for too long and the result was class conflict and social disintegration. Lawrence's discourse on instinct represented an attempt to redress this imbalance. The working class (especially working-class men), because of their closer relationship to the land, the natural world and the daily realities of labour, were still bearers of some of the older feelings. Hence the crucial importance of the rooted, instinctual working-class male in Lawrence's oeuvre – Mellors in *Lady Chatterley's Lover* is probably the best-known example.

Lawrence turned these antinomies between reason and nature, mind and body against many of his 'shallow' and 'superficial' middle-class acquaintances. Immediately prior to the break, Lawrence condemned Russell for being 'full of repressed desires, which have become savage and anti-social'.[39] A few months later he linked this charge to his own philosophy of the blood:

the tragedy of this, our life, and of your life, is that the mental and nerve consciousness exerts a tyranny over the blood-consciousness and that your will has gone completely over to the mental consciousness, and is engaged in the destruction of your blood-being or blood-consciousness, the final liberating of the one, which is only death in result.[40]

Lawrence went on to contrast Russell's 'mental consciousness' with his own sexually liberating practice:

> On the other hand, when I take a woman, then the blood-precept is supreme, my blood-knowing is overwhelming. There is a transmission, I don't know of what, between her blood and mine, in the act of connection. So that afterwards, even if she goes away, the blood-consciousness exists between us, when the mental consciousness is suspended; and I am formed then by my blood-consciousness, not by my mind or nerves at all.[41]

Supporting quotations could easily be multiplied here and Lawrence did not significantly shift from these positions during the rest of his life. The later novels, especially *Kangaroo* (1923) and *The Plumed Serpent* (1926), play out these themes. For Lawrence, husband and wife were 'two rivers of blood . . . two distinct streams', which communed and renewed each other through sexual intercourse. Without the phallus no such commingling was possible; 'the phallus is the connecting-link between the two rivers, that establishes the two streams in a oneness, and gives out of their duality a single circuit . . . the bridge to the future is the phallus, and there's the end of it. But not the poor, nervous counterfeit phallus of modern "nervous" love. Not that.'[42]

The crisis of the First World War forced Lawrence to elaborate his ideas explicitly; his abortive collaboration with Russell, as should by now be apparent, was immensely important in this respect. But they had informed his earlier work in more oblique ways and can be clearly discerned in *Sons and Lovers*. There is a crucial exchange towards the end of the novel between Paul Morel and his lover, Clara. It is worth quoting in full:

> One evening, as they were coming home over the fields, she startled him by asking:
>   'Do you think it's worth it – the – the sex part?'
>   'The act of loving, itself?'
>   'Yes; is it worth anything to you?'
>   'But how can you separate it?' he said. 'It's the culmination of everything. All our intimacy culminates then.'
>   'Not for me,' she said.
>   He was silent. A flash of hate for her came up. After all, she was dissatisfied with him, even there, where he thought they fulfilled each other. But he believed her too implicitly.

'I feel,' she continued slowly, 'as if I hadn't got you, as if all you weren't there, and as if it weren't me you were taking——'

'Who, then?'

'Something just for yourself. It has been fine, so that I daren't think of it. But is it me you want, or is it It?'

He again felt guilty. Did he leave Clara out of count, and take simply woman? But he thought that was splitting a hair . . .

'If I start to make love to you,' he said, 'I just go like a leaf down the wind.'

'And leave me out of count,' she said.

'And then is it nothing to you?' he asked, almost rigid with chagrin.

'It's something; and sometimes you have carried me away – right away – I know – and – I reverence you for it – but——'

'Don't "but" me,' he said, kissing her quickly, as a fire ran through him.

She submitted and was silent.

It was true as he said. As a rule, when he started love-making, the emotion was strong enough to carry with it everything – reason, soul, blood – in a great sweep, like the Trent carries bodily its back-swirls and intertwinings, noiselessly. Gradually the little criticisms, the little sensations, were lost, thought also went, everything borne along in one flood. He became, not a man with a mind, but a great instinct.[43]

Clara is the strong modern woman par excellence. She is able to take advantage of the opportunities afforded by Nottingham's diversified local economy and achieves a measure of financial independence through employment in the hosiery industry.[44] We are told that she is a feminist and a member of the Women's Social and Political Union, but once again Lawrence provides no details of this association in the novel.

The WSPU was a radical women's suffrage organization founded by Emmeline Pankhurst in Manchester in 1903, then moved to London by Emmeline and her daughter Christabel in 1906. From that year it became an increasingly militant, middle-class and elitist body. There was also a rival, more explicitly proletarian organization, the National Union of Women's Suffrage Societies, founded in London in 1897, which was much more open and democratic. Clara would certainly have known about the conflicts between these groups, though we can only speculate from the text. Women organized suffrage groups in specific localities, held meetings, read and discussed the feminist press, gave papers, attended demonstrations. Estimating support for this campaign among working-class women is difficult, though in the spring of 1901 the North of England Society for Women's Suffrage collected the signatures of 30,000 women workers from the cotton towns of Lancashire. There was also a good deal of cross-over and mutual support between branches of the Women's Co-operative Guild and suffrage societies, as modern feminist historians have discovered.[45]

This history is important because it is this experience as well as her financial independence, I suggest, that makes it possible for Clara to ask her question so boldly and voice her dissatisfaction: 'Do you think it's worth it – the – the sex part?' Paul translates this into a euphemism: 'The act of loving'. Millett has rightly argued that Paul, the character through which Lawrence explores his own formation, uses women in *Sons and Lovers* – his mother, Miriam and Clara – as means to his own personal development.[46] The most interesting and revealing thing about this passage though is that the sexual politics inscribed in the Clara–Paul relationship are so visible. In Lawrence's later work this theme is treated much more one-sidedly. Clara's fear is that Paul is in the relationship not for her whole self but for sex, a fear prompted by Paul's sexual selfishness. Lawrence's authorial voice acknowledges this possibility but disposes of it in a thoroughly unconvincing manner: 'Did he leave Clara out of count, and take simply woman? But he thought that was splitting a hair.' Paul's obsession with his own pleasure is manifest – 'I just go like a leaf down the wind' – and he quickly closes this threatening conversation with a 'spontaneous' kiss, to which Clara of course submits. A grand and metaphysical authorial intervention closes the exchange; here Lawrence describes lovemaking as a great flood of emotion, relentlessly carrying all before it, 'reason, soul, blood', like the River Trent. And no longer is Paul a thinking and feeling human being but 'a great instinct'. This is unfortunate for Clara to say the least: 'They did not often reach again the height of that once when the peewits had called', Lawrence remarks pathetically in the next paragraph.

Clearly then Lawrence's attitudes toward and prescriptions regarding male and female sexuality cannot and should not be separated from his representation of 'community'; Klaus Theweleit's *Male Fantasies* (1987) helps us to unravel this mentality more fully. Theweleit has explored the positioning and imaging of women by German Freikorps officers after the First World War via a study of proto-fascist and fascist autobiographies, diaries and novels. Key themes are the dread of Communism and the fear and attraction of female sexuality; the most dangerous combination being of course floods of 'red women'. Theweleit argues that within Western society in the modern period, women have been frequently represented, in written and visual forms of communication, through water imagery: rivers, seas and oceans. Similarly female sexuality and desire has been likened to watery flows, streams and floods. According to Theweleit, a central part of the making of modern bourgeois civilization involved the damming-up and careful channelling, by men, of these flows; hence his argument relates not only to a group of fascist men, but to the construction of modern patriarchal relations generally. He writes:

> A river without end, enormous and wide, flows through the world's literatures. Over and over again: the woman in the water; woman as water, as a stormy, cavorting ocean, a raging stream, a waterfall. . . . And every one of those flowing places goes by the name of Woman: Congo, Nile, Zambesi, Elbe, Neva ('Father Rhine' doesn't flow – he is a border). Or the Caribbean Sea, the Pacific, the Mediterranean, *the* ocean that covers two-thirds of the earth's surface and all its shorelines. . . . What is really at work here, it seems to me, is a specific (and historically relatively recent) form of the oppression of women. . . . It is oppression through exaltation, through a lifting of boundaries. . . . Here again, women have *no names*.[47]

This exaltation, Theweleit continues, is 'coupled with a negation of women's carnal reality'.

Time and time again in Lawrence we find a similar employment of metaphor. Here is Lawrence in the 'Study of Thomas Hardy' (1914): 'For a man who dares to look upon, and to venture within the unknown of the female, losing himself, like a man who gives himself to the sea . . . feels, when he returns, the utmost gladness of singing. This is certainly the gladness of a male bird in his singing.'[48] And again in 'Matriarchy' (1928): 'No good trying to stem the tide. Woman is in Flood.'[49] Lawrence did not wish to dam up female sexuality absolutely, or indeed rise erect above the swirling flow to the safety of the dry male plateau, as did the Freikorps officers, according to Theweleit.[50] Instead he wished momentarily to join the flood, which became a single river of blood during intercourse, at least for the duration of his own masculine pleasure. This commingling was necessary if the hegemony of the 'blood-consciousness' was to be preserved and the 'correct' ordering of the sexes achieved; it was the vital foundation for the maintenance of male dominance and the creation of 'community'. But at least in *Sons and Lovers* – and again this is one of its major strengths – Clara's awkward question momentarily subverts the narrative.

It is easy to dismiss Lawrence, as should by now be apparent. But what makes the life and the work compelling still perhaps is the context within which he wrote and tried to make himself into an 'author'. As we saw in the introduction, to break through to a particular middle-class reading public Lawrence needed the support of individuals with specific intellectual and literary connections, such as Heinemann, Edward Garnett, Ford Madox Ford and Edward Marsh. However, he never really made enough from commercial sales and his letters are full of references to fairly small sums, money owed for particular work, requests for donations from friends. Many of these were aristocratic aesthetes, especially women like Lady Cynthia and Lady Ottoline Morrell (later famously satirized in *Women in Love*) and Lawrence was heavily dependent on their patronage – they provided money, accommodation, connections – throughout his career. These 'conditions of production' are vital for a proper understanding of Lawrence's life and work. Eschewing a career as a 'populist' author, especially after the controversy which surrounded the publication and suppression of *The Rainbow* in 1915, his later work would not have been possible without this support network. In his final year Lawrence remarked upon the living writing had afforded:

> It is 17 years since I gave up teaching and started to live an independent life of the pen. I have never starved, and never even felt poor, though my income for the last 10 years was no better, and often worse, than it would have been if I had remained an elementary school teacher.
>
> But when one has been born poor a very little money can be enough. Now my father would think I am rich, if nobody else does. And my mother would think I have risen in the world even if I don't think so.[51]

Lawrence's precarious financial position and his dependent position within patronage relations fuelled his continuing class antagonism and class consciousness.

If we consider for a moment Lawrence's reception by the middle-class literary and intellectual elite during his own lifetime as well as their memories of him after his death in 1930, especially those produced by the fraction of intellectuals that inhabited the Cambridge and Bloomsbury nexus, we can get a better idea of the importance of class. Bertrand Russell invited Lawrence up to Cambridge to meet this set in the spring of 1915, and Lawrence was bitterly disappointed. He later wrote to Russell that 'Cambridge made me very black and down. I cannot bear its smell of rottenness, marsh-stagnancy. I get a melancholic malaria. How can so sick people rise up? They must die first.'[52] A decade after their break William Gerhardi mentioned Lawrence in Russell's presence and later remembered that 'the look of serenity fade[d] in his large wise eyes, and a note of intellectual fastidiousness crept into his voice, and he said "Lawrence has no mind"'.[53]

This was not merely a local and personal reaction. Many middle-class intellectuals, of both conservative and liberal political persuasions, were to attack Lawrence's status as an 'author' after his death, and the grounds for their attack was invariably Lawrence's supposed lack of 'mind' or formal education. In *After Strange Gods* (1934) T.S. Eliot remarked: 'The first [aspect of Lawrence] is the ridiculous: his lack of sense of humour, a certain snobbery, a lack not so much of information as of the critical faculties which education should give, an incapacity for what we ordinarily call thinking.'[54] Eliot reiterated this opinion a few years later and added an illuminating gloss: 'Lawrence, even had he acquired a great deal more knowledge and information than he ever came to possess, would always have remained uneducated.'[55] In other words, the door to the citadel of high middle-class culture would always have been barred to the collier's son, regardless of effort or achievement. Lawrence was defended against these charges by F.R. Leavis, who reminded Eliot in the pages of *Scrutiny* that Lawrence did not lack an 'intellectual and social training', but that his training was different from the norm; it was rooted in the religious traditions of Nonconformity and shaped by the exigencies of northern working-class life and labour.[56] In a later memoir the economist J.M. Keynes rehearsed the dominant structure of feeling, and stated that Lawrence was merely 'jealous' of the Cambridge/Bloomsbury 'civilization' that 'Bertie' had exposed him to.[57] Lawrence's rejection of this fraction as a narrow, snobbish and exclusive middle-class elite could not be taken seriously by this 'aristocracy of intellect'.[58]

Lawrence glimpsed this world, was repulsed, could not return to his working-class home and lived out a double estrangement. His peculiar 'imagined community', understandably deformed and partial, acted as a kind of suture which could sometimes knit together the different parts of his self. In an 'Autobiographical Sketch' written in 1929 Lawrence tried to make sense of it all in this way:

> It is since coming back from America that I ask myself seriously: why is there so little contact between myself and other people whom I know? Why has the contact no vital meaning?
>
> And if I write the question down, and try to write the answer down, it is because I feel it is a question that troubles many men.
>
> The answer, as far as I can see, has something to do with class. Class makes a gulf, across which all the best human flow is lost. It is not exactly the triumph of the middle classes that has made the deadness, but the triumph of the middle-class thing.
>
> As a man from the working class, I feel that the middle class cut off some of my vital vibration when I am with them. I admit them charming and educated and good people often enough. But they just stop some part of me from working. Some part of me has to be left out.[59]

This sense of estrangement has been a shared experience for an increasing number of working-class scholarship boys and girls since the Second World War who have found it difficult to internalize middle-class values and patterns of behaviour unproblematically.[60] Despite his confusions and excesses, Lawrence remains one of the first who managed both to climb the educational ladder and articulate (however inarticulately) the feelings of anger and disgust which accompanied this transformation.

A few reflections on another scholarship boy and 'author', one nearer to our own time, will serve as an appropriate coda. Raymond Williams, son of a railway signalman from Pandy on the Welsh borders, offered a highly sympathetic reading of Lawrence in his first published work. In *Culture and Society* (1958) Williams acknowledged the charges which could be levelled at Lawrence (the belief that 'sex solves everything'; 'a precursor of the fascist emphasis on blood') but dismissed them as the result of 'ignorance'.[61] Later, however, Williams himself became increasingly impatient with Lawrence and could not bear to read most of his work by the late 1970s, though he never gave up on him entirely.[62] I would suggest that Williams's long fascination with Lawrence drew on two main sources: they both experienced social mobility and reacted to that experience in 'class' ways; and the idea of 'community' was also a common reference point. Finally, then, it would be helpful to draw out some of the major parallels and differences between them.

Williams, like Lawrence, went to Cambridge, but as an undergraduate student in 1939. Nearly 40 years later he described his first encounter with academics and fellow students – the kind of people who had been 'put down [for Cambridge] at birth'.[63] The veneer of learning and civilization failed to impress the stranger from rural Wales who recalled:

> The class which has dominated Cambridge is given to describing itself as well-mannered, polite, sensitive. It continually contrasts itself favourably with the rougher and coarser others. When it turns to the arts, it congratulates itself, overtly, on its taste and its sensibility; speaks of its poise and tone. If I then say that what I found was an extraordinarily coarse, pushing, name-ridden group, I shall be told that I am showing class-feeling, class-envy, class-resentment. That I showed class-feeling is not in any doubt. All I would insist on is that nobody fortunate enough to grow up in a good home, in a genuinely well-mannered and sensitive community, could for a moment envy these loud, competitive and deprived people. All I did not know then was how cold that class is. That comes with experience.[64]

This passage is as bitter and angry as anything we encounter in Lawrence. Williams himself was one of the 'coarser others' at Cambridge and must have appeared rather uncouth and certainly unpolished to many of his peers. Note how he turns that charge – a defining feature of social distinction – against the dominant class; it is they who are ill-mannered and coarse. Interestingly, this class also lacks emotion and is 'cold' and probably sly. The idea of 'community' – and Williams is referring here of course to the working-class community he had come from himself – is used to criticize this ultimately shallow and depressing milieu.

The story of Williams's intellectual engagement with F.R. Leavis is well known[65] but one formative moment is of particular interest in the present context. A lecture by Professor L.C. Knights on the meaning of the word 'neighbour' in Shakespeare made a deep impression, for Knights was defending the Cambridge line at the time; that it was impossible for a twentieth-century person to grasp the full significance of the word 'neighbour' in its Shakespearian sense, for that world (or 'organic community') had completely disappeared. Leavis 'was leaning against the wall and nodding vigorously' and the whole audience was in full agreement, Williams recalled. And then Williams ran out of patience.

> Well, then I got up, straight from Pandy, so to say, and said I knew perfectly well what 'neighbour' in that full sense means. That got hissed – it was a remark so against the common sense that here was something in literature which was not now socially available: the notion of that kind of recognition of certain kinds of mutual responsibility.[66]

Williams knew full well what neighbours were for he had been surrounded by them at home; directly after this passage he recalls how his father had to stop people in the local pub from organizing a collection for him before he went up to Cambridge. One thing they did understand about Cambridge, Williams remembered, was that it would cost a lot of money, 'so a collection was taken up, to try to look after me'.

Neighbourliness made the community work in Pandy, held it together, according to Williams at least. He did not maintain that no conflicts or oppositions were to be found back home but rather that 'there was a level of social obligation which was conferred by the fact of seeming to live in the same place and in that sense to have a common identity'. This rural and fairly stable settlement fed into his early views on 'community' and informed, for example, the romantic, idealist prescriptions which close his first major work. Over time though, as we have seen, Williams became very critical of the blanket use of 'community', and argued for a much more differentiated understanding which took full account of the historical and political determinations of 'community'. The pit villages on the other side of the Black Mountains offered an alternative model:

> it did come to seem to me that a very different kind of community was actually physically quite close to where I'd grown up, but

which I'd not known so well. A community that didn't depend at all on this sense of relative stability, relative custom, but a community that had been hammered out in very fierce conflict, the kind of community that was the eventual positive creation of struggles within the industrialisation of South Wales.[67]

Williams came to the conclusion that the making of 'communities' was an intensely political process, bound up with the level of formal as well as informal organization among working people, and their ability to articulate their own interests and provide their own self-definitions of 'community'. In 1985, for example, he argued that the miners' strike represented not 'the last kick of an old order' but 'one of the first steps towards a new order'. This was because the miners and their families had appropriated and redefined their 'communities' against 'the logic of a new nomad capitalism'.[68]

Unlike Lawrence then, Williams insisted that working-class men and women could create a democratic and egalitarian future for themselves, a future which had been prefigured in some senses by working-class associations – namely trade unions, the Labour Party, and the Co-operative movement.[69] After he had taught for a number of years in adult education and written two major works of cultural and social criticism, Williams eventually returned to Cambridge to take up a lectureship at the university in 1961. The facilities afforded by the institution gave him the time and space to develop into the most important British Marxist theorist since William Morris. As Williams later remarked, 'it was very important to me to work out my particular argument in Cambridge',[70] but he remained an isolated figure and if anything his isolation increased over time: 'What is formed and forming, at the centre of it, is as alien now as at any time in my life', he wrote six years before his retirement in 1983.[71]

Williams had already worked his way through the emotional difficulties thrown up by the prospect of a full-time academic career before he took up the post at Cambridge, on paper at least. His first novel *Border Country*, which was published in 1960, had been an obsession for many years; Williams had rewritten it seven times between 1947 and 1960.[72] Like *Sons and Lovers*, *Border Country* presented an imagined community modelled on the author's birthplace, but at the centre of the novel Williams placed the impact the General Strike of 1926 had on the lives of his family and friends. Moreover – and this is the final contrast I wish to draw – Williams deliberately refused the available narrative of individual escape. Matthew Price, the scholarship boy in the novel, is forced to question the significance of his own experience of social and geographical mobility when his father becomes ill and eventually dies. A university lecturer in economic history living in London, Matthew had been working on patterns of migration into the Welsh valleys in the mid-nineteenth century. This intellectual project had been blocked by Matthew's inability to make sense of the human and emotional meaning of crude statistics: 'It was a problem of measurement, of the means of measurement, he had come to tell himself.'[73] The solution to this problem, as elaborated in the novel, involved a difficult and continuous confrontation between past and present. As Matthew remarks on the final page: 'Only now it seems like the end of exile. Not going back, but the feeling of exile ending. For the distance is measured, and that is what matters. By measuring the distance, we come home.'[74] For Williams, 'measuring the distance' was vital in order to begin to connect the community that had produced him to the kind of society he wanted to help create in the future.

The view that 'imagined communities' only or mainly exist in the nostalgic narratives of first-generation intellectuals or exiles must be rejected; they have also been made through the practices and representations of the majority of working-class people in their everyday lives. By means of his political example[75] and writings Williams indicated that we should avoid any simplistic celebration of working-class community as a point of method: 'Right back in your own mind, and right back inside the oppressed and deprived community, there are reproduced elements of the thinking and feeling of that dominating centre', was how he once expressed it.[76] But he also insisted that certain forms of popular 'practical knowledge'[77] embedded within particular 'imagined communities' – traditions of cooperation and mutuality especially – can inform both 'the possibilities of common life' and, by extension, the 'many socialisms' which might still replace nomad capitalism.[78]

WORKING MEN, OLD CHARTISTS AND THE CONTAGIOUS DISEASES ACTS

BERTRAND TAITHE

Josephine Butler's writings of the early years of the twentieth century have marked most historical accounts of the agitation for the repeal of the Contagious Diseases Acts (CDA, 1864, 1866, 1869).[1] Historians have since stressed the role of a particularly vocal group, the Ladies National Association (LNA), which, in the light of later suffragette agitation and feminist movements, seemed close to forms of gendered politics with which they could empathize.[2] As the Acts were essentially promoting a double standard of morality, registering prostitutes and submitting them to compulsory medical examination in eighteen military and naval bases of the country, it seemed logical that women should be the standard bearer of equality before the law.[3] It was a handful of men, the National Association, however, who really started the campaigning in 1869 and who were also instrumental in obtaining the complete repeal of 1886. Moreover, eleven other male-dominated organizations came into existence over this single issue.[4] Josephine Butler thus had a very peculiar role, perhaps that of a 'religious preacher', as American feminist Cady Stanton described her, but she was in no way representative of a feminine leadership.[5] Many organizations actually appeared independently from her and without the consent or supervision of the original Ladies National Association.

Two such organizations were the Working Men's League for the Repeal of the Contagious Diseases Acts and the City of London Committee. I will argue that these two less well-known organizations played a very important role in reshaping the message of the repeal campaigns and in fostering the social purity campaign that emerged in the 1880s. I will also argue that the Working Men's League may well have been one of the last incarnations of radical politics of the 1840s.

The City of London Committee is perhaps the least well-known group of the repeal agitation. It numbered fewer than fifty members and limited its activities to the publication of pamphlets in London and to the publishing of the *Protest* after 1878. These businessmen involved in social purity should not be dismissed as a group of useless 'well-meaning' sentimentalists.[6] They showed more political sense and were more radical than most other anti-CDA organizations. In 1879 Alfred S. Dyer, one of its founding members, created a twin organization, the City Committee Against the Traffic of White Slaves. These two marginal groups were linked with, and supported financially by, the Working Men's National League, thus making for the unlikely alliance of city businessmen and old radicals. Superficially it would seem that the Working Men's League had come in answer to earlier calls from the repeal movement leadership, an example of which is from an 1872 pamphlet:

Working Men of England! Use every legal effort to compel the speedy and total repeal of these Laws. Return no man to Parliament who will not give a pledge to vote for repeal, and by petitions and letters to your parliamentary representative, insist on immediate repeal of acts which oppress only the daughters of the poor.[7]

Yet the Working Men's League was started belatedly, and independently from other organizations. It was even perceived as a threat to other political leagues. An ageing former Chartist leader, Edmund Jones started the movement from his home town of Liverpool. From 1875, to his terminal invalidity in 1879, he spoke relentlessly for the cause. With twenty 'old comrades' Jones began canvassing Liverpool and Birkenhead with mixed success, attracting from 100 to 500 people per meeting. At each gathering the speeches lasted for about an hour and were followed by a vote. In Liverpool, on 4 July 1877 for instance, a van displaying posters canvassed the streets and then stopped. The cart was used as a platform with the horse still harnessed and ready to move on. A little crowd gathered and, after an eloquent denunciation, a motion against the CDA was voted on. Five hands rose against the motion, three of which were instantly denounced as belonging to 'police spies'.[8] Other meetings were held in Bristol at the Temperance Hall, and in London (Lawrence Hill and Black Lane) the same month. The League started publishing its journal, the *National League Journal* monthly in 1875. It moved down to London in 1876 and the *National League Journal* was then backed by the Dyer brothers' publishing house. On Edmund Jones's retirement in 1878, Benjamin Lucraft, another old Chartist, became the Working Men's League's second paid secretary. Greater names were called but without success, chiefly because of the advanced age of most 'historical' Chartists by the end of the 1870s.

> Dr William Lovett, the well known Chartist Leader whose death has occurred during the past month, on being applied to by Mr Edmund Jones, as a fellow labourer in Chartism, for his co-operation in the Repeal agitation answered that he was too old and too ill to engage himself in any agitation but that he was sure that in moving the heart and mind of this country, they will be able to affect (its policies), in spite of Aristocratic powers and influence. . . .[9]

William Lovett's message shows best the historical importance of the Chartist legacy for a movement such as the Working Men's League. The leaders were still chosen on the grounds of old companionship and 'fight' solidarity dating from the 1840s. The Chartist agitation, the Anti-Corn Law League and the Reform League provided examples of mass movements to repealers. There was this considerable popular political energy waiting to be channelled, ready to find yet another platform to carry on the struggle after the anticlimax of the 1867 electoral reform. The League reflected these origins and was ostensibly democratic. Under the elected president sat a committee of members of the City Committee such as Sheldon Amos, and Benjamin Scott, the chamberlain of the City of London and president of the City Committee. At the level under this executive committee of fifteen members (nine from London, two from the south and three from the north) the National Council met on the first Wednesday of every month. A branch (minimum six people) could elect as many candidates as they could fund: there was a fee of 5s per councillor. The League was built on the same lines as trades councils, and copied their structure. It recruited enough people to have councillors from the following cities and towns from 1877: Bath, Birmingham (2), Blackburn (2), Boston, Bristol (2), Burslem, Chatham, Clerkenwell, Ellensborough, Feuton, Glasgow (9), Greenwich, Hansley, Henley (3), Leamington, Leeds (4), Leek, Leicester (2), Lincoln, Liverpool (9), London (6), Maidstone, Manchester, Merthyr Tydfil, North Leith, Norwich, Nottingham, Oldham, Rotherhithe (2), Sheffield, Stockport, Stoke (4).[10] This broad pattern of recruitment reflects the fact that, like all other repeal movements, the League recruited predominantly in urban areas, but also that it was able to disseminate its message very quickly through pre-established channels such as trade unions. Membership being at 6d or free, the League's financial system was very precarious (c. £150 a year, about the same as the London Trades Council) and depended on the donations of a few people and on the sales of the National League Journal (6,000 copies in 1877).

The most influential people in the League were Edmund Jones, before he became too ill, Benjamin Lucraft and the Dyer brothers, publishers of the paper. George Dyer, a radical politician, was elected to the council for Battersea, while his brother Alfred S. Dyer was on the London Representation Committee. These two young Quakers were prominent figures in the repeal campaign and in the fight against regulation. The aim of the Working Men's League was to infiltrate unions, co-operatives and friendly societies, to convert them to repeal and enlist their members on the national roll. In 1877 the League had 12,000 nominal members, 7 major unions and the trades councils of Birmingham and Liverpool affiliated.[11] Thomas Burt MP had joined the organization nominally.[12] Direct contributors were quoted while the others, whose union had affiliated them, were not. In 1884 the League claimed the support of '50,000 members including 1,600 secretaries and officers of Trades and other Working Men's Societies'[13] and could reflect on its action after the TUC publicly decided to support its cause: 'The League has worked with diligence, and, as the recent resolution of the TUC,[14] the Parliament of Labour, shows, with considerable success in arousing the Working Class to a sense of the injustice and immorality of the retrograde legislation against which we are fighting.'[15]

The Working Men's League also contributed to gathering 8,190 petitions representing 1,968,379 signatures against the Contagious

Diseases Acts. By comparison, the organization in favour of the Acts had only 43 petitions and 3,578 signatures, most of which were from influential clergymen, medical practitioners and other members of the establishment.

To gather momentum through public meetings, the old Chartists started by using the street as a legitimate political space before retiring to the more established network of rooms, temperance halls and mechanics' institutes or even public house back rooms. Their second and most important tactic was to infiltrate other working-class movements and use them as a platform to convert fellow working men to their cause. This aspect of the agitation was backed by the use of pamphlets written purposely: '*Why should I attend a meeting for the Repeal of the Contagious Diseases Acts?* This tract will be found very useful in the organization of public meetings, as the facts narrated are eminently suited to arouse indignation and provoke further enquiry. 100 for 2s 6d.'[16]

This almost cynical use of the audience's indignation could not be more plainly exposed. Chartists were good at propaganda and at hijacking other meetings. This transfer of knowledge confirms recent theses that Chartism durably impregnated working-class political practices and perceptions.[17] The liberal tradition and the Anti-Corn Law League tradition also met in the organization of elections. At the 1880 Tower Hamlets parliamentary election, Benjamin Lucraft was an alternative 'Liberal' candidate. On this occasion the Working Men's League and the City Committee supported him and he campaigned almost exclusively on the subject of the repeal of the Contagious Diseases Acts. To finance his campaign Lucraft also organized a great 'bazaar', reminiscent of the Anti-Corn Law League bazaar of 1842.

This brand of repeal agitation was not in the mainstream politics of the movement and originally escaped the sphere of influence of its Liberal middle-class leaders. While Josephine Butler had always wished to lead a popular crusade, the LNA had failed because of its patronizing attitude and its strongly middle-class oriented class discourse. The League on the other hand had a leadership of working-class people and middle-class extreme radicals, a well-established reformist combination. The repeal discourse it produced integrated most of the previous radical political discourse and synthesized forms of social purity that were already part of the working-class tradition. The Electoral Union and the Northern County League did not react well to the creation of the Working Men's League and Wilson, their main electoral organizer, attempted to prevent its formation and asked Josephine Butler to stop it.[18] In his otherwise comprehensive chronological records of the repeal agitation Wilson left no entry relating to the Working Men's League and its publications.[19] While directly supporting the Working Men's League and its journal, Alfred S. Dyer started publishing the *Sentinel* (1877), a lively weekly involved in the repeal, the fight against prostitution and, from 1879, the 'white slave traffic'. This campaign in self-fulfilling expectations started with the case of Annie Swan who had escaped from a brothel in Brussels.[20] Dyer went off on the trail of what he believed to be a large-scale traffic in 'white slaves'.[21] He did discover further examples of young British girls detained against their will in Belgium. Most of them had been prostitutes before they left England, though Dyer was convinced of the opposite. From this 'logical' extension of the fight against regulation, came another, even more controversial, campaign against masturbation between 1880 and 1885. This was an exemplary evolution of a crusade, from the repeal of the CDA to the fight against a 'white slave traffic' and against unrestrained male sexuality.[22] The drift of Dyer's political agenda was not uncommon in the first years of the 1880s and the whole repeal campaign led directly to one of social purity, which eventually contributed to the perpetuation of the coercive provisions of the CDA.[23]

One of the vectors of this drift towards social purity within the Working Men's League and City Committee was through the glorification of patriarchal working-class values. Working-class men were determined as tropes of morality, simplicity, generosity and rustic virility:

> To BRITISH WORKING MEN it is comparatively easy to meet an open enemy. We can combine against the tyranny of capital; our ranks provide defence against foreign foes; those grim horrors, Famine or Want, do not deprive us of our sympathy towards each other, nor can they rob us of our integrity or virtue; but when a secret attack is made against the liberty and virtue of our wives, daughters and sweethearts, there is danger to our most sacred instincts and institutions. When all else have failed us, the sacred name of mother, the lofty faith of our wives, and the simple virtue of our sisters, have been our pride and glory.[24]

The patriarchal ideals mixed with self-glorification and sentimentalization in a happy cocktail of images, many of which were borrowed from more traditional radical papers:

The fact is however that England never was more Christian than at the present moment, and that as the power of proud and intolerant ecclesiastics to control the minds of the people and the policy of state has diminished, True Religion has grown and flourished. . . . Then the Universities in addition of being hotbeds of bigotry and seminaries of the most nauseous funkeyism and servility, are also regular training schools of sensuality, rowdyism and blackguardism of the most hideous and demoralising kind.[25]

This stereotypical address from *Reynold's News*, for instance, put the emphasis on the 'old corruption' of the upper classes. Benjamin Lucraft could not have put it better.

The contribution of the Working Men's League to a class discourse of social purity was not novel, but it was qualitatively different from earlier populist attempts within the repeal movement. Josephine Butler and Francis Newman had already used many a radical form of expression and political reference since 1869. What the Chartists did within the repeal movement was to increase the number of these references and give them authenticity and the weight of history. One of their most important contributions to the repeal discourse was the categorization of the Contagious Diseases Acts as a familiar form of class exploitation: the resurgence of the 'old corruption'. The meaning of corruption is here taken very literally as symptomatic of venereal diseases. This unbalanced presentation of legislation, as defending aristocratic interests and privileges, was particularly resilient and appears to have been the common stock of all popular politics until at least the end of the 1880s:

Two men in plain clothes (Police Spies) called at the house of the girl's father in his absence. One of them said he had come for Sarah. . . . The brutal Spy began to get impatient and rough . . . she was dragged upstairs and because she cried and refused to go voluntarily, the spy called her 'a sulky little b——'. She then had to submit to a surgical outrage too horrible and indecent for description.[26]

The Acts were thus interpreted as the expression of police brutality, class exploitation and the protection of debauchery and 'state harlotry'. Public figures like Daniel Cooper, president of the Rescue Society, expressed the conviction in 1869 that debauchery, an upper-class vice, was prevalent among the aristocrats of France, if not of England.[27] Debauchery implicitly referred to sexual practices incompatible with reproduction. Debauchery, like sodomy[28] to which it was closely related, was represented as an upper-class practice developed from school or university days. At the other end of the spectrum, the neo-Chartist discourse emphasized self-rehabilitation, political and moral improvement or nostalgia. Recent works also show how deeply ingrained the ideals of domesticity were into their quest of respectability.[29] During the Chartist era, the emphasis had been on melodrama and the class dimensions of domesticity.[30] To deal with morality as a class issue proved very self-indulgent. The repealers pretended, without any evidence, that venereal diseases were rife among the upper classes of France. By analogy, the English upper class would also fail to protect themselves from it. In the context of the British CDA, the argument seems irrelevant as the class of 'consumers' the Acts intended to protect belonged principally to the ranks of the British armed forces. Yet the appeal of the 'class exploitation' pattern was immense and avoided difficult judgements on prostitutes.

Working-class attitudes to prostitutes were ambiguous.[31] On the one hand there was a rhetoric of mercy for the poor fallen girl,[32] as found in most popular melodrama, and on the other there was the resentment at the unjustified consideration and treatment provided through the Acts: 'Are these buildings of "comfortable hospitals" providing regular care for – those persons who have deserved well from their country? – No! – professional prostitutes, who for the protection of male debauchees in their debauchery must be petted and pattered after and practised upon.'[33] This differentiation between the poor girl and the professional was purely a figure of speech rather than a practical classification. However, it opened the door to class-hatred towards the servants of the 'old corruption'. The publication of prostitutes' petitions in 1874 reinforced the image of a freely chosen servitude. The intervention of prostitutes themselves in favour of the CDA substantially increased this process of separation of 'prostitutes', as a debased caste, from their social context. It prefigured the semi-criminalization of prostitution by the 1885 Criminal Law Amendment Act. Judith Walkowitz argues convincingly that this Act sealed the definitive segregation of prostitutes from their social background and their criminalization.[34] From a popular standpoint this moral condemnation was certainly not new, but it became the condemnation of a political betrayal:

In England, during the last three years, upward of one million, seven hundred thousand signatures to petition have been presented to Parliament, praying for the unconditional repeal of these Acts which are now in force in 18 English and Irish towns, and in wide areas around these towns. Fearing that the Government would bow to the great expression of public feeling, the doctors and Police who carry out these Laws and receive high salary for their work got up petitions signed *exclusively* by prostitutes, praying that the acts might be retained because their repeal would be a *calamity to those women* and a *misfortune to the country at large.* These unprecedented petitions were received by the House of Commons with CHEERS and LAUGHTER whilst the petition of hundreds of thousands of religious and moral persons was scarcely noticed.[35]

This text recalls the frustration of most mass petitioning, including the great Chartist ones of 1847–8. Humiliating laughter trivialized the debate and called into question parliamentary morality. That prostitutes might petition was scandalous in many ways, especially as, when they actually expressed a view, they defended their trade as if it were normal business.[36] This dissociation of the infantilized 'girls' who deserved to be defended from 'common prostitutes' proceeded with the sentimentalization of the 'fallen girl' into a victim of seduction. The working-class woman eventually joined the working-class man in this idealization. The Chartist discourse provided the kind of respectable imagery necessary to Manichaean identifications of prostitutes. Self-representation was very explicitly idealistic and detailed:[37]

The husband and father, a man of honest, manly face, a member of the Working Men's League, whose brawny frame and labour stained hands bespeak a genuine son of toil is exercising his skill in making some article connected with his trade, and which is destined for the Lucraft fancy fair.

The wife and mother, a kind matronly looking woman, whose heart burns with indignation . . . is knitting away some article for the Lucraft Fair . . . her daughter in all the beauty of young womanhood . . . the elder son, a young man of eighteen, uncorrupted thank God! . . . when he speaks to his companion in the workshop of the infamous Laws that sacrifice women to men's bestial passions his eyes burn like fire. . . . As they are all busy at work, the other and younger son, a lad of 14 is reading aloud the life of some truly Great men,[38] William Lloyd Garrison, Joseph Sturge, Elihu Burritt. . . .[39]

This nostalgic vision of English cottage life prior to industrialization was also often found in temperance and teetotal literature. Like the repeal literature, the temperance literature had a sufficiently vague religious undertone to be open to extremes, including Catholics.[40] The temperance movement had mostly kept the ritual atonement of religion through the pledge and the conversion of drinkers to temperance or teetotalism.[41] To many sceptical working-class observers these rituals and the accompanying self-righteousness could be perceived as a threat,[42] yet teetotal intransigence was an early form of authoritarian reforming particularly relevant to the fight against prostitution. The most common explanation pattern was based on 'solid research' and implied a material agent, alcohol, in the process of the fall.

'Drunkenness sinks the *man* below the brute; leading to the destruction of his health, the ruin of his domestic peace, the wretchedness of his family, and the deterioration of society, by his neglect, his incapacity and corrupt example.'[43] This reflection was largely anterior to the repeal campaigns, but it came specifically from one of the people who articulated the social ideology of the repeal agitation at its beginnings. The fall into prostitution was thus often tracked down to parental neglect and intemperance.[44] Social determinism left intact the difficult question of the girls' free choice and responsibility. To members of the Working Men's League the teetotal faction provided the model of an 'elite of working men and radicals' coup.[45]

Underlining the teetotal discourse was the call for a sudden and total prohibition by means of law. The teetotal project was the close forerunner of the social purity project. The structure, the implication and even the political personae were the same. Working Men's League leaders, like Benjamin Lucraft,[46] were also actively fighting for teetotalism. In both movements, there was a strong emphasis on self-help and on the adoption of petit-bourgeois attitudes towards sexuality and alcohol.[47] In the 1870s the temperance movement became the hotbed of social purity in its most puritan forms. The White Cross Army, designated after a code of colour like the temperance Blue Ribbon Army, was under the patronage of the Bishop of Durham and the effective direction of Ellice Hopkins. It originated from the diocesan temperance movement of the Anglican Church but soon recruited Nonconformists as well. This organization, like various Anglican revival associations, inspired the Dyer brothers and the Working Men's League in their drift towards prohibitionist policies.

Prohibitionists had some other past connections in the Lord's Day Observance Society[48] which had a clearly authoritarian attitude towards leisure.[49] This tradition was implicitly referred to in the repeal discourse. For the 'regenerated' working-class family, Sunday had a considerable religious and family importance.[50] Repealers usually avoided meeting on Sundays and pointed out that regulationists used Sunday lectures for their propaganda.[51] The Sabbatarian movement was a controversial extreme of religious inflexibility to which it was difficult to refer openly. Radicals and even Christian working-class men found Sabbath observance and rational recreations difficult to combine.[52]

Politically, it is perhaps worth recalling Brian Harrison's argument that 'the temperance movement was, in fact, one of the transitional organizations channelling religious energies into party politics: "instead of making Radicalism Christian, it ended by secularising Christianity"'.[53] In that context the forms taken by much repealer propaganda go in Harrison's direction. The religious tone remained but the main topic of discussion was not religion but the causes of prostitution. The new scenario of the prostitute's fall, as described in Alfred Dyer's reports from Belgium, revolutionized the apportionment of guilt: male lust became the cause of prostitution, and was assisted by alcohol. Alcohol directly provoked lust in man but also served his evil deeds by weakening his 'preys'. Seduction was often associated with alcohol or even narcotics in popular literature.[54] This popular literary trick structured the storyline of most of the anecdotes related in the *National League Journal* or the *Sentinel* (which merged in 1884). Using popular stories to reinforce their case enabled Dyer and his friends to achieve the ultimate ambition of the repeal movement: the popularization of the cause. Other repealers had obtained their maximum audience very early and then stagnated. The Dyers took the debate further and the Working Men's League, after the early days of activism, turned into a morally arousing yet titillating literature distribution network, rather than into a mass demonstration movement.

The role of the audience in all repeal movements had been limited. Few manifestations of their presence were encouraged; discreet anger and indignation were some of them. The audience was understood to be supportive of the speakers. A religious silence or a respectful 'Hear, Hear' were common, but on the whole the audience was soberly dignified. Noise belonged to the enemies' crowd, composed of roughs and pimps: 'I wish to state, while I may, justly complaints of the conduct of the "noisy louts" who attended the meeting with evident intention of drowning my voice at every point. . . .'[55] 'It must be observed that these [Colchester "roughs"] were not of the class of honest working people, but chiefly a number of hired roughs and persons directly interested in the maintenance of the vilest of human institutions.'[56]

The decent working-class audience of the repeal speakers behaved, the enemies' crowd did not and implicitly belonged to the residuum. The accusations of hiring the working-class men attending the pro-CDA meetings, or luring them with free beverages, were practices denounced as part of the 'old corruption'.[57] Even if the audience of the repeal was idealized, especially for its working-class elements, the fact remains that it endured tedious speeches. The repealers' discourse was repetitive and monotonous. Beyond a short window of political opportunities in 1873, the chances of repeal faded and the propagandists were obliged to look abroad for more lurid material. The *Medical Enquirer* in 1879 justified its change from monthly to quarterly on the grounds that everything important had already been said. Those who wished to go further than simply reading the repeal literature were invited to diffuse it: 'Complaints have been made in the Newspapers of the circulation, sometimes even without being enclosed in envelopes, of letters and papers relating to an Act dealing with a subject of which all respectable and decent women must be of necessity totally ignorant!'[58] There are no details of who actually handed out these pamphlets, but we know of the existence of stalls at the entrance to churches and during repeal meetings. The written support aimed at enforcing the effect of the speeches and at stimulating the audience to echo it afterwards. The repeal material was written with the idea that it was to be used by the reader as an instrument of propagation; this is certainly one of the reasons why the style is often emphatic and close to that of speeches. Very often these letters were actually nothing but speeches, a practice quite common in politics at the time. In general the pamphlets were not too encumbered with figures or facts and used a single case to build a generalization. Statistics were rather uncommon and, as Wilson hand-wrote on the back of one report, they were

'Rather too technical to arrest the attention of the ordinary reader'. The Working Men's League went even further in the dismissal of statistical evidence: 'That statistics may be made to prove anything is the current belief of every one who knows much about them, with the exception perhaps of the Statistical Society.'[59] A general study of the pamphlets issued throughout the period actually shows a falling interest in technical debates and a concentration on the few anecdotes and scandals relevant to the cause. The volume of publication is difficult to establish: an average of 5,000 copies[60] per paper seems possible, with probably more for the *Shield*, the *National League Journal*, the *Sentinel* and less for the *Medical Enquirer* and the *Protest*. Pamphlets had a much higher circulation, from 6,000 for a pamphlet[61] destined for clergymen to 500,000 and more for social purity pamphlets.[62] Even these impressive figures do not hide the facts that penny tracts provided weak support for the repeal propaganda, that many were handed out free of charge and that they did not create an event by themselves. As in meetings, the repeal movement was confined to a limited audience and had difficulty in achieving any public recognition in the 1870s. In that context it is not surprising that the repealers responsible for the propagation of repeal ideas, i.e. publishers like the Dyers or the Methodist publicist Hugh Price Hughes, looked eagerly for new uses of the media. In the late 1870s and at the beginning of the 1880s, there were two models the repeal could follow or associate with: the Salvation Army and 'new journalism'.

The Salvation Army was the fastest growing religious movement in the late 1870s and 1880s. For the repealers the Salvation Army presented several arresting features: it was able to stir elite artisans and to win support in the remotest parts of London. It seemed to be achieving in a few years what city missionaries had been trying to do since the 1840s. The way they conducted their 'offensives' created a lot of interest among the journalists close to the repeal campaign. The 'Invasion of Darlington' in 1879 was led by two women officers, both illiterate and one of whom was under the age of 18. No fewer than 2,000 people attended each of their meetings.[63] In the case of the 'Invasion of Darlington' the 'contagion' of salvation seemed to be at its most effective since Wesley, and was a model for the repeal movement as well. The Salvation Army's enemies, the so-called 'Skeleton Army' which started in the East End of London around 1879, was also of the kind that the repealers liked to think of as their enemies. The Skeleton Army, like the 'Yellow Ribbon Army'[64] (opposing the 'Blue Ribbon

Army') was supported by brewers and publicans and picked its recruits from the ranks of the 'roughs', the pimps and the 'criminal classes'.[65] Here again the salvationists courted martyrdom. Before meeting the repealers the Salvation Army had not been involved in any form of rescue work. As a religious movement, the Salvation Army scrupulously avoided any areas of theological division and had good relations with churchmen of most denominations, including Archbishop Tait.[66] The movement was particularly good at regularly organizing grand demonstrations of power, such as their march on the East End, their conferences held in converted and renovated music halls and the successful sales of their literature. The greatest achievement of the Salvation Army was certainly economic, and it seems to have been one of the few movements able to expand its financial base.

One of the most powerful tools of this expansion was *War Cry*, which was one of the greatest 'journalistic' successes in the 1880s. First produced in 1879 with modest sales of 17,000, the paper grew from strength to strength and to a circulation of over 500,000 copies a week in 1883. It aimed to be 'a paper to arouse anybody against sin, chiefly by telling how the fight was . . . carried on and how the devil was being conquered throughout our ranks'. The type of material presented in the columns was relatively simple and usually referred to the melodramatic salvation of a sinner or the martyrdom of some other salvationist. *War Cry* was lavishly illustrated by contemporary standards, with pictures of martyrs or miracles: '5 people sent to prison for a week for yelling about Salvation in the streets of Crediton',[67] or 'Perfect eyesight miraculously restored to Captain Repkin ADC of the Northern Division'.[68] In many ways the *War Cry* did not take the place of a 'newspaper' but that of the 'penny dreadfuls'. The stories were simple, the endings stereotyped: salvation or death in misery, the advice was practical and, all in all, the *War Cry* related more closely to daily experience than 'penny dreadfuls' did. It also targeted more particularly women. This fitted with their model of conversion coming from the humble to the powerful, from women to men. The pattern of gender promoted in the Salvation Army was very similar to the one promoted through the repeal movement.

The Dyers were certainly impressed by the Salvation Army but in many ways the repeal movement had been a precursor and had much to teach salvationists. Bramwell Booth and the Salvation Army's leadership learned very early on of Alfred Dyer's private crusade against an international trade of prostitution and from 1882 the *War*

Cry reported missing persons.[69] At about the same time the *National League Journal* began to advertise practical rescue work in their columns: 'A situation is sought for a young French woman who has been rescued from a licensed house of prostitution. Please write to the Dyer Brothers.'[70]

Bramwell Booth and his wife also drove the Salvation Army into the repeal cause and rescue work complementary to that carried on by repealers like Josephine Butler or Ellice Hopkins.[71] Some of the rescued fallen women went from Butler's rescue home to another one managed by the Salvation Army.[72] In the 1880s there was an exchange of help and information between the repealers and the Salvation Army. Yet, in many ways, the Salvation Army was what the repeal movements had failed to be. The Salvation Army had a teleological vision of its mission; it fitted into a wider Messianic and millenarian tradition and went beyond petty political struggles.

Repealers and salvationists shared the same melodramatic reformist style. This style was a novelty to the pious reader of the Victorian era. As Altick pointed out in his classic study of the *English Common Reader*, readership in the nineteenth century was strictly segregated according to religion.[73] In 1864, temperance and religious magazines sold 2,700,000 copies monthly, at least three times more than all the other magazines and monthlies put together. On a weekly basis there was a parity between religious and secular newspapers. After the creation of the *War Cry* the balance was probably tipped in favour of religion again. As Ensor noted, religious publications by far outnumbered any secular publications at a ratio of about three to one.[74] In that context, one easily perceives that the yellow paperbacks of W.H. Smith[75] had only a limited readership, and that a large fraction of the population had no access to fiction and melodrama. This restricted access to melodrama was largely the result of self-censorship rather than of limited availability. Repeal pamphlets could be read in lieu of fiction, their supposed authenticity increasing their attractiveness.

The main practical objections remained that just as melodrama was a debased form of theatre, so was repeal journalism not taken seriously and so was its distribution too restrained to dissenting religious communities.[76] The upmarket model of the 'new journalism' was the only alternative channel of communication. This term was coined in the 1880s to describe the changes initiated by a small but influential evening newspaper, the *Pall Mall Gazette* (*PMG*).[77] At the origins of the 'revolution' of the 'new journalism' was a young editor, William T. Stead. Stead had been the main editor of a successful regional paper since 1873: the *Northern Echo*.[78] Like many northern papers it was rather favourable to the cause of repeal and gave frequent short notices of the repealers' meetings. In 1880, Morley, the owner and editor of the *Pall Mall Gazette* made Stead his assistant editor. By 1883 Morley retired and Stead had become the sole editor of the *PMG*.[79] Described as an 'earnest Puritan', Stead had powerfully supported Gladstone's 'Bulgarian Atrocities' campaign. His personal importance was disproportionate to the circulation of his newspaper which sold only about 9,000 copies, compared with the 50,000 of *The Times,* or the 60,000 of its direct rival the *Globe,* or the 250,000 of the *Daily Telegraph*. The Liberal press was quite limited with only two morning papers (the *Daily Chronicle* and the *Daily News*) and one evening paper, the *Echo*, while the Tory Party was supported by four major morning papers and three evening papers.[80] Radical papers such as *Lloyd's* or *Reynold's* were too unreliable in their support. In this context the *PMG* had no real competition among Liberal readers and soon proved to be one of the most attractively presented newspapers on the stand. Its small format and illustrations were a novelty in the daily press. In 1881, Stead invented catchy cross heads on several columns.[81] The style of the writing was just as vivid and inspired and somehow very close to that found in A.S. Dyer's newspapers. Biblical in tone and indignant on many burning issues, Stead brought some passion and sensationalism to a rather dull press.[82]

The *Bitter Cry of Outcast London* in 1883 started Stead's social purity campaign. This pamphlet emanated from the Congregationalist Union of London. The author Andrew Mearns ran it as a series of leaders in the *PMG* from 16 to 23 October 1883.[83] This campaign presents two interesting points if looked at from a repealer's perspective. The campaign was initiated by a private committee and amplified through the media. In a way Stead was purely instrumental in the scandal. Technically this was a precedent which could be repeated by repealers to assure the definitive repeal of the Contagious Diseases Acts and for their social purity campaign. The second interesting aspect was the impact of this environmentalist denunciation of London's immorality and poverty. With chapter headings such as: 'Non-attendance to worship', 'The Condition in which they live', 'Immorality, Poverty, and Heart-breaking Misery', the link was easily established between poverty[84] and immorality.[85]

In 1883 Alfred Dyer fed Stead his stories of an international traffic of nubile virgins.[86] The intermediary between Dyer and Stead was Benjamin Scott, of the City Committee and Working Men's League. Dyer and Scott objected to the *Bitter Cry* story. It notably stated that London was actually a centre of immorality even compared with other capital cities such as Paris or Brussels. Scott published a pamphlet to re-establish the correct exchange mechanism as Dyer saw it: pornography came from abroad into England while virgins travelled from England to regulationist countries like France and Belgium.[87]

Stead had been exposed to the 'facts' collected by Dyer on the fate of half a dozen prostitutes locked in Belgian brothel houses. None of these women was actually under 16, but Dyer's theory was that another traffic of pre-pubescent girls existed. This hypothesis remained unproved, so Stead decided to create some concrete evidence. He entered into a contract with Bramwell Booth to obtain a converted procuress named Rebecca Jarrett. Jarrett, being freshly rescued, was asked to buy a girl from her parents for the explicit purpose of prostitution. She bought Eliza Armstrong on 3 June 1885,[88] and took her to a notorious abortionist who certified her a virgin. Eliza was then sedated and put to bed. Stead tiptoed into the bedroom in disguise and woke her up. Stead subsequently left the room very shaken by the effect he had had on the little girl. The girl was later cross-checked by a doctor and testified again as a virgin as evidence of Stead's good behaviour. The whole of this enquiry was heavily documented for two purposes: the publication of articles in July and a cross-examination by a committee or even a trial.

Eliza was sent to salvationists in France, proving another of Dyer's points about the international traffic of virgins. Stead started his series of articles which ran from 6 to 15 July. The headings of the first articles were: 'The Violation of Virgins', 'The Confessions of a London Brothel Keeper', 'How Girls are Bought and Ruined', and 'A Child of 13 Bought for £5'. The story's heroine was nicknamed Lily. On the first day the newspaper sold out, and high sales carried on all the way through the series. Stead published yet more stories of kidnapping, abduction, rape, and incest (the third chapter of the series). The readership was scandalized and shocked but also delighted at this intrusion of the melodramatic pathos into the realm of the real. The journalistic venture turned into a proper sensation as early issues were sold second-hand. The *Globe* led a campaign against sensationalism, while *Lloyd's* was on the trail of the disappearance of Eliza Armstrong

(9, 16 and 23 August). *Lloyd's* investigation led to the conviction of Stead and his accomplice for kidnapping.

For Alfred Dyer and his friends of the Working Men's League the 'Maiden Tribute to Modern Babylon' was a complete success. Their message broke through into mainstream journalism. It provided another platform after the partial repeal of the Contagious Diseases Acts in 1883 and it seemed then that the Working Men's League could be integrally subsumed into their new Social Purity League. The Salvation Army organized a massive petition campaign in conjunction with the repeal associations. The 400,000 signatures collected in three weeks made for a 2½-mile-long petition which was taken to parliament in a procession on the shoulders of eight salvationists. At this point public emotion was running high and political power was particularly weak. The Criminal Law Amendment Bill (which had been defeated in 1883 and 1884) was reintroduced, heavily amended and passed unanimously in the House of Commons on 7 August 1885. This union of repealers, Salvation Army, social purity and politics remained to be consolidated under the leadership of Stead. The giant Hyde Park demonstration on 22 August attempted to seal this alliance.

This triumphalist phase was to be marred by the Stead trial. From the outset of his enquiry Stead had accumulated his evidence with a trial in mind:[89] 'We challenge prosecution, we court enquiry, we have reluctantly been driven to the only mode – that of publicity – for arousing men to a sense of the horrors which are going on at this very moment.' Stead had organized a committee[90] of personalities supportive of the repeal cause to examine his evidence and give him the seal of respectability.[91] The real trial took place later. *Lloyd's* enquiry into Eliza Armstrong's disappearance proved that 'Lily' and Eliza were really one person. *Lloyd's* claimed to champion the rights of the working class, in this case Eliza Armstrong's parents. On 24 August 1885, Eliza was returned to her parents and soon afterwards, Rebecca Jarrett surrendered to the police. Bramwell Booth, Mrs Combe, a salvationist, Jarrett and Stead were charged with abduction; Mrs Mourez, the abortionist, Stead and Jarrett were charged with indecent assault. Jarrett had bought the girl from her mother but had neglected to inform the father, who struggled to recover his daughter. The contrast between the drunken Armstrong family and the group of mostly teetotal middle-class men was striking. Stead used the trial to orchestrate more propaganda. He published his defence as a pamphlet which was distributed among most of the remaining repeal and social purity associations. Stead was sentenced to three months of gaol. Jarrett and Mourez served six months. The latter died in prison. The doctor who had practised a similar inspection of Eliza's genitals was not prosecuted. Stead posed as the victim of misinformation and put the blame on Jarrett. Year after year he would wear the prison uniform to commemorate his heroic defence of purity.

In fact the whole trial backfired, and the show of unity put up at the mass demonstration in Hyde Park crumbled. The hijacking of trade unions by social purity groups came to a halt and the Working Men's League disappeared. The message had been so adulterated by the new sensationalistic and melodramatic forms it had assumed that it became further estranged from the real debates on the economic causes of prostitution. Far from giving working men 'a moral purpose and a sense of agency', melodrama could also become derivative, voyeuristic and the vehicle of unwanted politics.[92] Stead's campaign transcended the repeal movement and helped to establish a political project wider than a simple rejection of an act of regulation, but this project ultimately failed. In social purity, the repeal had found its end and its future, the project of repealers was stretched to the extreme in the radical purification of society. Dyer had shown the way towards prohibition but he remained a part of the repeal movement. The social purity programme of the Vigilance Association was no longer a part of the original repeal project. The melodramatic element, introduced into the repeal movement as an instrument of propaganda, had taken it over. The popular media we still live with and their ways of repressing while also shocking and transgressing came into existence after this episode. The real social questions raised by sexual exploitation, pornography and violence against under-age children were trivialized by the media coverage the repeal movements had been trying to obtain for so long. In achieving the dubious status of transgressive entertainment, repealers and propagandists of social purity lost the radical political backing they had once enjoyed. The Committee of the London Trades Council's resolution of 1885 best illustrates the divorce between radical and social purity agendas: 'It was well known that many who were loudest in their clamour for this "new crusade" were notorious for imposing upon their workpeople all the industrial conditions which made social purity simply impossible. . . . It has not yet appeared that this "Social Purity League" has attempted, or intends, to attack any one of the great causes which produce social impurity, and merely tinkering with the effects is neither worthy of the energy nor time of earnest social reformers.'[93]

The Working Men's League was, indeed, one of the last incarnations of the radical politics of the 1840s, and the social purity campaign may have temporarily linked it with the wider middle-class movement against the Contagious Diseases Acts. Yet the essential conflict of interests over morality, work and employment meant that the Working Men's League and the middle-class groups eventually moved in opposite directions.

NOTES

INTRODUCTION

1. P. Wood, 'Finance and the Urban Poor Law', in M.E. Rose (ed.), *The Poor and the City: The English Poor Law in its Urban Context 1834–1914* (London, 1988).

2. J. Lewis, *The Voluntary Sector, the State and Social Work in Britain: The Charity Organisation Society and Family Welfare Association since 1869* (Aldershot, Edward Elgar, 1995).

3. *Reading Observer*, 23 January 1912, quoted in S. Yeo, *Religion and Voluntary Organisation in Crisis* (Brighton, Harvester, 1976), p. 211.

4. Even that excellent standard text D. Fraser, *The Evolution of the British Welfare State* (London, Macmillan, 1973), and its second edition produced in 1984, tends to accept this approach.

5. J. Harris, 'Society and State in Twentieth-century Britain', in F.M.L. Thompson (ed.), *The Cambridge Social History of Britain 1750–1950, Vol. 3, Social Agencies and Institutions* (Cambridge University Press, 1990), p. 68; J. Harris, *Private Lives, Public Spirit: A Social History of Britain 1870–1914* (Oxford, 1993).

6. H.P.R. Finberg, 'Local History', in *Approaches to History* (London, 1962), p. 121.

7. R. Frankenberg, *Communities in Britain: Social Life in Town and Country* (London, 1971), p. 238.

8. B. Anderson, *Imagined Communities: Reflections on the Origin and Spread of Nationalism* (London, 1991); D. Gilbert, 'Imagined Communities and Mining Communities', *Labour History Review*, vol. 60, no. 2 (1995).

9. J. Bourke, *Working-class Cultures in Britain 1890–1960* (London, 1994); R. Hoggart, *The Uses of Literacy* (London, 1957).

10. R. Colls, 'Save our Pits and Communities', *Labour History Review*, vol. 60, no. 2 (1995); T. Nicholson, 'Community and Class: The Cleveland Ironstone Field, 1850–1914', *Labour History Review*, vol. 60, no. 2 (1995).

11. F.K. Prochaska, 'Philanthropy', in F.M.L. Thompson (ed.), *The Cambridge Social History of Britain 1750–1950, Vol. 3, Social Agencies and Institutions* (Cambridge University Press, 1990).

12. *Help*, vol. 4, no. 2, November 1908.

13. K. Laybourn, *The Guild of Help and the Changing Face of Edwardian*

Philanthropy: The Guild of Help, Voluntary Work and the State 1904–1919 (Lampeter, Edwin Mellen Press, 1994); K. Laybourn, *The Evolution of British Social Policy and the Welfare State* c. *1800–1993* (Keele, Keele University Press, 1995), chapter 8.

14. P. Thane, 'Old People and Their Families in the English Past', in M. Daunton (ed.), *Charity, Self-interest and Welfare* (University College London, 1996), pp. 113–38.

15. R. Humphreys, *Scientific Charity in Victorian London: Claims and Achievements of the Charity Organisation Society 1869–1890* (London, London School of Economics and Political Science, Working Papers in Economic History, 1993).

16. A. Digby, *British Social Policy* (London, 1994), p. 43.

17. R. Holt, 'Football and the Urban Way of Life in Nineteenth-century Britain', in J.A. Mangan, *Pleasure, Profit and Proselytism: British Culture and Sport at Home and Abroad 1700–1914* (London, Cass, 1988).

CHAPTER 1

1. *Help*, (journal of the Bradford Guild of Help), vol. 4, no. 2, November 1908.

2. Borough of Poole League (later Guild) of Help, *Sixth Annual Report, 1912–1913*, 27 October 1913.

3. Bradford City Guild of Help, minutes, 1903–6, beginning.

4. *Yorkshire Daily Observer*, 21 September 1904.

5. *Help*, vol. 1, no. 1, October 1905.

6. *The Helper* (journal of the Halifax Citizens' Guild), vol. 2, no. 3, May 1910.

7. J. Sutter, *Britain's Next Campaign* (London, 1903), p. 274.

8. *Yorkshire Daily Observer*, 27 September 1904.

9. *Halifax Evening Courier*, 26 November 1909 referring to the speech of J.H. Howarth, Chairman of the Halifax Citizens' Guild at its fourth Annual General Meeting.

10. *Help*, vol. 1, no. 2, November 1905 and vol. 2, no. 3, December 1906, incorporating the Second Annual Report, p. 3.

11. *Help*, vol. 1, no. 2, November 1905 and vol. 2, no. 3, December 1906, incorporating the Second Annual Report; *Dudley Herald*, 17 November 1909.

12. *Report of the Proceedings, National Association of the Guild of Help, 1908*, appendix; K. Laybourn, *The Guild of Help and the Changing Face of Edwardian Philanthropy: The Guild of Help, Voluntary Work and the State, 1904–1919* (Lampeter, Edwin Mellen Press, 1994), pp. 5–6.

13. *Report of the Proceedings, National Association of the Guilds of Help, 1911*, appendix; M.J. Moore, 'Social Work and Social Welfare: the Organisation of the Philanthropic Resources in Britain 1900–1914', *The Journal of British Studies* (Spring, 1977), 94.

14. M. Brasnett, *Voluntary Social Action, a History of the National Council of Social Services 1919–1969* (London, National Council of Social Services, 1969), pp. 1–18.

15. Laybourn, *Guild of Help*, pp. 6–7.

16. Borough of Poole (later Guild) of Help, *Second Annual Report, 1908–9*, p. 5.

17. S. Yeo, *Religion and Voluntary Organisation* (London, 1976), p. 229.

18. Mr. T. Francis, of Middlesbrough, noted how the 1911 National Insurance Act had brought an 'entirely different outlook on health' which meant that there was

'a lighter burden on the Guild', *Croydon Borough Guild of Help Magazine*, 20 July 1912.

19. Bradford City Guild of Help, casebooks 1603, 1620, 1908, 2205, 2359, 2523 and 3378.
20. B.S. Rowntree, 'Social Symposium 1: The Social Worker', *Friends Quarterly Examiner*, xxxviii (1904), 73.
21. *The Helper* (Halifax), vol. 2, May 1910, quoting P. Bagenal of Halifax, a Local Government Board inspector for the Poor Law.
22. *County Borough of Croydon Guild of Help*, no. 12, June 1909, reporting on the National Conference of the Guild of Help held at Birmingham and quoting the Revd A.G. Lloyd.
23. G.R. Snowden, *Report to the President of the Local Government Board on the Guild of Help in England* (Cd. 56664, 1911), p. 9.
24. *County Borough of Bolton Guild of Help Magazine*, vol. 3, no. 3, March 1909.
25. Bradford City Guild of Help, *Seventh Annual Report*, 1910–11, and *Fifteenth Annual Report* 1918–19, which listed 31,723 names.
26. *Croydon Borough Guild of Help Magazine*, no. 3, July 1910, pp. 18–19.
27. Ibid., 6 October 1917, p. 460.
28. *County Borough of Bolton Guild of Help Magazine*, vol. 5, no. 8, June 1911, reporting on the annual conference of the Guild held at Birmingham, and summarizing the paper of the Revd A.G. Lloyd, 'Mutual Registration of Assistance'.
29. *The Citizen* (Reading), vol. 1, no. 4, January 1913.
30. Snowden, *Guilds*, pp. 8–9.
31. *Croydon Borough Guild of Help Magazine*, vol. 3, July 1910, p. 18.
32. Ibid.
33. *County Borough of Bolton Guild of Help Magazine*, vol. 5, no. 8, June 1911, pp. 182–4.
34. Ibid., 29 October 1913.
35. Snowden, *Guilds*, p. 2.
36. Borough of Poole Guild (formerly League) of Help, *Fifth Annual Report 1911–1912*, pp. 16–17; Middlesbrough Guild of Help, minutes, 5 February 1913.
37. *Croydon Borough Guild of Help Magazine*, no. 12, June 1911.
38. *Help*, vol. 4, no. 3, December 1908. A report in *Help*, vol. 3, no. 10, July 1908 suggests that it was three women and one man; Miss Newcombe in Division A, Miss E.T. Brailsford in Division B, Mrs Moser in Division C and W. Milledge (Central Office) in Division D.
39. *County Borough of Bolton Guild of Help Magazine*, vol. 5, no. 8, June 1911, pp. 176–7.
40. Ibid., reporting on the Annual Conference of the Guild of Help, Birmingham, 1911.
41. Ibid., vol. 5, no. 8, June 1911.
42. Bradford City Guild of Help, *Seventh Annual Report*, 1910–11.
43. *Help*, vol. 5, no. 8, June 1911, p. 179.
44. *Help*, vol. 2, no. 3, December 1906, in the Second Annual Report of the Bradford City Guild of Help.
45. *County Borough of Bolton Guild of Help Magazine*, vol. 4, no. 12, October 1910, p. 110.
46. *The Citizen.*, vol. 1, no. 4, January 1913.
47. *County Borough of Bolton Guild of Help Magazine*, vol. 4, no. 12, October 1910, p.109.
48. Laybourn, *Guild of Help*, pp. 89–90; The Warrington Citizens' Guild of Help,

First Annual Report, 31 December 1910; Middlesbrough Guild of Help, minutes, 3 October 1910, 9 October 1911; Plymouth Civic Guild of Help, *Fourth Annual Report to 31 August 1911*, p. 5 and *Sixth Annual Report 1912–13*, p. 5.

49. *The Helper* (Bolton), vol. 6, no. 4, April 1912.
50. Ibid., p. 49.
51. *Help*, 19 December 1907.
52. *The Helper* (Bolton), vol. 8, no. 4, April 1914, pp. 59–61.
53. *Help*, vol. 2, no. 3, December 1906.
54. Middlesbrough Guild of Help, minutes, 13 February 1911.
55. Ibid., 3 October 1911.
56. *Help*, vol. 4, no. 3, December 1908.
57. *County Borough of Bolton Guild of Help Magazine*, vol. 4, no. 5, March 1910, p. 49; *Wakefield Express*, 24 December 1909.
58. Sixth Annual Conference of the Guild of Help, Halifax, quoted in *The Helper* (Bolton), vol. 7, no. 10, October 1913, p. 92.
59. *The Helper*, vol. 8, no. 2, February 1914, pp. 22–3.
60. *Croydon Borough Guild of Help Magazine*, no. 12, June 1911; Borough of Poole League (later Guild) of Help, minutes, 14 and 20 January 1908.
61. First Annual Report of the Bradford City Guild of Help, 11 October 1905, quoted in *Help*, vol. 1, no. 2, November 1905.
62. *The Helper* (Halifax), vol. 1, no. 1, January 1909 and vol. 1, no. 3, February 1909, p. 8.
63. Report on the Fourth National Conference of the Guilds of Help, Birmingham, *The Helper* (Halifax), vol. 3, no. 3, May 1911.
64. Halifax Citizen's Guild of Help, *Fifth Annual Report 1909–10*, p. 10; *Sixth Annual Report 1910–1911*, p. 11; *Seventh Annual Report, 1911–1912*, p. 12.
65. W.H. Beveridge, *Unemployment* (London, 1912), p. 190.
66. *The Helper* (Halifax), vol. 1, no. 8, October 1909, p. 9.
67. Ibid., vol. 1, no. 7, July/September 1909, p. 4.
68. Ibid., vol. 1, no. 3, March 1909.
69. Ibid., vol. 1, no. 7, July/September 1909, p. 4.
70. Ibid., vol. 2, no. 2, March 1910, p. 7.
71. Ibid., vol. 3, no. 3, May 1911, p. 8.
72. Ibid., vol. 3, no. 3, May 1911, p. 8.
73. *County Borough of Bolton Guild of Help*, vol. 5, no. 9, July 1911, pp. 190–7.
74. *The Helper* (Bolton), vol. 6, no. 6, July–August 1912, pp. 72–3.
75. *The County Borough of Bolton Guild of Help Magazine*, vol. 2, no. 6, March 1908.
76. Bradford City Guild of Help, *Annual Report*, 1912, p. 6.
77. Laybourn, *Guild of Help*, pp. 46–65.
78. Brasnett, *Voluntary Social Action*, p. 6; Moore, 'Social Work', pp. 91–2.
79. *Croydon Guild of Help Magazine*, 20 July 1912, p. 98.
80. Bradford City Guild of Help, minutes, 22 December 1903 and 8 January 1904.
81. *Help*, vol. 2, no. 5, February 1907.

CHAPTER 2

1. K. Laybourn, *The Guild of Help and the Changing Face of Edwardian Philanthropy* (Lampeter, Edwin Mellen Press, 1994), p. 9.
2. Pat Thane, *The Foundations of the Welfare State* (London, Longman, 1982), p. 209.

3. F.K. Prochaska, 'Philanthropy', in F.M.L. Thompson (ed.), *The Cambridge Social History of Britain 1750–1950, Vol. 3; Social Agencies and Institutions* (Cambridge University Press, 1990).
4. Thane, *Foundations*.
5. P.F. Clarke, *Lancashire and the New Liberalism* (Cambridge University Press, 1971).
6. Laybourn, *Guild of Help*.
7. M. Brasnett, *Voluntary Social Action, a History of the National Council of Social Services 1919–1969* (London, National Council of Social Services, 1969).
8. Michael Cahill and Tony Jowitt, 'The New Philanthropy: The Emergence of the Bradford City Guild of Help', in *Journal of Social Policy*, vol. 9, no. 3, 1980, p. 370.
9. Ibid.
10. Julie Sutter, *Britain's Next Campaign* (London, R. Brimley Johnson, 1903).
11. Ibid.
12. *The Yorkshire Daily Observer*, 2 September 1904.
13. G.R. Searle, *The Quest for National Efficiency. A Study in British Politics and Political Thought, 1900–1914* (London, Ashfield Press, paperback edn, 1990).
14. B.S. Rowntree, *Poverty: a Study of Town Life* (1901).
15. Michael J. Moore, 'Social Work and Social Welfare: The Organisation of Philanthropic Resources in Britain, 1900–1914', *Journal of British Studies*, Spring 1977.
16. *Help*, vol. 1, no. 2, 1905.
17. *The Yorkshire Daily Observer*, 21 September 1904.
18. Cahill and Jowitt, 'The New Philanthropy'.
19. Walter Milledge, *Bradford City Guild of Help Handbook*, 1911.
20. Moore, 'Social Work'.
21. *Help*, vol. 1, October 1905.
22. Cahill and Jowitt, 'The New Philanthropy'.
23. *Help*, vol. 4, no. 2, November 1908.
24. Ibid., vol. 1, October 1905.
25. *Forward*, 10 March 1906.
26. Ibid., 24 March 1906.
27. Cahill and Jowitt, 'The New Philanthropy'.
28. Brasnett, *Voluntary Social Action*, p. 6.
29. Moore, 'Social Work'.
30. Milledge, *Handbook*.
31. Ibid.
32. *Help*, vol. 1, no. 6, March 1906.
33. Bradford City Guild of Help, casebook 2436.
34. Jane Lewis, *Women and Social Action in Victorian and Edwardian England* (Stanford University Press, 1991).
35. Laybourn, *Guild of Help*.
36. Milledge, *Handbook*.
37. Ibid.
38. Ibid.
39. Bradford City Guild of Help, casebook 2636.
40. Ibid., casebook 4456.
41. Milledge, *Handbook*.
42. Ibid.
43. Milledge, *Handbook*.
44. Bradford City Guild of Help, casebook 2436.

45. Ibid., casebook 3536.
46. Laybourn, *Guild of Help*.
47. *Help*, vol. 1, no. 2, November 1905.
48. Ibid., casebook 2476.
49. Laybourn, *Guild of Help*.
50. Ibid.

CHAPTER 3

1. Editorial Notes, *The County Borough of Bolton Guild of Help Magazine*, vol. 1, no. 9 (June 1907).
2. John Gould (Medical Officer of Health for the Borough of Bolton), 'A Cleaner Bolton', an address to Guild Helpers, *County Borough of Bolton Guild of Help Magazine*, vol. 1, no. 8 (May 1907), p. 101.
3. Ibid.
4. County Borough of Bolton Guild of Help, *Fifth Annual Report*, November 1910, p. 11.
5. Ibid.
6. For an extensive survey of the period see K. Laybourn, *The Guild of Help and the Changing Face of Edwardian Philanthropy. The Guild of Help, Voluntary Work and the State, 1904–1919* (Edwin Mellen Press, 1994) and G. Finlayson, *Citizen, State and Social Welfare in Britain, 1830–1990* (Clarendon Press, 1994).
7. J. Lewis, *The Voluntary Sector, The State and Social Work in Britain: The Charity Organisation Society/Family Welfare Association since 1869* (Aldershot, Elgar, 1995), p. 69.
8. John Gould, 'Consumption: The Preventive Measures Adopted in Bolton', *County Borough of Bolton Guild of Help Magazine*, vol. 5, no. 11 (December 1910), p. 9.
9. C. Lawrence, *Medicine in the Making of Modern Britain, 1700–1920* (Routledge, 1994), p. 72.
10. S. Webb and B. Webb, *The State and the Doctor* (1910), ibid., p. 74.
11. See M. Worboys, 'The Sanatorium Treatment for Consumption in Britain, 1890–1914', in J.Pickstone (ed.), *Medical Innovations in Historical Perspective*, (Macmillan, 1992).
12. See J. Lewis, 'Infant Welfare in Edwardian England', *Journal of Social Policy*, vol. 9 (1980).
13. Lawrence, *Medicine in the Making of Modern Britain*, p. 75.
14. Ibid.
15. Worboys, 'Sanatorium Treatment for Consumption', p. 48. The figures are those cited by the anti-TB movement, *c.* 1900. They are for Great Britain, excluding Ireland. At this time it was the convention to multiply the number of deaths by five to estimate the number of sufferers; by 1910 the convention was to multiply by ten.
16. L. Bryder, *Below the Magic Mountain: A Social History of Tuberculosis in Twentieth-century Britain* (Clarendon Press, 1988), p. 1; see also W.P.D. Logan, 'Mortality in England and Wales from 1848 to 1947', *Population Studies* (1950), 132–78.
17. Ibid.
18. Ibid.
19. Bryder, *A Social History of Tuberculosis in Twentieth-century Britain*, p. 3.

20. S. Delepine, *Astor Committee Final Report, ii*, Cd. 6654 (1913), ibid., p. 27.

21. Bryder, *A Social History of Tuberculosis in Twentieth-century Britain*, pp. 4–6.

22. Ibid., pp. 5–6.

23. *British Medical Journal* (1898), p. 1899. The British initiatives were part of a much wider international movement; France had established an anti-TB association in 1891, Germany in 1895, America in 1904. While regular international conferences were held throughout the period, the International Central Bureau for the Campaign against TB was founded in 1902 with its headquarters in Berlin.

24. *Transactions of the 18th Annual Conference of the National Association for the Prevention of Tuberculosis* (1932), p. 17.

25. NAPT, *Catalogue of Exhibits at the Tuberculosis Exhibition*, Town Hall, Reading, 11–16 September 1911, p. 9.

26. *British Medical Journal* (1912), p. 875.

27. This idea was developed at some length in a paper given at the TB Exhibition organized and managed by the Guild on behalf of the NAPT, C.W. Paget Moffatt, 'Healthy Homes', *County Borough of Bolton Guild of Help Magazine*, vol. 5, no. 11 (December 1910), p. 14.

28. 'A Letter to the Editor', *County Borough of Bolton Guild of Help Magazine*, vol. 2, no. 5 (February 1908), pp. 62–3.

29. John Gould, 'Consumption. Preventive Measures adopted in Bolton', *County Borough of Bolton Guild of Help Magazine (Tuberculosis Exhibition Number)*, vol. 5, no. 11 (December 1910), p. 9.

30. Ibid.

31. *Bolton Medical Officer of Health Annual Report for 1911–12*, p. 34.

32. Ibid., *Annual Report for 1913–14*, p. 27.

33. Ibid., *Annual Report for 1910–11*, pp. 26–7. Between 1905 and 1910 1,226 cases were brought to the attention of the MOH as a result of compulsory notification.

34. Figures compiled from the *Annual Reports* of the County Borough of Bolton Guild of Help, 1906–12. To supplement beds at the Meathop and Wilkinson sanatoria the Guild also had access to beds in Blair's Hospital, a convalescent home on the outskirts of Bolton, and six beds were also maintained for children in the North of England Children's Sanatorium in Southport.

35. County Borough of Bolton Guild of Help, *Third Annual Report*, November 1907–8, p. 8. The Guild was also able to send 60 children to Southport for 14 days in the summer in conjunction with Pearson's Fresh Air Fund, which had been established and was run by a Guild member.

36. 'A History of Preventive Measures', *Bolton Medical Officer of Health Annual Report for 1909–1910*, p. 52. The article was a summary of a report produced at the request of the Local Government Board as to the operation of Section 52 of the Bolton Corporation Act, 1905, which sanctioned the compulsory notification of pulmonary TB.

37. Ibid., pp. 50–1.

38. Ibid., p. 51.

39. Ibid.

40. *Bolton Medical Officer of Health Annual Report for 1912–13*, p. 35.

41. Ibid.

42. The Act provided that a sum of 1s 3d per insured worker was set aside for sanatorium benefit. A further 1d was added by the Treasury to fund research. This cover was extended to the dependants of the insured following the

recommendations of the Astor Committee (*Departmental Committee on Tuberculosis*, Cd. 6164) which was set up to determine the best way of administering anti-TB initiatives. In addition local authorities were made responsible for treating the insured, with half the cost being redeemable from the Treasury. Every TB sufferer, man, woman, and child was, therefore, entitled to some form of treatment as a consequence of the 1911 Act. While this may appear to represent a radical departure in social policy, it really meant little on paper.

43. NAPT, *Catalogue of Exhibits at the Tuberculosis Exhibition*, Town Hall, Reading, 11–16 September 1911, p. 1 in Bryder, *A Social History of Tuberculosis in Twentieth-century Britain*, p. 27.

44. T.N. Kelynack (ed.), *Tuberculosis Year-book and Sanatoria Annual, 1913–14*, (London, 1914).

45. Ibid., p. 29.

46. Worboys, 'Sanatorium Treatment for Consumption', p. 56.

47. C.W. Paget Moffat, 'Healthy Homes', *County Borough of Bolton Guild of Help Magazine (Tuberculosis Exhibition Number)*, vol. 5, no. 11 (December 1910), p. 15.

48. See M.A. Crowther, *The Workhouse System 1834–1929: The History of an English Institution* (London, 1981), pp. 57–8.

49. W. Farnworth, 'Bolton's Sanatorium', *County Borough of Bolton Guild of Help Magazine*, vol. 2, no. 5 (February 1908), pp. 65–6.

50. Mrs W. Haslam, 'A Lay Opinion on Remedial Measures', *County Borough of Bolton Guild of Help Magazine (Tuberculosis Exhibition Number)*, vol. 5, no. 11 (December 1910), p. 55.

51. County Borough of Bolton Guild of Help, *Third Annual Report*, November 1908, p. 7.

52. Ibid., p. 8.

53. Ibid.

54. J.K. Fowler, *Problems in Tuberculosis* (1923), p. 5.

55. County Borough of Bolton Guild of Help, *Sixth Annual Report*, November 1911, p. 9.

56. W. Farnworth, 'The After-care of Consumptives', *The County Borough of Bolton Guild of Help Magazine*, vol. 5, no. 11 (October 1911), p. 212.

57. *Journal of the NAPT*, vol. 3, no. 1 (1904); p. 83 in Bryder, *A Social History of Tuberculosis in Twentieth-century Britain*, p. 33.

58. J.D. Marshall, 'Sanatorium Life and Treatment', *County Borough of Bolton Guild of Help Magazine*, vol. 5, no. 11, December 1910, p. 38.

59. J. Cunningham-Browne, *Lancet*, Pt 2 (1910), p. 1040 in Worboys, 'Sanatorium Treatment for Consumption', p. 58.

60. Mrs W. Haslam, 'A Lay Opinion on Remedial Measures', *County Borough of Bolton Guild of Help Magazine (Tuberculosis Exhibition Number)*, vol. 5, no. 11 (December 1910), p. 50.

CHAPTER 4

1. See A.S. Wohl, *Endangered Lives, Public Health in Victorian Britain* (London, Methuen, 1983) and F.B. Smith, *The People's Health, 1880–1910* (London, Croom Helm, 1977).

2. Since the late 1970s a plethora of influential local and regional surveys have

emerged in Britain. The most definitive studies are by M.E. Pooley and C.G. Pooley, 'Health, Society and Environment in Victorian Manchester'; R. Woods, 'Mortality and Sanitary Conditions in Late Nineteenth-century Birmingham'; B. Luckin, 'Evaluating the Sanitary Revolution: Typhus and Typhoid in London, 1851–1900'; B. Thompson, 'Infant Mortality in Nineteenth-century Bradford'. All these studies are in a collection edited by R. Woods and J. Woodward, entitled *Urban Disease and Mortality in Nineteenth-century England* (London, Batsford Academic and Educational, 1984). Public health, housing and sanitation in the north-east area of Teesside is also dealt with in detail in A.A. Hall's doctoral study of *Working-class Living Standards in Middlesbrough and Teesside, 1870–1914* (Middlesbrough, Teesside Polytechnic, 1979).

3.   All figures are derived from the Huddersfield MOH's *Annual Reports* between 1877 and 1914. The reason for the first terminal date being 1877 as opposed to the more rounded date of 1870 is because the MOH's *Annual Reports* are not published consistently until then.

4.   C. Chinn, *They Worked All Their Lives: Women of the Urban Poor in England, 1880–1939* (Manchester University Press, 1989), p. 134.

5.   D.V. Glass, *The Town and a Changing Civilisation* (London, Bodley, Head and Chivers, 1935), p. 5.

6.   J. Lewis, *The Politics of Motherhood: Child and Maternal Welfare in England, 1900–1939* (London, Croom Helm, 1980), p. 196.

7.   Chinn, *They Worked All Their Lives*, p. 135.

8.   Ibid., p. 134.

9.   Lewis, *The Politics of Motherhood*, p. 199.

10.   Ibid., p. 196.

11.   A.S. Wohl, *Endangered Lives*, p. 38.

12.   J.M. Winter, 'The Decline of Mortality in Britain, 1870–1950', in T. Barker and M. Drake (eds), *Population and Society in Britain, 1850–1980* (London, Batsford Academic and Educational, 1982), p. 100.

13.   R.I. Woods, P.A. Watterson and J.H. Woodward, 'The Causes of Rapid Infant Mortality Decline in England and Wales, 1861–1921 Part I', *Population Studies*, vol. 42, 1988, and 'The Causes of Rapid Infant Mortality Decline in England and Wales, 1861–1921 Part II', *Population Studies*, vol. 43, 1989.

14.   Writers include C. Parton, 'The Infant Welfare Movement in Early Twentieth Century Huddersfield', *Journal of Regional and Local Studies*, vol. 3, 1983, and H. Marland, 'A Pioneer in Infant Welfare: the Huddersfield Scheme, 1903–1920', *Society for the Social History of Medicine*, 1993.

15.   Marland, *Society for the Social History of Medicine*, p. 25.

16.   In 1887 there was a peak of 125 deaths from measles and 61 from whooping cough.

17.   The only significance of the Longwood district as the choice for the scheme was that Longwood was Broadbent's native village.

18.   Marland, *Society for the Social History of Medicine*, p. 37.

19.   R. Brook, *The Story of Huddersfield* (London, MacGibbon and Kee, 1968), p. 189.

20.   The acceptance of the national 1907 Notification of Births Act in Huddersfield reduced the notification time to 36 hours.

21.   Marland, *Society for the Social History of Medicine*, p. 38.

22.   Wohl, *Endangered Lives*, pp. 12–13.

23.   M. Llewelyn Davies, *Maternity – Letters from Working Women* (London, Virago, 1989), p. 5.

24. J. Burnett, *Plenty and Want: A Social History of Food in England from 1815 to the Present Day* (London, Routledge, 1989).

25. J.B. Eagles, *John Benson Pritchett: First Medical Officer of Health for Huddersfield* (Huddersfield, Local History Workshop Series, 1984), p. 6.

26. Wohl, *Endangered Lives*, p. 34.

27. N. Porritt, *Cornered*, c. 1880, pp. 62–6. In the purely fictional case a young child was suffering from fits and Nancy Bell, the 'female medicine man, midwife, and oracle of the neighbourhood', was called in as the mother could not afford to seek relief from the parish doctor. The nurse diagnosed that the child was suffering from 'brownkitus and hinflaymation' and prescribed two drops of gin, half a teaspoon of syrup of vierlets, and five drops of Indian brandy to be administered every three hours. On following these instructions, the child's condition deteriorated and the mother was forced to call the doctor, who informed her that her child was suffering from the effects of narcotic poisoning.

28. E. Roberts, 'Working Wives and their Families', in Barker and Drake, *Population and Society*, pp. 155–6.

29. Eagles, *John Benson Pritchett*, p. 6.

30. Roberts, 'Working Wives', p. 156.

31. Ibid., p. 156.

32. Chinn, *They Worked All Their Lives*, p. 136.

33. W.V. Hole and M.T. Pountney, *Trends in Population, Housing and Occupancy Rates, 1861–1961* (London, HMSO, 1971), p. 5.

34. One problem of interpretation has emerged regarding any estimate of overcrowding figures in relation to the population; the 1891 and 1901 figures could be deemed inaccurate as they only enumerate dwellings with under five rooms. Thus any figures stated must be seen as an underestimate. Nevertheless the figures are fairly accurate as it could be argued that those persons occupying tenements with five rooms or more would not usually have a family exceeding ten individuals and therefore would not live in overcrowded conditions.

35. Hall, *Working-class Living Standards*, p. 400.

36. Charles Henry Jones was also the first mayor of the new Huddersfield Municipal Borough.

37. T.W. Woodhead, *History of the Huddersfield Water Supplies* (Huddersfield, Wheatley, Dyson and Son, 1939), p. 63.

38. Wohl, *Endangered Lives*, p. 128.

39. Huddersfield MOH, *Annual Report*, 1979, p. 40.

40. The privy midden system was the most unhygienic and filthy method used nationally in the late Victorian and Edwardian period, and it was not completely phased out in Huddersfield until after the First World War.

41. Huddersfield MOH, *Annual Reports*, 1878 and 1914.

42. Ibid., *Annual Report*, 1910.

43. Ibid., p. 60.

44. The chief sanitary inspector's *Annual Reports* are housed within the Huddersfield MOH's *Annual Reports*.

45. Brook, *The Story of Huddersfield*, p. 189.

46. Huddersfield MOH, *Annual Report*, 1894.

47. The total number of deaths from *all types of fever*, not *enteric fever* individually, in five-yearly groups are: 1877–81 = 149, 1882–6 = 64, 1887–91 = 70, 1892–6 = 52, 1897–1901 = 68, 1902–6 = 69, 1907–11 = 44 and 1912–14 = 14* (* 1912–14 only represents a three-year group).

48. Huddersfield MOH, *Annual Report*, 1892, p. 59.

49. Between 1877 and 1897, the technique involved was the counting of the duration of seven minutes of black smoke per hour produced by the chimneys, and after 1898 the technique changed to a limit of three minutes of black smoke per half-hour. It was not until 1944 that a more sophisticated technique emerged.
50. It must be remembered that in 1898 the period of taking observations was reduced from an hour to half an hour which could partly explain the sudden increase in the number of smoke observations after 1898.
51. Wohl, *Endangered Lives*, p. 340.

CHAPTER 5

1. Old Age Pensions Act 1908, Section 3b, in J. Betty, *English Historical Documents* (London, 1983), pp. 1–5.
2. Herbert F. Stead, *How Old Age Pensions Began to Be* (London, 1910), p. 299.
3. D. Fraser, *The Evolution of the British Welfare State* (London, Macmillan, 1984), pp. 150, 154.
4. M. Bruce, *The Coming of the Welfare State* (London, 1968), p. 18.
5. D. Vincent, *Poor Citizens. The State and the Poor in Twentieth Century Britain* (London, 1991), pp. 40, 41.
6. P. Thane, 'The Development of Old Age Pensions in Britain', unpublished PhD thesis (London School of Economics, 1970) p. 20.
7. Asquith in his budget speech to the House, 1908, quoted in Stead, *How Old Age Pensions*, p. 249.
8. H. Hoare, *Old Age Pensions: Their Actual Working and Ascertained Results in the United Kingdom* (London, 1915), p. 151.
9. Thane, 'The Development of Old Age Pensions', p. 272.
10. Ibid., pp. 269, 271, 280.
11. Salisbury City Council: Clerk's Letter Book: 1908–1919 (G23/21715) [S/CLB] 9 November 1909, 3 September 1915.
12. Derived from the *Annual Report of His Majesty's Customs and Excise Board: 1910–1914, 1916–1919* [CEB], and the *52nd Report of Commissioners of His Majesty's Inland Revenue*, October 1908–March 1909 [IR].
13. The figures for Tables 5.2, 5.3 and 5.4 are taken from Salisbury City Council: Register of Claims 1918–1919 (G23/217/8) [SIRC].
14. A. Wilson and G.S. Mackay, *Old Age Pensions* (London, 1941), p. 46.
15. Hoare, *Old Age Pensions*, p. 35.
16. Ibid., p. 34.
17. *Annual Report of His Majesty's Customs and Excise Board: 1910–1914, 1916–1919* [CEB] 1912, p. 79.
18. Salisbury City Council: Minutes of the Old Age Pensions Committee: 1908–1919 (G23/217/1–4) [S/OAP], 14 June 1916.
19. S/OAP Committee 2, 30 December 1908.
20. Hoare, *Old Age Pensions*, pp. 17, 18.
21. S/OAP, 22 November 1911.
22. Ibid., 24 January 1912.
23. S/CLB 29 August 1916.
24. S/OAP, 1 February 1911.
25. Ibid.
26. Hoare, *Old Age Pensions*, p. 27.

27. S/OAP, 11 December 1911.
28. Hoare, *Old Age Pensions*, p. 20.
29. S/OAP, 2 January 1911.
30. Ibid., 29 March 1911.
31. Hoare, *Old Age Pensions*, pp. 25, 28.
32. S/CLB, 10 July 1911. Francis Hodding served as clerk to the Salisbury Pension Committee for the whole period 1908–19. His letters show that he was a go-between among the various parties in a claim which often went beyond his formal duties.
33. Hoare, *Old Age Pensions*, p. 16.
34. Ibid., p. 19.
35. S/OAP, 13 November 1918.
36. Thane, 'Development of Old Age Pensions' p. 318.
37. 52nd Report of Commissioners of His Majesty's Inland Revenue: October 1908 –March 1909 [IR] p. 196.
38. S/OAP, 12 February 1913.
39. S/CLB, 24 January 1919.
40. Hoare, *Old Age Pensions*, p. 55.
41. S/OAP, 30 December 1908.
42. S/CLB, 8 June 1911.
43. Thane, 'Development of Old Age Pensions', p. 264.
44. IR, p. 197.
45. S/CLB, 30 June 1913.
46. Hoare, *Old Age Pensions*, p. 54.
47. CEB, 1912.
48. M.A. Crowther, 'Family Responsibility and State Responsibility in Britain before the Welfare State', *The Historical Journal*, 36 (1992), p. 132.
49. Hoare, *Old Age Pensions*, p. 48.
50. S/CLB, 26 March 1909.
51. Ibid., 20 January 1912.
52. IR, p. 197.
53. S/CLB, 27 July 1917.
54. Ibid., 26 March 1909.
55. Ibid., 20 January 1912.
56. Ibid., 3 September 1915.
57. Hoare, *Old Age Pensions*, p. 75.
58. P. Thane (ed.), *The Origins of British Social Policy* (London, 1978), p. 14.
59. Hoare, *Old Age Pensions*, p. 107.
60. Thane, 'Development of Old Age Pensions', p. 279.
61. Hoare, *Old Age Pensions*, p. 108.
62. S/OAP, 14 December 1910.
63. Ibid., 8 April 1914.
64. Ibid., 2 October 1912, 10 June 1914, 27 February 1918.
65. CEB, 1912, p. 79.
66. S/OAP, 16 November 1910, 1 February 1911.
67. Hoare, *Old Age Pensions*, p. 112.
68. See E.P. Thompson, *Whigs and Hunters* (London, 1975), chapter 10 for a discussion of the deterrent effect of the law in imposing discipline.
69. Thane, 'Development of Old Age Pensions', p. 306.
70. CEB, 1911, p.78.
71. Ibid., 1911, p. 78. The Pension Officers received much praise from the

Commissioners for the 'loyal and efficient manner' in which they had responded to the extra work.

72.   Hoare, *Old Age Pensions*, pp. 84–5.
73.   Thane, 'The Development of Old Age Pensions', p. 275.
74.   S/RC, 9 December 1908.
75.   Hoare, *Old Age Pensions*, p. 89.
76.   W. Beveridge, *The Beveridge Report* (London, HMSO, 1942), p. 131.
77.   S/OAP, 2 January 1911.
78.   CEB, 1911, p. 78.
79.   S/OAP, 29 March 1911.
80.   Ibid., 26 April 1911.
81.   S/CLB, 3 May 1911.
82.   S/OAP, 29 August 1911, Hannah Bailey.
83.   Ibid., 29 April 1911.
84.   CEB, 1912, p. 80.
85.   Hoare, *Old Age Pensions*, p. 93.
86.   S/CLB, 9 November 1909.
87.   S/OAP, 18 December 1908, 24 April 1909, 27 March 1918, 16 November 1910, 29 August 1917.
88.   Quoted from *Hansard* in Thane, 'Development of Old Age Pensions', p. 223.
89.   Quoted in Thane, 'Development of Old Age Pensions', p. 302.
90.   Ibid., p. 339.
91.   J. Harris, 'Political Thought and the Welfare State 1870–1940: An Intellectual Framework for British Social Policy', *Past and Present* (1992), p. 117.
92.   Quoted in Stephen Yeo, 'Working-class association, private capital, welfare and the state in late nineteenth and twentieth centuries', in *Social Work, Welfare and the State*, edited by Noel Parry, Michael Rustin and Carole Satyamurti (London, 1979), p. 49.
93.   CEB, 1911, p. 78.
94.   D. Ashford, *The Emergence of the Welfare State*, Oxford, 1986, pp. 14, 27, 37, 43.
95.   P. Corrigan and D. Sayer, *The Great Arch* (Oxford University Press, 1985), p. 119.
96.   I. Gough, *The Political Economy of the Welfare State* (London, 1979), p. 66; Corrigan and Sayer, *Great Arch*.

CHAPTER 6

1.   For a fuller discussion of certain themes raised in this chapter and their wider context, see D. Taylor, *Crime, Conflict and Control: the Advent and Impact of the New Police* (Manchester University Press, 1997).
2.   *The Times*, 24 December 1908, pp. 6, 7.
3.   M.V. Dixon, *Constabulary Duties: A History of Policing in Picture Postcards* (Market Drayton, SB Publications, 1990), p. 33.
4.   R. Reiner, *Chief Constables* (Oxford University Press, 1992), p. 112.
5.   Ibid., p. 111.
6.   Ibid., pp. 110–11.
7.   It is interesting to note that in the Report of the 1962 Royal Commission on the Police roughly two-thirds of policemen, in what has been seen as the golden age of policing, said they had 'severe difficulties' in making friends outside the force

while only slightly fewer, just under 60 per cent, felt that the general public was either reserved, constrained in conversation or suspicious in their dealings with the police. Other evidence collected around the same time revealed that policemen's wives, when on holiday, were unhappy to tell others of their husbands' work, while a survey in the early 1970s found that the majority of policemen and their families felt cut off from the community. M.E. Cain, *Society and the Policeman's Role* (London, Routledge & Kegan Paul, 1972), chapter 4.

8. C. Steedman, *Policing the Victorian Community: the Formation of English Provincial Police Forces, 1856–80* (London, Routledge & Kegan Paul, 1984), p. 27.

9. This is most graphically seen at the time of the Swing Riots. The vast majority of contemporary pamphlets, seeking to explain the machine-breaking and arson attacks, paint a picture of an organic community and of innocent labourers. 'Evil' comes from without, corrupts the natural innocence of the villagers and brings dissension and conflict. See, for example, *An Address to the Men of Hawkhurst* and *The Tale of Turvey Down*. Similar sentiments are to be found in the address of the Baron Vaughan to the Grand Jury of the Special Assize at Winchester in 1831.

10. C. Reith, *A New Study of Police History* (London, Oliver & Boyd, 1956), p. 140.

11. Ibid., p. 142.

12. Flora Thompson, *Lark Rise to Candleford* (London, Penguin, 1973), p. 484.

13. Alun Howkins, *Poor Labouring Men: Rural Radicalism in Norfolk, 1870–1923* (London, Routledge & Kegan Paul, 1986), p. 239.

14. H. Hopkins, *The Long Affray: the Poaching Wars in Britain* (London, Macmillan, 1986), p. 239.

15. *Essex Weekly News*, 9 November 1888, cited in M. Scollan, *Sworn to Serve: Police in Essex* (Chichester, Phillimore, 1993), p. 43; see also J. Woodgate, *The Essex Police* (Lavenham, Dalton, 1983), especially photograph on p. 69. Such communal protest was not new. Two unpopular policemen in Eaton Bray, Bedfordshire, were subjected to 'rough music', following the sentencing of eight men found guilty of assaulting the police. C. Emsley, 'The Bedfordshire Police, 1840–1856', *Midland History*, vol. 7, 1982. But this was as nothing when compared to the welcome received by PC Thomas Griffiths, one of 'Paddy Mayne's Grasshoppers', as the Staffordshire County Police were known, when he visited the Old Three Pigeons in Nesscliff. He was lifted bodily into the air and thrown on to the open fire. On his escape from the fire he was kicked under a cupboard whence he was rescued by the timely intervention of the landlady. Such were Griffiths's injuries that he did not return to work for three months: D.J. Elliot, *Policing Shropshire, 1836–1967* (Studley, Brewin Books, 1984), pp. 26–7.

16. M. Hann, *Policing Victorian Dorset* (Wincanton, Wincanton Press, 1989), pp. 31, 43–4, 50, 54, 107.

17. This is also the conclusion of Steedman, *Policing*, and D. Foster, 'The East Riding Constabulary in the Nineteenth Century', *Northern History*, vol. 21, 1985.

18. AA, *Country Coppers: the Story of the East Riding Police* (Hornsea, Arton Books, 1993), p. 47; Hann, *Policing Victorian Dorset*, p. 4. Transfers were also used for disciplinary purposes.

19. 4 August 1866, cited in C. Emsley, *The English Police: a Social and Political History* (Hemel Hempstead, Wheatsheaf Harvester, 1991), p. 63.

20. V.A.C. Gatrell, 'The Decline of Theft and Violence in Victorian and Edwardian England', in V. Gatrell, B. Lenman and G. Parker (eds), *Crime and the Law* (London, Europa, 1980).

21. S. Petrow, *Policing Morals: the Metropolitan Police and the Home Office, 1870–1914* (Oxford University Press, 1994), p. 294, fn. 2.

22. Elizabeth Cass, a dressmaker, had been arrested and charged with soliciting but the case was dismissed at the Marlborough Street Police Court following the evidence given by her employer that she was a respectable young woman. The situation was inflamed by the comments of the magistrate, Mr Newton, who declared that he was sure that she had gone out for immoral purposes and, if she were honest, she would not have been walking in Regent Street at night. Ibid., p. 139.

23. Madame Eva d'Angely was a Frenchwoman arrested for 'riotous and indecent behaviour', having been seen accosting gentlemen in Regent Street. Again, the case was dismissed but the magistrate, Mr Denman, did not criticize the police but made it clear that he felt that an unescorted woman walking in Regent Street must be soliciting. Ibid., p. 139.

24. Attitudes towards prostitution varied considerably across the country. In some areas, such as the West Riding of Yorkshire, the question did not give rise to major problems. In other areas, especially where there was a powerful local moral purity lobby, there could be considerable difficulties with the police trapped in the middle. The most spectacular example took place in Liverpool in 1890 when the chief constable, Nott Bower, found himself at odds with the local Watch Committee over the question of the wholesale prosecution of prostitutes and brothel-keepers.

25. C. Booth, *Religious Influences*, vol. 1, pp. 52–3, cited in D. Woods, 'Community Violence', in J. Benson (ed.), *The Working Class in England, 1870–1914* (London, Croom Helm, 1985), p. 184.

26. P. Cohen, 'Policing the Working-class City', in Bob Fine et al. (eds.), *Capitalism and the Rule of Law* (London, Hutchinson, 1979); J. White, *The Worst Street in North London: Campbell Bunk, Islington between the Wars* (London, Routledge & Kegan Paul, 1986); S. Humphries, *Hooligans or Rebels? An Oral History of Working-class Childhood and Youth, 1889–1939* (Oxford, Blackwell, 1984).

27. Cited in White, *Worst Street*, p. 116.

28. Such attitudes were not confined to Campbell Bunk, as White notes. Personal testimony from older members of the author's family confirms that similar attitudes were to be found in the poorer districts of Kentish Town and Tottenham around the turn of the century.

29. S. Reynolds and B. and T. Woolley, *Seems So! A Working-class View of Politics* (London, Macmillan, 1911), p. 86.

30. Ibid., pp. 86–7.

31. Ibid., p. 87.

32. Humphries, *Hooligans or Rebels?*, especially chapters 6, 7.

33. Robert Roberts, *The Classic Slum: Salford Life in the First Quarter of the Century* (London, Penguin, 1971), pp. 93–4, 99–100, 162.

34. J.E. King, '"We Could Eat the Police": Popular Violence in the North Lancashire Cotton Strike of 1878', *Victorian Studies*, vol. 28, 1985; Bob Dobson, *Policing in Lancashire, 1839–1989* (Staining, Blackpool, Lundy, 1989).

35. J.H. Morgan, *Conflict and Order: the Police and Labour Disputes in England and Wales, 1900–39* (Oxford University Press, 1987); B. Weinberger, *Keeping the Peace? Policing Strikes in Britain, 1906–1929* (Oxford, Berg, 1991).

36. Humphries, *Hooligans or Rebels?*, p. 206. Such attitudes were not restricted to the early twentieth century. During the 1950s policemen's children, easily identified because of the distinctively painted houses in which they lived, were often treated with grave suspicion and subject to verbal, if not outright physical, abuse. From a number of people I have interviewed on the subject, this appears to have been true of village as well as town life.

37. Cited in J. Davis, 'From "Rookeries" to "Communities": Race, Poverty and Policing in London, 1850–1985', *History Workshop Journal*, no. 14, 1987, p. 69. This section draws heavily on Davis's analysis.

38. *Middlesbrough Weekly News*, 8 October 1864. For a fuller discussion of the development of policing in this north-eastern town see D. Taylor, *'A Well-chosen Effective Body of Men': the Middlesbrough Police Force, 1841–1914*, Teesside Papers in North-Eastern History No. 6, Middlesbrough, University of Teesside, 1995.

39. *Middlesbrough Weekly News*, 6 January 1865.

40. Ibid., 8 December 1875.

41. Woods, 'Community Violence', p. 182.

42. B.D. Butcher, *'A Movable Rambling Force': An Official History of Policing in Norfolk* (Norwich, Norfolk Constabulary, 1989), p. 62.

43. K. Mourby, *The Social Effects of Unemployment on Teesside, 1919–1939* (Manchester University Press, 1985), chapter 4.

44. A. Davies, 'The Police and the People: Gambling in Salford 1900–39', *Historical Journal*, vol. 34, 1991.

45. Colin McInnes, *Mr Love and Justice*, p. 21 cited in S. Box, *Deviance, Reality and Society* (London, Holt, Rinehart & Winston, 1981), p. 175.

CHAPTER 7

1. A. Howkins, 'The Discovery of Rural England', in R. Colls and P. Dodd (eds), *Englishness, Politics and Culture 1880–1920* (Beckenham, Croom Helm, 1986).

2. G. Boyes, *The Imagined Village. Culture, Ideology and the English Folk Revival* (Manchester University Press, 1993), chapters 2, 4.

3. For discussion of topophilia in modern sport, see J. Bale, *Sport, Space and the City* (London, Routledge, 1993) and *Landscapes of Modern Sport* (London, Leicester University Press, 1994).

4. The statistics of match attendances are taken from B. Taberner, *Through the Turnstiles* (Hadfield, Yore, 1992). Though Taberner may be criticized for an over-reliance on newspaper estimates of crowds before 1914, no other work has so readily accessible data about the match attendances for all Football League clubs.

5. D.H. Woods and A. Crabtree, *Bristol City. A Complete Record 1894–1987* (Derby, Breedon, 1987), pp. 22, 238.

6. *Yorkshire County Cricket Club Twelfth Annual Issue, Twentieth Annual Issue*; the figures for Essex are calculated from Essex CCC *Annual Reports* 1904, 1914.

7. P.A. Greenhalgh, 'The History of the Northern Rugby Football Union, 1895–1915', Lancaster University, unpublished PhD thesis, 1992, p. 279.

8. *Warrington Guardian*, 29 March 1905.

9. A.J. Arnold, *A Game That Would Pay. A Business History of Professional Football in Bradford* (London, Duckworth, 1988), p. 59.

10. R. Fletcher and D. Howes, *Rothman's Rugby League Yearbook 1983–84* (London, Queen Anne, 1983), pp. 408–9.
11. L. Allison, 'Association Football and the Urban Ethos', *Stanford Journal of International Studies*, vol. 13 (1978); R.J. Holt, 'Football and the Urban Way of Life in Nineteenth-century Britain', in J.A. Mangan, *Pleasure, Profit, Proselytism. British Culture and Sport at Home and Abroad 1700–1914* (London, Cass, 1988).
12. J. Walvin, *Victorian Values* (London, Cardinal, 1988), pp. 108–9.
13. J.K. Walton and R. Poole, 'The Lancashire Wakes in the Nineteenth Century', in R.D. Storch (ed.), *Popular Culture and Custom in Nineteenth-century England*, (London, Croom Helm, 1982), p. 100.
14. For details of the shareholdings of football clubs, see W. Vamplew, *Pay Up and Play the Game. Professional Sport in Britain 1875–1914* (Cambridge University Press, 1988), pp. 295–9; for Northern Union clubs, see Greenhalgh, thesis, p. 190.
15. Arnold, *A Game that Would Pay*, p. 59.
16. *Nelson Leader*, 25 September 1903.
17. *Northern Daily Telegraph*, 13 May 1897.
18. *Nelson Leader*, 29 May 1903.
19. *Blackburn Times*, 7 April 1883.
20. *Warrington Guardian*, 3 May 1905.
21. *Northern Daily Telegraph*, 27 April 1914.
22. *Blackburn Times*, 18 March 1882; J. Hill, 'Rite of Spring: Cup Finals and Community in the North of England', in J. Hill and J. Williams (eds), *Sport and Identity in the North of England* (Keele University Press, 1996), discusses the role of cup final celebrations in northern popular culture.
23. *Blackburn Times*, 7 April 1883.
24. *Northern Daily Telegraph*, 1 April 1890.
25. *Nelson Leader*, 25 September 1903.
26. *Warrington Guardian*, 13 May 1905.
27. J. Hill, 'League Cricket in the North and Midlands, 1900–1940', in R. Holt (ed.), *Sport and the Working Class in Modern Britain* (Manchester University Press, 1990), p. 131.
28. Names and addresses of the representatives of the First Division clubs are given in *Bolton and District Cricket Association Handbook 1914*.
29. *Warrington Guardian*, 3 May 1905.
30. Holt, 'Football and the Urban Way of Life', pp. 77, 81.
31. R. Roberts, *The Classic Slum. Salford Life in the First Quarter of the Century* (Manchester University Press, 1971), p. 3.
32. For contemporary reports of how the Barnsley tactics were perceived, see T. Mason, 'Football, Sport of the North?' in J. Hill and J. Williams (eds), *Sport and Identity in the North of England* (Keele University Press, 1996).
33. See Taberner, *Through the Turnstiles*, for seasonal attendances; P. Soar and M. Tyler (eds), *Encyclopedia of British Football* (London, Willow, 1983) provides seasonal league placings.
34. *Northern Daily Telegraph*, 11 May 1897.
35. *Darwen News*, 22 April 1899.
36. Ibid., 23 March 1912. For a history of Darwen FC see R.W. Lewis, 'The Development of Professional Football in Lancashire, 1870–1914', Lancaster University unpublished PhD thesis, (1993), chapter 5.
37. J. Vernon, *Politics and the People. A Study in English Political Culture, c. 1815–1867* (Cambridge University Press, 1993), p. 49.

38. Ibid., p. 54.
39. *Northern Daily Telegraph*, 21 June 1897.
40. *Bury Times*, 22 April 1903.
41. *Warrington Guardian*, 13 May 1905.
42. *Blackburn Standard*, 7 April 1883.
43. *Blackburn Times*, 24 March 1883.
44. Holt, 'Football and the Urban Way of Life', p. 80.
45. *Farnworth Weekly Journal* concentrated on the activities of the two cricket clubs from Farnworth. In the winter Bolton Wanderers dominated its football reporting. A. Metcalfe, 'Sport and Community: a Case Study of the Mining Villages of East Northumberland, 1800–1914', in Hill and Williams, *Sport and Identity*, p. 35.
46. *Blackburn Times*, 1 April 1882.
47. *Northern Daily Telegraph*, 31 March 1890.
48. R. Taylor, *Football and its Fans. Supporters and their Relations with the Game, 1885–1985* (Leicester University Press, 1992), p. 7; T. Mason, *Association Football and English Society 1863–1915*, (Brighton, Harvester, 1980), pp. 152–3.
49. Scrapbook of press cuttings relating to Blackburn Rovers, Blackburn Public Library.
50. Greenhalgh, thesis, p. 293.
51. *Warrington Guardian*, 3 May 1905.
52. Ibid.
53. *Northern Daily Telegraph*, 25 April 1912.
54. Taylor, *Football and its Fans*, p. 7.
55. S. Inglis, *The Football Grounds of Great Britain* (London, Willow, 1987), pp. 73, 209, 213.
56. Hill, 'League Cricket', p. 131.
57. Inglis, *Football Grounds*, p. 12; P. Cullen, *Bury FC 1885–1985* (Manchester, Mike Andrews, 1895), pp. 25, 28.
58. Blackburn Rovers scrapbooks.
59. *Blackburn Rovers Grand Bazaar Brochure*.
60. P.J. Waller, *Town, City and Nation. England 1850–1914* (Oxford University Press, 1983), p. 78.

CHAPTER 8

1. For the origins of the Cleveland workforce see B.J.D. Harrison, 'Origins of East Cleveland and Rosedale Ironstone Miners from the 1871 Census', *Cleveland and Teesside Local History Society Bulletin*, 19 (1972–3). Also T. Nicholson, 'The Growth of Trade Unionism amongst the Cleveland Ironstone Miners, 1850–76' (unpublished MA dissertation, Teesside Polytechnic, 1982).
2. The following account of Mary Ward's murder is taken from various newspaper accounts of the local court hearings. See for example *North-Eastern Daily Gazette*, 7 January 1874.
3. Census Enumerators' Books, Eston district 1851. HO/107 – 2375.
4. A copy of the ballad has been given to the author and will be deposited in Cleveland County Archives.
5. There are a range of newspapers which provide a valuable insight into social conditions in the new mining communities. See, for example, *Middlesbrough News and Cleveland Advertiser*; the *Miners' Advocate and Record*;

Middlesbrough Weekly Exchange; the *North-Eastern Daily Gazette*; *The Guisborough Weekly Exchange*; *Northern Echo*.

6. *North-Eastern Daily Gazette*, 3 September 1873 and 8 September 1875, contains some interesting police reports of shebeens given to Guisborough Brewster Sessions. See also *Guisborough Weekly Exchange*, 8 July 1875, for a general complaint of their prevalence and *Guisborough Exchange*, 11 March 1876 for details of a police raid.

7. See, for example, *Middlesbrough Weekly News*, 27 July 1861; *Middlesbrough Weekly Exchange*, 18 July 1872.

8. *Guisborough Weekly Exchange*, 6 May 1875, gives one example. See the same paper for 12 June 1873 for an editorial discussion on the troubled relationship between police and public in the mining district.

9. A number of elopement cases involving lodgers and miners' wives were reported in the local press. Examples in *Middlesbrough Weekly News*, 18 August 1865; *Middlesbrough Weekly Exchange*, 20 August 1869.

10. *North-Eastern Daily Gazette*, 16 March 1875, contains editorial comment on wife beating. There is one (as far as I can tell) unique case of a local miner being beaten by his wife in the same paper for 24 March 1875.

11. Assaults featured regularly in the petty sessional courts of the area, but more formal 'prize fights' attended by large crowds of miners could also be staged; for example, *Middlesbrough Exchange*, 8 April 1870.

12. Pitch-and-toss cases are featured in *Middlesbrough Weekly News*, 19 February 1876 & 13 May 1876. Reference is also made to betting rings in a more general article, 'Habits of Pitmen', which appeared in *Middlesbrough Weekly News*, 15 March 1867. This piece was cut and pasted from other north-eastern papers, but a more accurate analysis of the Cleveland district was provided in 'Among the Cleveland Miners' in *Guisborough Weekly Exchange*, 12 June 1873.

13. See *Guisborough Weekly News*, 25 March 1875; *Middlesbrough Weekly News*, 13 March 1868, which commented on the landlord using a rabbit-coursing meeting to draw 'many roughs and low characters together'.

14. The term, 'dog-men' was used by the radical, working-class editors of the *Miners' Advocate and Record* to describe the roughest and most feckless sections of local mining society. See the *Advocate*, 31 May 1873.

15. The tensions between landowners and mineowners are illustrated nicely in the evidence given by representatives from both groups in *Minutes of Evidence taken before the Select Committee of the House of Lords on the Cleveland Railway Bill*, 2 August 1859.

16. The three model settlements were at Hutton Lowcross, New Marske and Skinningrove. Full-time temperance missionaries were employed by the Peases in each of these communities. The *Middlesbrough Weekly Exchange*, 4 July 1872, includes an account of a testimonial to one such missionary, J.M. Browne.

17. The 'Skelton and Brotton UDC Minutes' DC/SB, Cleveland County Archives, illustrate the important role of J.T. Wharton, the local 'squire' of Skelton Castle, in the creation and development of this particular local authority. J.T. Ward's 'West Riding Landowners and Mining in the Nineteenth Century', *Yorkshire Bulletin of Economic and Social Research*, XV (1963), provides similar evidence from another mining district. At a broader level F.M.L. Thompson's *Landed Society in the Nineteenth Century* (1963) still offers an excellent overview.

18. *Middlesbrough Weekly News*, 26 July 1867.

19. Records of the 'Hope to Prosper' Lodge, North Skelton. Copies to be deposited in Cleveland County Archives.

20. Raymond Williams's *The Long Revolution* (1961) is a founding text which establishes this basic point through what he calls 'the structure of feeling'; see particularly chapter 2, 'The Analysis of Culture', pp. 57–88. See also J. Clarke, C. Critcher and R. Johnson (eds), *Working-class Culture: Studies in History and Theory* (1979) for the application of this analysis to the experience of the workplace.

21. Keith McClelland's article, 'Masculinity and the "Representative Artisan" in Britain, 1850–80', *Gender and History*, vol. 1, no. 2 (1989), pp. 164–77 offers a pioneering study of masculine identity. It is reprinted in M. Roper and J. Tosh (eds), *Manful Assertions: Masculinities in Britain since 1800* (1991). S. Rose, 'Respectable Men, Disorderly Others: The Language of Gender and the Lancashire Weavers' Strike of 1878 in Britain', *Gender and History*, vol. 5, no. 3 (1993), pp. 382–97, develops some of the themes introduced by McClelland.

22. See Harrison 'Origins' and J. Lambelle, 'The Origins of the Cleveland Ironstone Miners from the 1861 Census', *Cleveland and Teesside Local History Society Bulletin*, no. 7. See also Nicholson, 'Growth of Trade Unionism'.

23. A.V. John, *By the Sweat of their Brow: Women Workers at Victorian Coal Mines* (1984), is probably the best general study of Victorian attitudes to women mine workers.

24. R. Moore, *Pitmen, Preachers and Politics: The Effects of Methodism in a Durham Mining Community* (1974), p. 66, records that Pease and Partners employed a recruiting agent in Lincolnshire. See also A.H. Hill, *Our Unemployed: An Attempt to Point out Some of the Best Means of Providing Occupation for Distressed Labourers* (c. 1869), and *Impediments to the Circulation of Labour* (1873), which provide an insight into the recruitment links between Cleveland mineowners and Hill, a London lawyer who sought better employment opportunities for dockyard workers. These links resulted in a major movement of East End dockers and their families into Cleveland during the early 1870s. See *Northern Echo*, 27 May 1870, for a miner's complaint that 'the pleasant village of Marske-by-the-Sea has, this week or two, been thrown into great excitement by being swarmed out by large batches of the unemployed dockyard labourers from the south. . .'. Recruiting agents were also employed in Cornwall; see *Middlesbrough Weekly News*, 13 September 1867.

25. The Cleveland Mineowners Association Minute Books, 25 March 1875: 'When a new mine was opened the manager thereof, to obtain miners, was almost obliged to offer prices which would yield higher wages than the average of the district. . . .'

26. *Report of Special Assistant Poor Law Commissioners on the Employment of Women and Children in Agriculture*, 1843. Evidence from the Guisborough Union.

27. *Report of Special Assistant Poor Law Commissioners on the Employment of Women and Children in Agriculture*, 1843. Evidence from Fylingdales.

28. See *Middlesbrough Weekly News*, 7 September 1866.

29. *Middlesbrough Weekly News*, 7 September 1866.

30. For a fuller discussion of the place of the 'hag system' in the Cleveland mines see Nicholson, 'Growth of Trade Unionism', chapter 2.

31. Most boys began work in the mines as either 'trappy-boys', employed to open and close ventilation doors as tubs went through, or as 'spraggers', employed to insert 'sprags' (primitive braking devices) into the wheels of tubs. A graphic account of these processes can be gained from the Tom Leonard Mining Museum, Skinningrove, Cleveland.

32. *Report on the Inspection of Cleveland Mines* (1873) – see section on the

Huntcliffe Mine for a complaint of shortages of wagons or tubs. See also *Middlesbrough Exchange*, 1 August 1872, for an official union view of these shortages.

33. Interview with Jim Easton, miner and overman of Lofthouse Mine, *c*. 1920–58. Recorded in 1988.

34. *Guisborough Weekly Exchange*, 25 April 1873.

35. Ibid., 18 April 1873.

36. Evidence of union concern over the behaviour of driver lads can be found in *Middlesbrough Exchange*, 1 August 1872: 'At some of the mines the boys employed as drivers had caused considerable trouble and did not work so agreeably as they might do. . . .' *Guisborough Weekly Exchange*, 20 June 1873, provides an account of an assault committed by a gang of driver lads on a mine horsekeeper. A strike of driver lads is recorded in *North-Eastern Daily Gazette*, 7 April 1875.

37. Many of the immigrants into Cleveland started to move out during a strike in 1874. See *Guisborough Weekly Exchange*, 14 May 1874. Emigration remained a prominent feature throughout the remainder of the 1870s. See *Middlesbrough Weekly News*, 6 April 1878, for a report of the 'hundreds of empty cottages' in the mining district.

38. *North-Eastern Daily Gazette*, 4 July 1893.

39. Ibid., 19 August 1872, in which Joe Shepherd complained of the ill-treatment of an experienced miner 'who had worked in a mine for eighteen years and was at length put into a hole fifty yards away from any ventilation. . .'.

40. The records of the 'Hope to Prosper' Lodge, North Skelton, contain numerous cases of negotiations between miners and managers on these 'consideration' issues.

41. See D. Douglas, 'The Durham Pitman', pp. 219–20 in R. Samuel (ed.), *Miners, Quarrymen and Saltworkers* (1977), for an excellent description of a similar set of independent values among the Durham colliers.

42. *North-Eastern Daily Gazette*, 27 May 1872.

43. Ibid., 19 August 1872.

44. Ibid., 15 June 1872.

45. Ibid.

46. *Guisborough Weekly Exchange*, 8 October 1874.

47. The level of linkage was relatively high. Of the 211 names listed in the Lodge Membership Book, 151 were linked to names in the 1881 Census Enumerator's Records for North Skelton. The analysis then worked on the assumption that all other miners and mine workers listed in census records for North Skelton were therefore non-unionists. It is possible that some of these men were members of other lodges, but such cases are not likely to have been many. The records of this lodge were salvaged by a local industrial archeologist some years ago and have remained in his private possession. The author was given access to these valuable records which have now been copied. The copies will be deposited in Cleveland County Archives.

48. *North-Eastern Daily Gazette*, 12 January 1874.

49. Ibid., 7 January 1874.

CHAPTER 9

An earlier version of this chapter was originally given as a lecture to students in the School of Cultural and Community Studies, University of Sussex, January 1989.

Place of publication is London unless specified otherwise.

1. Benedict Anderson, *Imagined Communities: Reflections on the Origin and Spread of Nationalism* (revised edn, 1991), p. 7; David Gilbert, 'Imagined Communities and Mining Communities', in *Labour History Review*, vol. 60, no. 2, 1995, pp. 47–55.

2. Joanna Bourke, *Working-class Cultures in Britain 1890–1960* (1994), pp. 136–51. The target of much of this criticism is Richard Hoggart's influential text, *The Uses of Literacy* (1957). See also Carolyn Steedman, *Landscape for a Good Woman: A Story of Two Lives* (1986), on this theme and Williams's incisive review of the latter reprinted in Neil Belton, Francis Mulhern and Jenny Taylor (eds), *What I Came To Say. Raymond Williams* (1989), pp. 30–5.

3. For able defences of 'community' from the left see Eileen and Stephen Yeo, 'On the Uses of "Community": From Owenism to the Present', in Stephen Yeo (ed.), *New Views of Co-operation* (1988); Robert Colls, 'Save our Pits and Communities!', *Labour History Review*, vol. 60, no. 2, 1995, pp. 55–66.

4. See Lawrence's 'Autobiographical Sketch' in Warren Roberts and Harry T. Moore (eds), *Phoenix II. Uncollected, Unpublished, and Other Prose Work by D.H. Lawrence* (1968; Penguin, 1978), pp. 592–4. On the historical invention of the 'author' see Roger Chartier, *The Order of Books* (1994), pp. 29–32.

5. David Vincent, *Bread, Knowledge and Freedom. A Study of Nineteenth-century Working Class Autobiography* (1981); David Vincent, *Literacy and Popular Culture. England 1750–1914* (Cambridge, 1989); Julia Swindells, *Victorian Writing and Working Women* (Cambridge, 1985).

6. Raymond Williams, *Marxism and Literature* (Oxford, 1978) p. 115.

7. Graham Holderness, *D.H. Lawrence: History, Ideology and Fiction* (Dublin, 1982), p. 25.

8. *Sons and Lovers* (1913; Penguin, 1977), p. 45.

9. Ibid., pp. 42–3.

10. Raymond Williams, *The English Novel from Dickens to Lawrence* (1971), p. 173.

11. As is well known, the antinomy between beauty and ugliness is central in Lawrence's work as a whole; the natural environment as well as the bodies and minds of the workers bore the scars of 'industrialism' and some of Lawrence's best writing attacks this related despoliation. The early chapter 'In the Train' in *Women in Love*, which describes the grey, oppressive London sprawl, is an excellent example. In 'Nottingham and the Mining Countryside' (1929) he wrote that: 'The real tragedy of England, as I see it, is the tragedy of ugliness. The country is so lovely: the man-made England is so vile.' See Edward D. McDonald (ed.), *Phoenix. The Posthumous Papers of D.H. Lawrence* (1936; Penguin, 1978), p. 137.

12. *Sons and Lovers*, pp. 61, 89, 111, 247.

13. Strict divisions between male and female worlds have been regarded as one of the defining features of mining communities. See Martin Bulmer, 'Sociological Models of the Mining Community', *Sociological Review*, vol. 23, 1975.

14. Note how this representation contrasts with the 'theoretical' and ahistorical description of gender relations within 'community' which informs Ferdinand Tönnies's seminal sociological work, *Gemeinschaft und Gesellschaft* (1887). In this text the opposition is reversed; women are bearers of 'natural will', while men alone are fully capable of 'rational will': 'women are usually led by the feelings, men more by intellect. Men are more clever. They alone are capable of

calculation, of calm (abstract) thinking, of consideration, combination and logic. As a rule women follow these pursuits ineffectively. They lack the necessary requirement of rational will' (1974 edn, p. 174). On this theme see also Hilary Simpson, *D.H. Lawrence and Feminism* (1982).

15. *Sons and Lovers*, pp. 313–14. For a later development of this argument see Lawrence's *Studies in Classic American Literature* (1923; Penguin, 1978), pp. 91–2.

16. On the links between Carlyle and Lawrence see Raymond Williams, *Culture and Society* (1958), pp. 199–200.

17. Harry T. Moore (ed.), *D.H. Lawrence's Letters to Bertrand Russell* (1948), p. 54. See also Lawrence's essay on 'Matriarchy' (1928): 'And give the men a new foregathering ground, where they can meet and satisfy their deep social needs, profound social cravings which can only be satisfied apart from women.' *Phoenix II*, p. 552. For a perceptive discussion of Lawrence's changing ideology see Holderness, pp. 190–219.

18. See the essay on 'Democracy' in *Phoenix*, p. 702; Roger Taylor, 'D.H. Lawrence and Fascism' (MA thesis, University of Sussex, 1968).

19. Francis Mulhern, *The Moment of Scrutiny* (1979).

20. In 'A Propos of "Lady Chatterley's Lover"', *Phoenix II*, p. 513.

21. Raymond Williams, *Politics and Letters. Interviews with New Left Review* (1979), p. 119. As Williams's interviewers remind him, after the First World War German fascists used the term *Volksgemeinschaft* as a key word in Third Reich propaganda.

22. For the Guild see Margaret Llewelyn Davies, *The Women's Co-operative Guild, 1883–1904* (Kirkby Lonsdale, 1904); Llewelyn Davies (ed.), *Life as We Have Known it* (1931); Catherine Webb, *The Woman With the Basket* (1927); Gill Scott, '"The Working Class Women's Most Active and Democratic Movement": the Women's Co-operative Guild, 1883–1950' (unpublished D.Phil thesis, University of Sussex, 1988).

23. Moore, *Lawrence's Letters*, p. 49, letter dated 8 June 1915.

24. Ibid., pp. 52–3.

25. Ibid., p. 17.

26. David Gilbert, *Class, Community, and Collective Action. Social Change in Two British Coalfields, 1850–1926* (Oxford, 1992), pp. 151–2.

27. Ibid., p. 173. For the different paths of development taken in other coalfields see Hywel Francis and David Smith, *The Fed. A History of the South Wales Miners in the Twentieth Century* (1980); Robert Colls, *The Pitmen of the Northern Coalfield. Work, Culture and Protest, 1790–1850* (Manchester, 1987).

28. Gilbert, *Class, Community, and Collective Action*, pp. 198–205.

29. 'Return to Bestwood', *Phoenix II*, pp. 262–3.

30. Ibid., p. 259.

31. Ibid., p. 260. Arthur Cook conducted an extensive campaign in the area from late August 1958 and soon praised the progressive attitude of local women: 'I cannot pay them too high a tribute. They are canvassing from door-to-door in some of the villages where some of the men had signed on. The police take the blacklegs to the pits, but the women bring them home. The women shame these men out of scabbing. . . . The women of Notts. and Derby have broken the coalowners'. *The Miner*, 28 August 1926, quoted by Gilbert, *Class, Community, and Collective Action*, p. 193. Gilbert observes that 'the Eastwood district was "completely quiet" during the General Strike.' Ibid., pp. 189–90.

32. Raymond Williams, *Culture and Society*, p. 212.

33. In the first local elections in Eastwood after the strike Labour candidates won seats which had been held securely by Conservatives. Gilbert, *Class, Community, and Collective Action*, p. 201. Note, however, Gilbert's observation that 'Eastwood was chronically divided at the end of the strike.' For another example of the struggle over 'community' see David Smith, 'Tonypandy 1910: Definitions of Community', *Past and Present*, 87, 1980, pp. 158–84.

34. Juliet Mitchell's influential *Psychoanalysis and Feminism* (1974) emphasizes Freud's insistence on 'culture' as an historical variable.

35. Moore, *Lawrence's Letters*, p. 31.

36. Ibid., p. 32.

37. 'The Real Thing', *Phoenix*, p. 196.

38. Ibid., pp. 196–7.

39. Moore, *Lawrence's Letters*, p. 59.

40. Ibid., p. 63.

41. Ibid., p. 64.

42. 'A Propos', *Phoenix II*, pp. 506–8.

43. *Sons and Lovers*, pp. 441–2.

44. For these opportunities and the contrast with South Wales where paid employment for women was much more scarce see Gilbert, 'Imagined Communities', pp. 52–3.

45. This phase in the history of the women's movement has been partially reconstructed by Jill Liddington and Jill Norris in *One Hand Tied Behind Us* (1978). See also Liddington, *The Life and Times of a Respectable Rebel. Selina Cooper 1864–1946* (1984).

46. Kate Millett, *Sexual Politics* (1969), p. 257. Note that even Miriam is allowed to articulate an implicitly feminist sensibility. See *Sons and Lovers*, pp. 191–2.

47. Klaus Theweleit, *Male Fantasies* Vol. I (Cambridge, 1987), pp. 283–4.

48. *Phoenix*, pp. 491–2.

49. *Phoenix II*, p. 550.

50. Theweleit, *Male Fantasies*, p. 249.

51. *Phoenix II*, p. 594. For a discussion of Lawrence and 'social mobility' see Holderness, *D.H. Lawrence*, pp. 146–7.

52. Moore, *Lawrence's Letters*, p. 43.

53. Ibid., p. 25.

54. Quoted by F.R. Leavis in 'Mr Eliot, Mr Wyndham Lewis and Lawrence' (1934), reprinted in *The Common Pursuit* (1952; Peregrine, 1962), p. 243.

55. Quoted by Leavis in 'The Wild, Untutored Phoenix' (1937), reprinted in ibid., p. 238.

56. Ibid., p. 236.

57. Quoted by Leavis in, 'Keynes, Lawrence and Cambridge', reprinted in ibid., p. 256.

58. Leonard Woolf's phrase; see Williams's analysis, 'The Bloomsbury Fraction' in *Problems in Materialism and Culture* (1980).

59. *Phoenix II*, p. 595.

60. For a classic study of this process from within the sociology of education see Colin Lacey, *Hightown Grammar* (1971).

61. Williams, *Culture and Society*, p. 199.

62. See his remarks in *The Country and the City* (1973), p. 271; *Politics and Letters*, pp. 125–7.

63. Raymond Williams, 'My Cambridge' (1977), reprinted in *What I Came to Say*, p. 5. The porter had made this remark to Williams's father during an advance

visit to Trinity College. Williams caustically remarks that: 'I remember sitting on the benches in hall, surrounded by these people, and wishing they *had* been put down at birth.'

64. Ibid., pp. 5–6. See too the first, largely disappointing, biography: Fred Inglis, *Raymond Williams* (1995).

65. This is a huge theme but see Terry Eagleton, *Criticism and Ideology* (1978); Eagleton (ed.), *Raymond Williams: Critical Perspectives* (Cambridge, 1987); Alan O'Connor, *Raymond Williams: Writing Culture Politics* (Oxford, 1989); Tony Pinkney, *Raymond Williams* (Cardiff, 1991).

66. Raymond Williams, 'The Importance of Community' (1977) reprinted in *Resources of Hope. Culture, Democracy, Socialism* (1989), p. 114.

67. Ibid.

68. Raymond Williams, 'Mining the Meaning: Key Words in the Miners' Strike' (1985) in *Resources of Hope*, p. 124.

69. The stress on the importance on working-class association can be found in the early work. See Williams's comments in *Culture and Society*, p. 327.

70. Williams, *What I Came to Say*, p. 12.

71. Ibid., p. 13. For his estrangement from Cambridge English see the essays in part four of his *Writing in Society* (1984).

72. For a useful insight into the origins and development of this work and Williams's fiction generally see *Politics and Letters*, pp. 271–302; John and Lizzie Eldridge, *Raymond Williams. Making Connections* (1994).

73. Raymond Williams, *Border Country* (1960; Readers Union, 1962), p. 9.

74. Ibid., p. 351. For subaltern intellectuals and the experience of exile see Edward Said, *Representations of the Intellectual. The 1993 Reith Lectures* (1994), p. 39.

75. On this point see Julia Swindells and Lisa Jardine, *What's Left? Women in Culture and the Labour Movement* (1990), p. 152.

76. Raymond Williams, 'The Importance of Community', reprinted in *Resources of Hope*, p. 117.

77. See Pierre Bourdieu, 'Doxa and Common Life', *New Left Review*, vol. 191, 1992, pp. 113–14, 118. In many respects Bourdieu has spent most of his academic life measuring the distance. See his remarks in ibid., p. 117: 'I try to put together the two parts of my life, as many first-generation intellectuals do. Some use different means – for instance, they find a solution in political action, in some kind of social rationalization. My main problem is to try and understand what happened to me. My trajectory may be described as miraculous, I suppose – an ascension to a place where I don't belong. And so to be able to live in a world that is not mine I must try to understand both things: what it means to have an academic mind – how such is created – and at the same time what was lost in acquiring it. For that reason, even if my work – my full work – is a sort of autobiography, it is a work for people who have the same sort of trajectory, and the same need to understand.'

78. Raymond Williams, 'The Practice of Possibility' (1987), reprinted in *Resources of Hope*, p. 322; and Williams, 'Towards Many Socialisms' (1986), reprinted in ibid., p. 297.

CHAPTER 10

1. J. Butler, *Personal Reminiscence of a Great Crusade* (London, Horace Marshall and Son, 1911), 2nd edn, published after her death in 1906.

2. E. Moberly Bell, *Josephine Butler, Flame of Fire* (London, Constable, 1962);

G. Petrie, *A Singular Iniquity, the Campaigns of Josephine Butler* (London, Macmillan, 1971); P. McHugh, *Prostitution and Victorian Social Reform* (London, Croom Helm, 1980); J. Walkowitz, *Prostitution and Victorian Society* (Cambridge University Press, 1980); L. Bland, *Banishing the Beast, English Feminism and Sexual Morality, 1885–1914* (Harmondsworth, Penguin, 1995), pp. 96–101.

3.   J.G. Gamble, 'The Origins, Administration and Impact of the CDA, from a Military Perspective', unpublished Ph.D thesis, University of Southern Mississippi, 1983.

4.   Existing in 1876: National Association, Midland's Counties Electoral Union, Northern Counties League, Friends' Association, Wesleyan Methodist Association, Congregational Committee, National Medical Association, North Eastern Association, Scottish National Association, British and Continental Federation for the Abolition of State Regulated Prostitution, Working Men's League, City of London Committee.

5.   E. Cady Stanton, *Eighty Years and More (1815–1897), Reminiscences of E. Cady Stanton* (New York, European Publishing Company, 1898), p. 368. 'Her style is not unlike that one hears in Methodist camp meetings.'

6.   McHugh, *Prostitution*, p. 115.

7.   *Letter from Edmond Beales Esq.* (LNA, 1872), p. 1.

8.   *Working Men's League Journal*, 4 July 1877, p. 4.

9.   *National League Journal*, 2 September 1877, p. 6.

10.   Ibid., 1 December 1877, p. 12.

11.   Ibid., 1 October 1877, pp. 13–14.

12.   Thomas Burt (1837–1922) had been the secretary of the Northumberland Miners' Association since 1865, and MP for Morpeth from 1874 until 1918.

13.   *National League Journal*, 1 July 1884, p. 5.

14.   R.M. Martin, *TUC: The Growth of a Pressure Group. 1868–1976* (Oxford, Clarendon Press, 1980), p. 56. Henry Broadhurst, 1840–1911, leader of the TUC 1875–90, MP 1874–98, was a partisan of the late period of the repeal agitation and social purity. In his autobiography any connections with the cause of social purity are not referred to, another example of the growing unpopularity of the cause in the late nineteenth century. Henry Broadhurst, *The Story of his Life: from a Stonemason's Bench to the Treasury Bench* (London, Hutchinson & Co., 1901).

15.   Benjamin Lucraft's editorial, *National League Journal*, January 1884, p. 1.

16.   *Working Men's League Journal*, August 1877.

17.   P. Pickering, 'Class Without Words: Symbolic Communication in the Chartist Movement', *Past and Present*, no. 112 (1986), pp. 144–62; J. Epstein and D. Thompson (eds), *The Chartist Experience: Studies in Working-class Radicalism and Culture, 1830–1860* (London, Macmillan, 1982).

18.   McHugh, *Prostitution*, p. 113.

19.   H. Bell and J. Wilson, *Copy of a Rough Record of Events and Incidents Connected with the Repeal of the Contagious Diseases Acts in the United Kingdom* (London, Association for Social Hygiene, 1906).

20.   Petrie, *A Singular Iniquity*, p. 241.

21.   The term 'White Slave' was coined by a Swiss preacher, the Pastor Borel, *The White Slavery of Europe*, tr. from the French (Halifax, London, Sheffield, J. Edmonson, Dyer Brothers and Banks, H.J. Wilson, 1876).

22.   E. Hopkins, *The Present Moral Crisis, an Appeal to Women* (Dyer Brothers, 1886), p. 10. Hopkins estimated that masturbation, the first manifestation of an

uncontrolled lust, concerned 90 to 95 per cent of the boys educated in boarding schools.

23. Walkowitz, *Prostitution*, p. 243.
24. E. Jones, *National League Journal*, 1 March 1876, p. 1.
25. Leader, *Reynold's News*, 8 March 1868.
26. *National League Journal*, 1 February 1878, p. 3.
27. D. Cooper, *The Remedy Worse than the Disease* (Rescue Society, 1869), p. 39. 'But if the form of the disease is, as has been proved, more prevalent among the upper classes in France (with stringent laws there existing to prevent its spread) than in England, of what use is it to attempt its suppression by the same line of legislation?'
28. On the construction of the homosexual see Jeffrey Weeks, *Sex, Politics and Society, the Regulation of Sexuality since 1800* (London, Longman, 1981, repr. 1989), pp. 96–108; *Against Nature, Essays on History, Sexuality and Identity* (London, Rivers Oram, 1991).
29. A. Clark, *The Struggle for the Breeches, Gender and the Making of the British Working Class* (London, Rivers Oram, 1995), pp. 220–32; J. Schwarzkopf, *Women in the Chartist Movement* (London, Macmillan, 1991).
30. On melodrama see P. Brooks, *The Melodramatic Imagination* (New Haven, Yale University Press, 1976), C. Crosby, *The Ends of History, Victorians and the 'Woman Question'* (London, Routledge, 1991), pp. 69–79, 91.
31. There is a shortage of studies of working-class attitudes to the business of sexuality in the nineteenth century. See M. Mason, *The Making of Victorian Sexuality* (Oxford University Press, 1994), pp. 37–103.
32. G. Ball, 'Practical Religion; a Study of the Salvation Army Social Services for Women 1884–1914', unpublished Ph.D thesis, Leicester, 1987.
33. Mrs Hume Rothery, *A Letter Addressed to the R.H.W. Gladstone, MP Touching the C.D.A. of 1866–1869* (Manchester, Abel Heywood, Simpkin and Marshall, 1870), p. 15.
34. J.R. Walkowitz, 'Male Vice and Feminist Virtue, Feminism and the Politics of Prostitution in 19th Century Britain', *History Workshop Journal*, vol. 13 (1982), 85; *City of Dreadful Delights, Narratives of Sexual danger in late-Victorian London* (Virago, 1992).
35. *Beware of State Harlotry* (National Association, 1874), p. 4.
36. Josephine Butler claimed that prostitutes going out of the Dover Lock Hospital were welcomed by a cheering crowd of friends and customers. Butler to the 1871 Parliamentary Commission. See Walkowitz, *Prostitution*, p. 68.
37. *National League Journal*, 1 November 1879, p. 13.
38. All published in a series of penny biographies by the Dyer brothers, Benjamin Lucraft's life included. See for instance: *A Hero from the Forge, a Biographical Sketch of Elihu Burritt* (London, Dyer Brothers, 1877).
39. A.Tyrell, *Joseph Sturge and the Moral Radical Party in early Victorian Britain* (London, Christopher Helm, 1987).
40. See H. Mayhew, *London Labour and the London Poor* (London, 3 vols, 1851), vol. 1, p. 181.
41. J. Greenwood, *The Seven Curses of London* (London, Stanley Rivers and Co., 1869), p. 370.
42. T. Wright, *Some Habits and Customs of the Working Classes, by a Journeyman Engineer* (London, 1867, repr. Cass, 1970), p. 134.
43. W. Lovett, *Social and Political Morality* (London, Simpkin Marshall and Co., 1853), p. 43.

44. See Thomas Beggs: 'The children of our neglected homes spread the contagion of their vices abroad. The little arab of the streets becomes a tempter in his turn. The outcast girl, who is cast upon the pavé by the intemperance or neglect of her parents becomes the seducer of our youth.' T. Beggs, *Juvenile Delinquency and Reformatory Institutions* (London, Social Science, 1857), p. 8.

45. B. Harrison, *Drink and the Victorians; the Temperance Question in England 1815–1872* (London, Faber and Faber, 1971), p. 131.

46. B. Harrison, *Dictionary of British Temperance Biography* (London, Society for the Study of Labour History, 1973).

47. The old debate on middle-class hegemony is particularly inadequate for the question of temperance. See P. Hollis (ed.), *Pressure from Without in Early Victorian England* (London, Edward Arnold, 1977).

48. On the Sabbatarian campaigns see P. Bailey, *Leisure and Class in Victorian England, Rational Recreation and the Contest for Control* (London, Methuen, 1978, repr. 1987); Brian Harrison, *Peaceable Kingdom; Stability and Change in Modern Britain* (Oxford, Clarendon Press, 1982), pp. 123–40.

49. See some of the earlier debates on the opening days of the great exhibition and other instances of rational recreation. Revd J. Hall, *The Sons of Toil and the Crystal Palace; in Reply to Mr Mayhew* (London, John Snow, 1853).

50. G. Crossick (ed.), *The Lower Middle Class in Britain 1870–1914* (London, Croom Helm, 1977).

51. W. Burgen, *The Dangerous Tendencies of Medical Alarmists*, Concert Hall, Liverpool, 31 January 1876 (Woolord, Thomson, Porter, Jones, 1876).

52. R. Malcolmson, *Popular Recreation in English Society 1700–1850* (Cambridge University Press, 1973).

53. Harrison, *Drink and the Victorians*, p. 31.

54. F. Barret-Ducrocq, *L'amour sous Victoria, sexualité et classes populaires à Londres au XIX siècle* (Paris, Plon, 1989), p. 141.

55. Burgen, *The Dangerous Tendencies*, p. i.

56. Butler, *Personal Reminiscence*, p. 27.

57. The *Sentinel*, July 1885.

58. The *Lancet*, 1883, vol. I, p. 486.

59. *National League Journal*, 8 December 1877, p. 8.

60. Ibid., 1 June 1877, p. 4.

61. *Methodist Protest*, 16 February 1878; of those 6,000 pamphlets 4,000 had been sent to the clergymen of the diocese of Canterbury alone.

62. A.S. Dyer, *Facts for Men on Moral Purity and Health* (London, Dyer Brothers, 50,000 copies, 1884); *Plain Words to Young Men upon an Avoided Subject* (London, Dyer Brothers, repr. 1884, repr. 1885, 70,000 copies, repr. 1899, 145,000 copies). J.A. Jones, *The Anxious Enquirer*, 600,000 copies; J. Varley, *A Lecture to Men*, 800,000 copies, etc. E. Hopkins material also sold in large numbers.

63. Salvation Army Archives, J. Fairbanks, 'The Salvation Army and the Maiden Tribute', unpublished paper given at the Stead Memorial Society Conference, 5 July 1985.

64. J. Greenwood, *Odd People in Odd Places, or the Great Residuum* (London, Frederick Warne and Co., 1883), p. 205.

65. V. Bailey, 'The Dangerous Classes, Social Disturbances at the End of the Victorian Era', unpublished D.Phil, University of Oxford, 1978, p. 137.

66. P.T. Marsh, *The Victorian Church of England in Decline; Archbishop Tait and the Church of England, 1868–1882* (London, Routledge & Kegan Paul, 1969), p. 65.

67. The *War Cry*, 11 May 1882.
68. Ibid., 23 May 1883.
69. G. Ball, 'Practical Religion', p. 122.
70. *National League Journal*, 1 September 1880, p. 9.
71. Catherine Booth, *The Iniquity of State Regulated Vice* (London, Dyer Brothers, 1884).
72. Salvation Army Archives, Rebecca Jarrett, *Memories*, second version, pp. 30–5.
73. R.D. Altick, *The English Common Reader, a Social History of the Mass Reading Public, 1800–1900* (University of Chicago Press, 1957), p. 122.
74. R.C.K. Ensor, *The Oxford History of Britain 1870–1914* (Oxford University Press, 1936, repr. 1992), p. 381.
75. Altick, *Common Reader*, p. 299.
76. See the Ladies National Association's *A Warning Voice to the Religious People of England, Scotland and Ireland* (London, LNA, 1871); *Important Testimonies of Eminent Divines and of Religious Conferences or Synods in Support of the Entire Repeal of the Contagious Diseases Acts* (London, Dyer Brothers, 1874).
77. The *PMG* was founded in 1865 by G.M. Smith, owner of the *Cornhill Magazine*, and was successively edited by a series of remarkable editors. Frederick Greenwood was the first editor and gave the paper a firm jingoistic and Tory tone until 1879, at which time Morley took control of the newspaper and assumed the editorship. The paper changed attitudes and became a fervent but critical Liberal paper. J.W. Robertson Scott, *Manchester Guardian*, 2 July 1949.
78. R.L. Shults, *Crusader in Babylon; W.T. Stead and the Pall Mall Gazette* (Lincoln, University of Nebraska Press, 1972), pp. 16–30; V.P. Jones, *Saint or Sensationalist? The Story of W.T. Stead* (Chichester, Gooday, 1988).
79. Stead left the *PMG* in 1889 and founded the *Review of Reviews* which he edited until his death on board the *Titanic* in 1912.
80. The Tory press empire was composed of *The Times*, the *Morning Post*, the *Standard*, the *Daily Telegraph*, the *Globe*, the *Evening Standard* and *St James's Gazette*. H.R.F. Bourne, *The English Newspapers, Chapters in the History of English Journalism* (2 vols, London, Chatto and Windus, 1887).
81. Cross-heads repeat some elements of the text as a kind of headline within the text. Headlines across several columns were also used by Stead.
82. Bourne, *The English Newspapers*, vol. 2, p. 392.
83. Mearns, *The Bitter Cry of Outcast London*, 1883, pp. 12–16.
84. G. Stedman Jones, *Outcast London, a Study in the Relationship between Classes in Victorian Society* (Oxford, Clarendon Press, 1971), pp. 231–41.
85. R.R. Sims, *How the Poor Live and Horrible London* (London, Chatto and Windus, 1888).
86. A.S. Dyer, *The European Slave Trade in English Girls* (London, Dyer Brothers, 1st edn 1880, 9th edn 1885).
87. B. Scott, *Is London More Immoral than Paris or Brussels?* (London, Dyer Brothers, 1883).
88. Shults, *Crusader in Babylon*, p. 130; W.T. Stead, *Speech at the Central Criminal Court* (London, Vickens, Moral Reform Union, 1885); *Why I went to Prison! Reprinted from the Review of Reviews* (London, *Review of Reviews*, 1911).
89. *Pall Mall Gazette*, 9 July 1885.
90. Shults, *Crusader in Babylon*, p. 143.
91. A similar enquiry happened in India where A.S. Dyer invited two middle-class and respectable American women to inspect his evidence and publish a report.

The ladies were from the World's Women Christian Temperance Union; one was the widow of a Methodist minister and the other was a qualified doctor. This readiness to be the subject of a public enquiry was one of the most powerful elements of propaganda in the nineteenth century, and one repealers used to their best advantage. K. Ballhatchet, *Race, Sex and Class under the Raj; Imperial Attitudes and Policies and their Critics, 1793–1905* (Weidenfeld & Nicolson, 1980), p. 69.

92. J. Vernon, *Politics and the People: a Study in English Political Culture* (Cambridge University Press, 1993), p. 389.

93. London Trades Council, *Annual Report*, 1885. The case was complicated by the fact that one of the Hyde Park demonstrators usurped the title of councillor on the LTC. See 'Minutes of the LTC', book 4, 6 August 1885, pp. 249–51.

INDEX